CHARISMA, HISTORY, AND SOCIAL STRUCTURE

Recent Titles in Contributions in Sociology
Series Editor: Don Martindale

Max Weber's Political Sociology: A Pessimistic Vision of a Rationalized World
Ronald M. Glassman and Vatro Murvar, editors

The Adventure of Reason: The Uses of Philosophy in Sociology
H. P. Rickman

Social Hierarchies: Essays Toward a Sociophysiological Pespective
Patricia R. Barchas, editor

Social Cohesion: Essays Toward a Sociophysiological Perspective
Patricia R. Barchas and Sally P. Mendoza, editors

Family and Work: Comparative Convergences
Merlin B. Brinkerhoff, editor

No Place to Hide: Crisis and Future of American Habitats
Manuel Marti, Jr.

Systems of Discourse: Structures and Semiotics in the Social Sciences
George V. Zito

Ideologies, Goals, and Values
Feliks Gross

People's Poland: Patterns of Social Inequality and Conflict
Wladyslaw Majkowski

Weeding Out the Target Population: The Law of Accountability in a Manpower Program
James Latimore

Social Responses to Technological Change
Augustine Brannigan and Sheldon Goldenberg, editors

Overload and Boredom: Essays on the Quality of Life in the Information Society
Orrin Klapp

CHARISMA, HISTORY, AND SOCIAL STRUCTURE

Edited by
Ronald M. Glassman and
William H. Swatos, Jr.

Contributions in Sociology, Number 58

GREENWOOD PRESS
New York • Westport, Connecticut • London

Library of Congress Cataloging-in-Publication Data

Main entry under title:

Charisma, history, and social structure.

(Contributions in sociology, ISSN 0084-9278 ; no. 58)
Bibliography: p.
Includes index.
Contents: Introduction / Ronald M. Glassman and William H. Swatos, Jr. — On the interpretation and misinterpretation of the concept of charismatic leadership. Charisma and bureaucracy : a philosophy of history / H.H. Gerth and C. Wright Mills — Reflections on charismatic leadership / Reinhard Bendix — [etc.]
1. Leadership. 2. Social structure. I. Glassman, Ronald M. II. Swatos, William H. III. Series.
HM141.C37 1986 303.3′4 85-17730
ISBN 0-313-24908-3 (lib. bdg. : alk. paper)

Library of Congress Catalog Card Number: 85-17730
ISBN: 0-313-24908-3
ISSN: 0084-9278

First published in 1986

Greenwood Press, Inc.
88 Post Road West, Westport, Connecticut 06881

Printed in the United States of America

The paper used in this book complies with the Permanent Paper Standard issued by the National Information Standards Organization (Z39.48-1984).

10 9 8 7 6 5 4 3 2

Copyright Acknowledgments

Permission to use material from the following sources is gratefully acknowledged:

The Introduction from *From Max Weber: Essays on Sociology*, edited and translated by H. H. Gerth and C. Wright Mills. Copyright 1946 by Oxford University Press, Inc. Renewed 1973 by Hans H. Gerth. Reprinted by permission of the publisher..

"Reflections on Charismatic Leadership," by Reinhard Bendix, which first appeared in *Asian Survey* and later in *Scholarship and Partisanship*, edited by Reinhard Bendix. © 1967, 1971 by The Regents of the University of California. Reprinted (with redaction) from *Scholarship and Partisanship*, pp. 170-87, by permission of The Regents.

In order to keep this title in print and available to the academic community, this edition was produced using digital reprint technology in a relatively short print run. This would not have been attainable using traditional methods. Although the cover has been changed from its original appearance, the text remains the same and all materials and methods used still conform to the highest book-making standards.

Contents

Introduction
Ronald M. Glassman and William H. Swatos, Jr. 3

PART I. On the Interpretation and Misinterpretation of the Concept of Charismatic Leadership

Chapter 1. Bureaucracy and Charisma: A Philosophy of History
H. H. Gerth and C. Wright Mills 11

Chapter 2. Reflections on Charismatic Leadership
Reinhard Bendix 17

Chapter 3. Charisma and Modernity: The Use and Abuse of a Concept
Joseph Bensman and Michael Givant 27

Chapter 4. Charisma and Illegitimate Authority
Richard S. Bell 57

PART II. Charisma and Religion

Chapter 5. Charismatic Calvinism: Forging a Missing Link
William H. Swatos, Jr. 73

Chapter 6. Hasidism and Moonism: Charisma in the Counterculture
Alan L. Berger 83

Chapter 7. Against Satan: Charisma and Tradition in Iran
Michael S. Kimmel and Rahmat Tavakol 101

PART III. The Fate of Charisma in the Modern World

Chapter 8. Manufactured Charisma and Legitimacy
Ronald M. Glassman 115

Chapter 9. The Disenchantment of Charisma: On Revolution in a Rationalized World
William H. Swatos, Jr. 129

Chapter 10. Hitler's Dictatorial Charisma
Arthur Schweitzer 147

Chapter 11. The Historic Fate of the Charisma of Reason
Peter Kivisto 163

Epilogue: Charisma and Social Structure—The Success or Failure of Charismatic Leadership
Ronald M. Glassman 179

Notes 205

Bibliography 223

Index 233

About the Contributors 239

CHARISMA, HISTORY, AND SOCIAL STRUCTURE

Introduction

RONALD M. GLASSMAN
and WILLIAM H. SWATOS, JR.

"Charismatic leadership" is perhaps the most creatively compelling ideal-typical tool in Max Weber's very extensive conceptual arsenal. In formulating the construct of "charisma," Weber drew upon historical examples of known leaders (persons acknowledged both in their own time and recognized as such by later generations), and then selected a *core of definitive characteristics* which appeared to explain the type of authority relationship between them and their followers that enabled them to rule. All actual cases of historical charismatic leadership will, of course, vary from the ideal type, but it serves as a theoretical yardstick by means of which empirical cases can be compared. "The term charisma," then, Weber writes,

> will be applied to a certain quality of an individual personality by virtue of which he is considered extraordinary and treated as endowed with supernatural, superhuman, or at least specifically exceptional powers or qualities. These are such as are not accessible to the ordinary person, but are regarded as of divine origin or as exemplary, and on the basis of them the individual concerned is treated as a "leader."[1]

Weber also distinguishes between the differing spheres of society from which charismatic leadership may emerge. For instance, the charismatic may emerge as a religious prophet, a war leader, or a great orator. In each of these spheres, human anxiety levels can run high, while signs from "the Beyond" attain increasing significance. We can in a broad sense, then, agree with Karl Loewenstein when he observes that "fundamentally . . . the locus of charisma is the world of religion"—or with Wolfgang Mommsen, when he writes that "charisma . . . is a form of spiritual energy oriented to other-worldly ideals which are in more or less sharp contrast to the facts of daily life."[2]

Our existential awareness of our own impending death or that of others, and our search for the meaning of life in an infinite, hostile universe, open us to charismatization by religious leaders who seem to create meaning and hope out of meaninglessness and hopelessness. Likewise, the dangers and horrors of war open us to the hero-worship of the successful war-leader who can bring us through the holocaust safely and triumphantly—"like a god." In times of crisis, in societies in which decision-making is open to public debate, the great orator can mesmerize us and sway us to his banner, speaking "like a god," lending us a feeling of confidence, cohesion, and moral superiority that had heretofore been lacking. Although Weber recognized significant differences between the institutional spheres of the military, politics, and religion, he also was careful not to divorce them.

Weber never focuses, then, on leadership divorced from the political, structural, and cultural context in which it functions. His ideal type, "charismatic leadership," is presented as one of his typified categories of *legitimate domination*. As such, "charismatic authority" becomes the main focus for Weber's analyses, and it is by means of this concept that Weber links the study of leadership with an analysis of legitimation and social structure. "History, biography, and social structure" become causally interrelated in a complex Weberian synthesis.[3]

GENUINE CHARISMA OR DEPERSONALIZED CHARISMA?

Weber adds another important category to the study of charisma. For, though charisma should logically be unique to the person of a specific leader, in actuality it may be transferred. Close associates of a charismatic leader, such as a brother or a son, may become charismatized in a leader role. More remarkable than this, charisma may, in fact, be conferred upon a whole *clan*, an entire *stratum*, or specific high-status *offices*.

Weber calls this "depersonalized" charisma, because the clan, stratum, or office creates the charismatic aura, rather than the incumbent's "gift of grace." However, these depersonalized charismata are not maintained without elaborate manufactured effects. Furthermore, though depersonalized charisma results in social cohesion, it is a different kind of cohesion from that produced by genuine charisma. Genuine charismatic authority produces a dynamic cohesion, breaking the petrification of jaded institutions, whereas depersonalized charisma engenders an institutional authority which rigidifies social structures and inhibits genuine charismatic leadership.[4]

THE ROUTINIZATION OF CHARISMA

Weber was concerned not only with the period of charismatic domination, but also with the routinization of charisma that follows the decline of charismatic authority. There are two dimensions of Weber's analysis that are of interest to us in this regard.

First, Weber makes it clear that the routinization of charisma may move in a traditional or a modern direction. This is especially important to theories of social change, because it means that a society in transition does not necessarily move "onwards" towards a progressive stage of development. Charismatic leadership may not always lead the way to the future; it may lead to a contemporized version of the past, or even "backwards" to a past unknown within a particular civilizational context. On a theoretical level this is important because it voids all unilinear theories of social change. Practically, it serves to remind us that "change" is not always "change for the better." To concretize this point, we have included analyses of both Hitler and the Ayatollah Khomeini.

Second, charisma may be routinized in a democratic or despotic direction. We are especially interested in the structural and cultural processes that lead a nation towards a democratic or despotic routinization. The causal processes involved in routinization are discussed in the epilogue to this volume, while the essay by Swatos on Calvinism and Berger's analysis of Hasidism provide case materials.

"HUMANISTIC" AND "EVIL" CHARISMATIC LEADERS

Weber makes no distinction as value-loaded as this one. On one hand he presents us with examples of berserk warrior leaders, linked obviously with the blood-lust, slaughter, rape, and pillage of conquest; on the other, religious prophets, linked with the extension of ethical codes and the inculcation of social justice.

Given the emergence of the murderous, yet genuinely charismatic, Hitler just after Weber's death, we believe that the distinction between the heinous and the humanistic charismatic leader is worth emphasizing and investigating. Even among warrior leaders one can find the demonic Attila or the relatively humanistic Alexander. Religious charismatics, too, can run the gamut from Jesus' pacifism to Khomeini's repression. Amongst great orators, Pericles and Alcibiades come to mind—the one enchanting the Athenians with the spirit of freedom and democracy, the other degrading them to acts of civil violence and foreign domination.[5] In the modern context, as Ann Ruth Willner has noted, both Hitler and Roosevelt enmeshed entire nations in their oratorical spells, but how can one ignore the differences in the character of the charismatic message?[6] Apparently, charismatic leaders may be possessed of the gift of the devil as well as the gift of grace.

Weber knew this. That is why his dream was the dream of the plebiscitarian charismatic leader, constrained within the confines of the law. But as Aristotle warned, where the bounds of law are exceeded, as they are definitionally in charisma, "the character of the beast" may emerge.[7] The good and the bad, the democratic and the despotic, the modern and the traditional—all these dimensions of charisma must be analyzed within the sociocultural structure in which the actual historical charismatic leader arises and declines.

THE FATE OF CHARISMA IN THE MODERN WORLD

As we enter the world of modernity, we enter a world in which charisma can be falsified and denigrated—falsified by its artificial manufacture, denigrated by the cynicism and disenchantment that permeate the rational approach to social life in our times. Modern societies are increasingly *run* by faceless managers, *impressed* by media celebrities whom we know only as faces, and *inhabited* by individuals who *retreat* into private spheres of narcissistic self-development.

Yet moderns still long for charisma. The world of modernity is one in which the individual is increasingly isolated from the mediating structures of family, community, religion, and even friendship.[8] In this "lonely crowd" existence of "familiar strangers" we feel a great need for connectedness to a leader who in some sense unifies us with an "imaged" society at large. Rather than finding genuine charisma, however, the isolated individual of modernity becomes a bystander to media campaigns by "superstars" attempting to sell ideology in the guise of camera-projected personalism.

The manufacture of charisma through the mass media creates a whole new category of leadership, carrying a pseudocharismatic aura. In modern social-technical settings even a genuine charismatic leader would have to seek the enhancing devices of the mass media to broaden the charismatic effect into a mass phenomenon of an all-encompassing kind. Hitler, ironically, was the first modern charismatic leader to utilize the mass media in this way. However, leaders lacking genuine charisma will turn to the mass media in order to attempt to manufacture pseudocharisma in its place. Though this manufactured charisma does not create the same cathectic bond that genuine charisma generates in the charismatized followers, it does create an aura of ever-present recognition and "star" status. The pseudocharismatic leader enters the world of media celebrities which appears to exist beyond the world of ordinary individuals and in this sense gains partial legitimacy.

Weber was very much interested in the process of charisma as it functioned in legal-democratic societies. The center of his attention was the plebiscitarian leader, who runs for office through popular vote by reaching out to the people directly in an attempt to gain constitutionally delineated power. Weber favored the American presidential system for this reason. Weber hoped that within a structure of legal authority a democratically elected leader could ascend to charismatic heights and lead the people against the petrifying growth of the modern bureaucratic state and economy. Unfortunately, as Mommsen and others have pointed out, charismatic-plebiscitarian leadership, when translated back into German, comes out "*führer* democracy"—a frightening specter indeed.[9] Yet, if we avoid Nietzschian nightmares, the phenomenon of electoral leadership in legal-democratic nation-states in this era of the mass media becomes one of the central foci of contemporary political analysis. Amplified by the mass media, electoral charisma—in both its genuine and manufactured forms—represents a new dimension in political leadership. The presidency of Ronald Reagan stands as a case in point ripe for Weberian analysis.[10]

In communist societies, too, after the era of genuine revolutionary charisma, and with the onset of stultifying bureaucratic administrations, attempts at the manufacture of pseudocharisma have been typical. The style in the communist nations has been more heavy handed than in the legal-democratic nations. Nonetheless, there is no doubt that the manufactured charisma created for the leaders has produced partial legitimation, especially within their own societies.

The manufacture of pseudocharisma and its consequences is taken up in greater detail in the essays by Bensman and Givant and by Glassman, with applications in rather different directions in Berger's analysis of the Unification Church's leader, the Reverend Moon, and Kivisto's essay on the Left.

In a world of rational-scientific perceptions and technical-managerial evaluations, finally, the magic is removed from charisma. A leader cannot be conceived as godly in an age which proclaims "God is dead." The irrational bond between leader and led becomes qualified. On the positive side, the modern individual is free of the superstition and blindness that accompany the magical worldview. On the negative side, however, faith in a humanistic ethic and spiritual unification of the universe are challenged by a nihilistic existentialism and cynical withdrawal into personal self-satisfaction.

In the same way as it is possible to manufacture charisma and hence create pseudocharisma, is it not also possible to manufacture enchantment? Might we not then speak of *pseudoenchantment* as the bureau-technic response to the ennui of disenchantment? To what extent is contemporary mass culture as a whole centered on the manufacture, distribution, and consumption of "enchantment" (i.e., pseudoenchantment)? As the core social institutions are differentiated, they are denuded of transcendent value for the individual. They become mere instruments of technical rationality. Meaning, commitment, and symbolism are centered on consumption, play, and "leisure." Work is largely amoral and devoid of significance beyond instrumental task-performance. Institutions of escape thus grow daily more entrenched in the market, while nostalgia for a return to "normal" is even more dangerous, for it can be based only on false consciousness and lead toward fascism in the political arena. The public sphere appears increasingly disenchanted, while "enchantment"—spurious though it may be—is a market commodity eagerly sought by millions. The demystification of the 1960s excised the last bits of pre-modern enchantment, and the latter decades of this century are in turn witness to a new phenomenon: the manufacture of "transcendent experiences."[11] The implication of these processes for revolutionary social change is assayed by Swatos in an essay interweaving charismatic authority and the process of disenchantment.

A NOTE ON WEBERIAN SOURCES

The bulk of Weber's treatment of charisma occurs in the essays that form the German text *Wirtschaft und Gesellschaft*, masterfully edited by Guenther Roth and Claus Wittich as *Economy and Society*. Unfortunately, Weber's entire corpus has yet to be translated, and with the exception of *Economy and Society*, what is available is not generally a consistent replication of the German collections. Essays forming a single German volume may be scattered into three or four in English, and an English volume may contain works from several German ones. In addition, some essays appear more than once in both German and English collections, with the possibility of several different editions of one or more of these. On the assumption that most of our readers will have English as their first or second language, we have attempted to minimize the confusion by (1) restricting citations to English-language texts of Weber's works wherever these are available and (2) citing the 1978 edition of *Economy and Society* whenever a passage appears therein and in multiple English-language texts as well. At times this latter convention may create a discrepancy between a quote in an essay here and as it appears in *Economy and Society*. These occasions have been marked in the notes. With very few exceptions, a reader who wishes to proof-text our authors' Weberian scholarship needs only *Economy and Society* and the Gerth and Mills collection, *From Max Weber*, to do the job.

PART I

On the Interpretation and Misinterpretation of the Concept of Charismatic Leadership

1

Bureaucracy and Charisma: A Philosophy of History

H. H. GERTH
and C. WRIGHT MILLS

The principle of rationalization is the most general element in Weber's philosophy of history. For the rise and fall of institutional structures, the ups and downs of classes, parties, and rulers implement the general drift of secular rationalization. In thinking of the change of human attitudes and mentalities that this process occasions, Weber liked to quote Friedrich Schiller's phrase, the "disenchantment of the world." The extent and direction of "rationalization" is thus measured negatively in terms of the degree to which magical elements of thought are displaced, or positively by the extent to which ideas gain in systematic coherence and naturalistic consistency.

The urge towards such a comprehensive and meaningful interpretation of the universe is ascribed to groups of intellectuals, to religious prophets and teachers, to sages and philosophers, to jurists and experimental artists, and finally, to the empirical scientist. "Rationalization," socially and historically differentiated, thus comes to have a variety of meanings. In this connection Weber makes a masterful contribution to what has come to be known as the "sociology of knowledge."[1]

Weber's view of "disenchantment" embodies an element of liberalism and of the enlightenment philosophy that construed man's history as a unilinear "progress" towards moral perfection (sublimation), or towards cumulative technological rationalization. Yet his skeptical aversion to any "philosophical" element in empirical science precluded any explicit constructions of historical time in terms of "cycles" of "unilinear" evolution. "Thus far the continuum of European culture development has known neither completed cyclical movements nor an unambiguously oriented 'unilinear development.' "[2] We nevertheless feel justified in holding that a unilinear construction is clearly implied in Weber's idea of the bureaucratic trend. Even so "inward" and apparently subjective an area of experience as that of music lends itself to a sociological treatment under Weber's concept of "rationalization." The fixation of clang patterns, by a more concise notation and the establishment of the well-tempered scale; "harmonious" tonal music and the standardization of the quartet of woodwinds and string instruments as the core of the symphony orchestra. These are seen as progressive "rationalizations." The musical systems of Asia, of preliterate Indian tribes, of Antiquity, and of the Middle East are compared in regard to their scope and degree of "rationalization." The same comparative focus is of course used in the account of religious systems, as may be seen in the typological sketch contained in "The Social Psychology of World Religions."

This process of rationalization is punctured, however, by certain discontinuities of history. Hardened institutional fabrics may thus disintegrate and routine forms of life prove insufficient for mastering a growing state of tension, stress, or suffering. It is in such crises that Weber introduces a balancing conception for bureaucracy: the concept of "charisma."

Weber borrowed this concept from Rudolf Sohm, the Strassburg church historian and jurist. Charisma, meaning literally "gift of grace," is used by Weber to characterize self-appointed leaders who are followed by those who are in distress and who need to follow the leader because they believe him to be extraordinarily qualified. The founders of world religions and the prophets as well as military and political heroes are the archetypes of the charismatic leader. Miracles and revelations, heroic feats of valor and baffling success are characteristic marks of their stature. Failure is their ruin. Although Weber is aware of the fact that social dynamics result from many social forces, he nevertheless places great emphasis upon the rise of charismatic leaders. Their movements are enthusiastic, and in such extraordinary enthusiasms class and status barriers sometimes give way to fraternization and exuberant community sentiments.[3] Charismatic heroes and prophets are thus viewed as truly revolutionary forces in history.[4]

Bureaucracy and other institutions, especially those of the household, are seen as routines of workaday life; charisma is opposed to all institutional routines, those of tradition and those subject to rational management. This holds for the economic order: Weber characterizes conquistadores and robber barons as charismatic figures. When used in a strictly technical manner, the concept of charisma is free of all evaluations. Stefan George as well as Jeremiah, Napoleon as well as Jesus Christ, a raving berserk warrior of Arabia as well as the founder of Mormonism—all these are typified as charismatic leaders, for they have in common the fact that people obey them because of faith in their personally extraordinary qualities.

A genuinely charismatic situation is direct and inter-personal. In the contrast of the everyday life of institutions with the personalized and spontaneous nature of charismatic leadership, one may readily discern the heritage of liberalism that has always confronted similar dichotomies: mass *versus* personality, the "routine" *versus* the "creative" entrepreneur, the conventions of ordinary people *versus* the inner freedom of the pioneering and exceptional man, institutional rules *versus* the spontaneous individual, the drudgery and boredom of ordinary existence *versus* the imaginative flight of the genius. In spite of the careful nominalism of his method, Weber's conception of the charismatic leader is a continuation of a "philosophy of history" which, after Carlyle's *Heroes and Hero Worship*, influenced a great deal of nineteenth-century history writing. In such an emphasis, the monumentalized individual becomes the sovereign of history.

Weber's conception of the charismatic leader is in continuity with the concept of "genius" as it was applied since the Renaissance to artistic and intellectual leaders. Within the confines of "moral" history, W. E. H. Lecky broadened the conception in such a way as to apply it to leaders of human conduct rather than merely to creators of symbols. Not only men of ideas but ideal men thus came into focus, as the following passage indicates:

> There arise from time to time men who bear to the moral condition of their age much the same relations as men of genius bear to its intellectual condition. They anticipate the moral standard of a later age, cast abroad conceptions of disinterested virtue, of philanthropy, or of self-denial that seem to have no relation to the spirit of their time, inculcate duties and suggest motives of action that appear to most men altogether chimerical. Yet the magnetism of their perfections tells powerfully upon their contemporaries. An enthusiasm is kindled, a group of adherents is formed, and many are emancipated from the moral condition of their age. Yet the full effects of such a movement are but transient; The first enthusiasm dies away, surrounding circumstances resume their ascendency, the pure faith is materialised, encrusted with conceptions that are alien to its nature, dislocated, and distorted, till its first features have almost disappeared. The moral teaching, being unsuited to the time, becomes inoperative until its appropriate civilisation has dawned; or at most it faintly and imperfectly filters through an accumulation of dogmas, and thus accelerates in some measure the arrival of the condition it requires.[5]

It is clear that Lecky was interested in the genius as an extraordinary man who transcends the bounds of everyday routines; and in this, his statement foreshadows one of the key theories of Weber: the routinization of charisma.

Like Lecky, Weber sees the genuine charismatic situation quickly give way to incipient institutions, which emerge from the cooling off of extraordinary states of devotion and fervor. As the original doctrines are democratized, they are intellectually adjusted to the needs of that stratum which becomes the primary carrier of the leader's message. If these ideas are not adaptable in this way, then, regardless of their intrinsic merit, either their message will fail to influence the conduct of everyday life or those whom they do influence will remain enclosed in a special way of life and alien to the larger social body. The religions of India, according to Weber, have very often ended up as the doctrines of such aristocracies of salvation.[6]

Emphasis upon the "sovereignty of the charismatic man" does not minimize the mechanics of institutions; on the contrary, by tracing out the routinization of charisma, Weber is able to assign a heavy causal weight to institutional routines. Thus he retains a social determinism by emphasizing charisma's routinization. His handling of this problem testifies to his constant endeavor to maintain a causal pluralism and to bring the economic order into the balance.

In general, Weber's construction of historical dynamics in terms of charisma and routinization is an attempt to answer the paradox of unintended consequences. For the charisma of the first hour may incite the followers of a warrior hero or prophet to forsake expediency for ultimate values. But during the routinization of charisma, the material interests of an increased following are the compelling factor.

A charismatic movement may be routinized into traditionalism or into bureaucratization. Which course is taken does not depend primarily upon the subjective intentions of the followers or of the leader; it is dependent upon the institutional framework of the movement, and especially upon the economic order. "The routinization of charisma, in quite essential respects, is identical with adjustment to the conditions of the economy, that is, to the continuously effective routines of workaday life. In this, the economy leads and is not led."[7] Just as in this particular context a leading role is given to the economy, so does the very title of his key work, *Economy and Society*,[8] bespeak an appreciation of the determining weight of the economic bases.

The "philosophical" element in Weber's construction of history is this antinomic balance of charismatic movements (leaders and ideas) with rational routinization (enduring institutions and material interests). Man's spontaneity and freedom are placed on the side of heroic enthusiasm, and thus there is an aristocratic emphasis upon elites ("virtuosos"!). This emphasis is intimately associated with Weber's attitude towards modern democracy, which we have already indicated.[9]

Yet Weber sees in the concept of "personality" a much-abused notion referring to a profoundly irrational center of creativity, a center before which analytical inquiry comes to a halt. And he combats this poeticized and romantic element.[10] For his conceptual nominalism and his pragmatic outlook are opposed to all reification of "unanalyzed" processes. The ultimate unit of analysis for him is the understandable motivations of the single individual. His concepts are analytical tools with which he reconstructs various mechanisms. They are not descriptive categories, with which one tries to "taste" the color and grasp the surface image of the "spirit of the times." They are not concepts that contemplate the supposed substances of great men and epochs. In fact, despite Weber's emphasis on charisma, he is not likely to focus on "the great figures of history." Napoleon, Calvin and Cromwell, Washington and Lincoln, appear in his texts only in passing. He tries to grasp what is retained of their work in the institutional orders and continuities of history. Not Julius Caesar, but Caesarism; not Calvin, but

Calvinism is Weber's concern. In order to understand this fully, we have to understand his conceptual tools: the constructed type, the typological series, the comparative method.

2

Reflections on Charismatic Leadership

REINHARD BENDIX

"The term 'charismatic leader' has recently attained widespread and almost debased currency. In the past, it was occasionally applied to Gandhi, Lenin, Hitler, and Roosevelt. Now nearly every leader with marked popular appeal, especially those of new states, is indiscriminately tagged as charismatic."[1] Difficulties in the use of this term arise not only from indiscriminate labeling but also from conflicting theories of societies. Two recent discussions are especially instructive in this respect.

In an assessment of Max Weber's political writings Karl Loewenstein has raised the question of whether or not the term "charisma" can properly be applied in contemporary politics. Charismatic leadership depends upon a widespread belief in the existence of extraordinary or supernatural capacities, but such beliefs are at a discount in secular contexts. Though democratization has increased the plebiscitarian component of modern politics, the qualities of personality which attract voters indicate the popularity, but not necessarily the charisma, of a successful political leader. Accordingly, Loewenstein feels that today "charisma" in the proper sense is likely to be found in those areas of the world in which a popular belief in supernatural powers is still widespread, as in some parts of Africa or Asia.[2]

Quite the opposite position has been formulated by E. A. Shils, who sees a charismatic element in all societies. Shils notes Weber's distinction between the disruptive or innovative effects of charisma and the continuous and routine character of tradition or the legal order; this parallels Loewenstein's distinction between the magico-religious contexts that encourage and the secular contexts that discourage charisma. As Shils points out, Weber himself did not confine his use of the term to magical or religious beliefs, and he analyzed the institutionalization of charisma through kinship, heredity, and office. But he also believed that the opportunities for genuine charisma had diminished in the course of an increasing rationalization and bureaucratization of Western society. Shils takes issue with this last point. He maintains that men in all societies confront exigencies of life which demand a comprehensive solution. Man's position in the cosmos, birth, death, marriage, basic ideas of equity are among these central concerns. The need for establishing some order with reference to these concerns may vary among men, but the point is that charisma attaches itself to those individuals or institutions which satisfy that need or promise to do so. Such ordering may involve philosophical or artistic representations, religious doctrines, interpretations of the law, or the authority of government. Charisma has necessarily a protean character, since it may become a focus of belief whenever ultimate concerns are given an authoritative ordering.[3]

This is not the place to discuss these larger questions substantively, but it is appropriate to refer briefly to one rather topical application of the term "charisma." The new nations provide a setting of rapid change in which charismatic leaders may achieve new forms of political integration. In his analysis of *Ghana in Transition*, David Apter has suggested that charismatic leadership helps to undermine tribal authority and thus helps to make way for the creation of secular legal institutions in a nation-state. He notes, however, that charismatic leadership is not easily reconciled with secular systems of authority. Perhaps a charismatic leader like Nkrumah can transfer some of the loyalty traditionally accorded to tribal chiefs to the agents and symbols of a secular government—as long as he is the leader. But then the problem is: How can the loyalties of a personal following be transferred to the institutions of government ("routinized" in Weber's terminology)? Without such transfer, governmental stability is not assured.[4]

In a critique of writings on Ghanaian and African politics Claude Ake has raised the basic question whether or not in the new nations charismatic leaders can fulfill any such constructive function. They often command a large percentage of the vote, but this may involve a fleeting acclamation or an engineered consent rather than widespread public support. Since in the new nations political instability is rife and integration difficult to achieve, any leader may at times obtain considerable political power, if he can command a certain degree of loyalty. Modern means of publicity can give such leadership all the appearance of charisma: the singular gifts of the leader and the unquestioning devotion of his followers. But such appearances can be misleading. The popular celebrations at Nkrumah's overthrow in 1966 suggest either that his charisma had disappeared by then, or that it had been on the wane for some time, or indeed, that there had been little of it in the first place. Such uncertainties only point up the evanescent qualities of "charisma," which may come to the fore in times of rapid change but which are neither a substitute for regular leadership nor easily reconciled with enduring political institutions.[5]

These contemporary uncertainties in the use of the term suggest that there are special hazards in drawing analogies between new nations, then and now. In his analysis of *The First New Nation* S. M. Lipset has noted that George Washington was a source of unity in the early years of the United States and that his commanding military success inspired widespread veneration of his person. But Lipset also notes that Washington was oriented to the rule of law, permitted the growth of an embryonic party system, and established a precedent for succession to office by voluntarily stepping down in favor of President-elect Adams. Genuine as Washington's charisma probably was, it was acted out in a framework of received political and legal institutions—and it is just the absence of such a framework which jeopardizes analogies between this early American and the contemporary experience in the new nations.[6]

I have cited the large interpretative questions raised by Loewenstein and Shils and the uncertainties of the contemporary application of the term because I believe that the proper definition and use of the concept "charisma" must be clarified before these larger issues can be addressed. My purpose in this paper is, therefore, to restate Weber's original formulation of the concept and emphasize its dynamic implications. Second, I shall comment briefly on some analytic problems which arise when the term "charismatic leadership" is applied to two Asian leaders whose careers illustrate different facets of the problem.

In referring now to Weber's specification of the term "charisma" I confine myself to the concept of "charismatic leadership," leaving out the "routinization of charisma" (through its association with kinship, heredity, and office) as well as the positive or negative relations between charisma and social structure. An analysis of individual political leaders need not be concerned with routinization, excpet insofar as it bears on the problem of succession. The leaders under consideration are politically active in societies undergoing rapid change, i.e., in contexts presumably favorable to charismatic appeals.[7]

Five specifications are added to Weber's basic definition of charisma.[8] Weber notes first that "charisma" is probably the greatest revolutionary power in periods of established tradition, and second that it typically neglects considerations of economic efficiency and rationality.[9] Third, he emphasizes that the charismatic leader and his followers constitute a congregation (*Gemeinde*); he has no officials assisting him, but rather disciples or confidants who have no career or qualifications in the bureaucratic sense—and no privileges. They are personally called by their leader based on his peremptory judgment of their own charismatic gifts; they may be as summarily dismissed whenever he judges that they have failed his trust in them.

Weber's fourth and fifth specifications are of special interest to us here. For that reason it may be best to quote him verbatim:

It is *recognition* on the part of those subject to authority which is decisive for the validity of charisma. This is freely given and guaranteed by what is held to be a

> "sign" or proof (*Bewährung*), originally always a miracle, and consists in devotion to the corresponding revelation, hero worship, or absolute trust in the leader. But where charisma is genuine, it is not this which is the basis of legitimacy. This basis lies rather in the conception that it is the *duty* of those who have been called to a charismatic mission to recognize its quality and to act accordingly. Psychologically this "recognition" is a matter of complete personal devotion to the possessor of the quality, arising out of enthusiasm, or of despair and hope.
>
> No prophet has ever regarded his quality as dependent on the attitudes of the masses toward him. No elective king or military leader has ever treated those who have resisted him or tried to ignore him otherwise than as delinquent in duty. . . .
>
> If proof of his charismatic qualification fails him for long, the leader endowed with charisma tends to think his god or his magical or heroic powers have deserted him. If he is for long unsuccessful, above all *if his leadershp fails to benefit his followers*, it is likely that his charismatic authority will disappear. This is the genuine charismatic meaning of the phrase "by the grace of God" (*Gottesgnadentum*).[10]

A first reading of this passage might suggest that a leader is charismatic when his followers recognize him as such, because they see "powerful results achieved in the absence of power."[11] But closer examination suggests that both the recognition by followers and the leader's own claims and actions are fundamentally ambivalent.

For the charisma of a leader to be present, it must be recognized by his followers, and in the ideal typical case this recognition is a matter of *duty*. But a personal devotion arising from enthusiasm, despair, or hope is easily contaminated by the *desire for a "sign"* which will confirm the existence of charisma. In turn, the leader demands *unconditional devotion* from his followers, and he will construe any demand for a sign or proof of his gift of grace as a lack of faith and a dereliction of duty. Yet his "charismatic authority will disappear, . . . if *proof of charismatic qualifications* fails him for too long." It appears then that charismatic leadership is not a label that can be applied but refers rather to a problematic relation between a leader and his followers which must be investigated. For it is in each case a question of fact: To what extent and in what ways has the followers' desire for a sign—born out of their enthusiasm, despair, or hope—interfered with, modified, or even jeopardized their unconditional devotion to duty? And similarly it is a question of fact: To what extent and in what ways has the leader's unconditional claim to exceptional powers or qualities been interfered with, modified, or even jeopardized by the actions which he construes as proof of his charismatic qualifications?

The following sketches of two political leaders in Asia may be considered with these questions in mind.

JAWAHARLAL NEHRU, INDIA (1889–1964)

Of the two leaders considered here, Nehru is one who is clearly a disciple and a publicly designated successor. Since in the eyes of his followers at least, Nehru's charisma was derived from Gandhi, we are obliged to examine the transfer of charisma from teacher to disciple, in order to assess the latter's charismatic appeal. Weber discusses the transfer of charisma as an aspect of "routinization." Since by definition charisma is out of the ordinary and dependent upon manifestions of strictly personal qualities, it exists in pure form only in the person in whom it originates. Yet the disciples of the leader and his followers at large share a strong desire to perpetuate that "gift of grace" and its real or presumed benefits, and efforts at such perpetuation come to the fore when the problem of succession must be solved. In this respect Weber distinguishes six typical alternatives; the one of interest here is that the original charismatic leader designates his own successor, who is then accorded recognition by the community.

Nehru's long schooling in England had prepared him to become a junior member in his father's legal firm, but he found this prospect dull. In 1919, at the age of thirty, he became actively involved in the Indian independence movement. The designation of Nehru as successor to Gandhi took place over a number of years. During this early period, Nehru emerged as a young, conspicuously Western, relatively wealthy, and intensely theoretical member of the inner circle of disciples. All the disciples were held together by their faith in Gandhi's political and moral leadership. Yet there were divisions among them, for the specific goals of Hindu-Moslem harmony, the elimination of untouchability, and the improvement of village life were broad enough to allow considerable variation with regard to means and ends. In the context of the movement for independence the most noteworthy division concerned nonviolence, which was a creed to some and a tactic to others. This tells us something about Gandhi's tolerance for diversity among his immediate followers, suggesting the permissive preaching of the *exemplary prophet* which "says nothing about a divine mission or an ethical duty of obedience, but rather directs itself to the self-interest of those who crave salvation, recommending to them the same path as he himself traversed."[12]

Nehru's tie to Gandhi was based on deep respect and acceptance of Gandhi's tactical skill, but these sentiments did not affect Nehru's own wide-ranging ideological and political explorations and commitments. Such world-political preoccupations separated Nehru from things Indian even in the midst of intense political activities. Gandhi commented in 1924 that Nehru was one of "the loneliest young men of my acquaintance in India."[13] This personal and cultural isolation was directly related to the articulation of Nehru's political position. His views on international affairs sharpened his conflict with the older Congress leaders including his father, but these views also enabled Nehru to appeal effectively to labor groups and radical youth, among whom some had lost faith in Gandhi. In this setting, Gandhi, choosing to withdraw from the Congress presidency in favor of Nehru (1930), used Nehru to keep the young rebels in line. Gandhi also induced his chosen disciple to accept policies that bewildered him so that Nehru was forced for the sake of party unity to represent as his own a position in which he did not believe. This pattern recurred during the long years of discipleship, from Gandhi's reconciliation between Nehru and his father in 1919 to the formal designation of Nehru as his political heir in 1942. For Nehru these were years during which he was pulled in several directons, dedicated to the man in whose charisma he believed, but at odds with him in style and judgments. Yet Nehru served him and the cause of independence with complete devotion despite the false positions and humiliating experiences into which Gandhi's tactics forced him from time to time.

A lesser man might have succumbed to the strain of that relationship, compounded as it was by Gandhi's alternately cooperative and antagonistic relations with Nehru's father. But Nehru was an intense and ebullient man, who apparently overcame the ambiguities of his position and his own ambivalence. He was aided not only by his courage and idealism for India but also by Gandhi's patient trust in his qualities of mind and character despite Nehru's outbursts of temper, doctrinaire views, and repeated clashes with other Congress leaders. Nehru's relationship with Gandhi reflected his ambivalence to India as a whole. Admiring Gandhi's tactical "magic" and his uniquely Indian means of achieving independence, Nehru still saw non-violence only as a tactic to achieve a political purpose; thus at the same time he identified with, and dissociated himself from, this symbol of India. While he endowed Nehru with his trust during the long years of discipleship, Gandhi still mixed expressions of confidence with fatherly admonitions, giving Nehru his blessing but withholding his mandate.

There is some suggestion in this context that Nehru's successful campaigns among the Indian masses were an escape from an enervating tutelage as well as a discovery of India. Contacts with the Indian people were a means of attaining confidence in his mission, for he witnessed the unconditional devotion with which they viewed him as the embodiment of Gandhi's charisma and recognized the charisma of his own sacrifices for independence. There is an almost tragic irony in the paradox that what his personality represented to the people was largely independent of what he said to them. Nehru's effect on the masses inspired his confidence in India while increasing the skepticism of his colleagues. Yet this mass enthusiasm and Nehru's continued isolation among the disciples provided Gandhi again and again with the opportunity to weld the factions of the Congress together.

At the age of fifty-three, once more in jail, Nehru learned from the book of an Englishman what it was that distinguished him from Gandhi. The book distinguished between the prophet, who pursues the truth relentlessly, and the leader, who strikes a compromise between truth and the views of the average man. Nehru thought his own role to be that of the leader but believed Gandhi had confused the two roles. Apparently Nehru did not recognize Gandhi's unique fusion of prophecy and teaching, which was a part of that specific charisma of India's holy men beyond his own grasp. By separating the teacher's role from the educative function of exemplary conduct, Nehru revealed his Western acculturation as well as the discrepancy between his self-image and the Indian people's recognition of his charismatic gift. He wanted to be their teacher, while they sought in him the exemplary prophet.

In this all too brief consideration I have emphasized the problem of succession, highlighted by the great charisma of Nehru's mentor. It may be noted that the charismatic appeal of Gandhi and of Nehru is entirely the by-product of their personal gifts in the context of the Indian independence movement. In turning now to a discussion of a leader of a Communist country, we must attempt to disentangle the relationship between the leader and his people from the manipulated representation of that relationship by the mass media.

KIM IL-SŎNG, NORTH KOREA (1919-)

It is difficult to separate fact from fiction in the life history of Kim Il-sŏng. Kim has concentrated in his hands all power of decision-making in the party, the government, and the army. To account for this fact, and to celebrate it, North Korean historians have written hagiological accounts which twist the story of Kim's childhood, his role as a guerilla leader, and the first phase of his party leadership into anticipations of his present preeminence. For that reason it becomes difficult to assess the rather meager descriptions of Kim's leadership.

The Korean party appears to model its mobilization of the people after a shock-troop pattern, giving its civilian appeals and organizational efforts the appearance of simulated combat under conditions of guerilla warfare. For example, Kim approaches production problems in the manner of a self-confident guerilla leader who himself masters whatever he asks of his soldiers and by his example encourages them to greater effort. He reportedly learns the technicalities of the factories or collectives he will visit, thus living up to the reputation of the omniscient leader. In this way he emphasizes by his example the party's mission as the teacher of the people.

Organized propaganda shows this leadership in action and seeks to enhance its exemplary effects by the testimony of "awed witnesses." But this inevitably raises questions, as does Kim's power to divert resources to those farms and enterprises which have been selected for exemplary success in their production efforts. Propagandistic manipulation of this kind can give a hollow ring to the claim of exceptional powers on behalf of the leader, and a mere joke or derisive comment aimed at such manipulation can turn a follower's devotion into a skeptic's "withdrawal of efficiency."[14]

Here we come to a lacuna in Weber's approach to charisma, due to the time at which his analysis was written (1913-14). He did not foresee fully how it would be possible to *simulate* publicly all aspects of charismatic leadership—the manifestations of the leader's extraordinary gift, the unconditional devotion of his disciples, and the awed veneration of his large following—saturating all channels of communication so that no one could escape the message. Modern dictatorships have used such centrally organized, public hagiology extensively; and given the possibilities of the "great lie" and the "will to believe," a widespread belief in charisma can be created under favorable conditions.

Yet the built-in limitations of "charisma by publicity" should not be overlooked. All hagiological writings contain paeans to the virtues of the saints; in the eyes of the believers the credibility of these writings is enhanced, rather than diminished, by stories showing "powerful results achieved in the absence of power," and such stories are also a regular feature of dictatorial propaganda. But then the authors of conventional hagiology were true believers themselves, who expressed their own sense of the miraculous for the edification of their readers, in the absence of any claim to be believed other than the authenticity of their own religious experience. In this respect, a manipulated hagiology differs. Where all media are saturated with news of the leader's great deeds and the devotion of his followers, ordinary people may begin to resist the message by various strategies which help them escape the din and the drive to mobilize them. For the saturation of the media *means* manipulation and can suggest even to the unlettered that "powerful results are 'achieved' in the presence of power" and hence in the absence of miracles.

Nevertheless, it would be mistaken to infer that charismatic leadership cannot occur under these conditions. First of all, central manipulation of news is still compatible with credibility. All totalitarian regimes have an interest, for example, in obtaining testimonials to the leader by prominent individuals with a reputation for probity and independent judgment. Whether or not pressure is used to obtain such testimonials, they can be turned to good account by the mass media—at least for quite a time. Again, the leader himself may use the media to project his supreme confidence in his mission, while pomp and circumstance can enhance the effect of that message. In this respect it is quite wrong to suppose that charismatic leadership implies the absence of deliberate manipulation on the part of the leader. On the contrary, a sense of personal mission will justify the manipulative enhancement of the charismatic appeal, so long as this does not conflict with the appeal itself.[15] Second, the leader's career may exemplify his charisma in the eyes of the people, and the mere fact of media manipulation will not necessarily undermine their belief in him. Indeed, a people's recognition of that charisma—born of "the will to believe" and manifest in their devotion to duty—may endure long after they have begun to discount the credibility of the leader's entourage or the whole apparatus of media manipulation.

CONCLUSION

It is now appropriate to reconsider the distinction between charismatic leadership and leadership *san phrase*. The term "charisma" is used indiscriminately because this distinction is difficult to make in practice, though not in theory. All types of leadership are alike in that they involve an ambivalent interaction between leaders and led. A leader demands unconditional obedience, because he does not want his performance to be tested against criteria over which he has no control. Such tests jeopardize his authoritative right to command. On the other hand, the led withhold ultimate surrender of their will (if only in the form of mental reservations), because they do not want to forgo their last chance for a quid pro quo—i.e., for a gain through effective leadership in exchange for the obedience shown. Yet to withhold unconditional obedience in this way always runs the risk that leadership will fail us, because we have not shown our ultimate devotion to duty.

The interactions between leaders and led probably trace an erratic path between Scylla and Charybdis. The hazards of cumulative causation (as actions and reactions reenforce each other) and the reluctance of most people to face the ultimate consequences of their acts frequently lead to a tempering of demands and expectations on both sides. By not claiming ultimate authority and by not demanding unconditional obedience leaders can avoid being challenged and yet hope to accomplish a modicum of success. And the led are ready to obey when no ultimate commitment is demanded of them, because a mixture of acquiescence and performance leaves them free to hope for benefits with only a moderate inconvenience to themselves.

In theory it is easy to see that "charisma" makes its appearance when leaders and led are convinced that these easy accommodations are no longer enough, when consummate belief, on one side, and the promptings of enthusiasm, despair, or hope, on the other, imperatively call for unconditional authority and obedience. In theory it is even easy to see that "charisma" appears to be present and yet is in jeopardy, when such convictions animate the leader *or* the led, but not both simultaneously. There are many historical examples of a leader who feels the call but cannot find a following, or of people at large searching in vain for a leader who will satisfy their longing for a miracle. Thus charisma frequently appears to occur because the search for it continues. But genuine charisma is a rare event, born as it is of a belief in the mysterious gift of one person which that person shares with those who follow him.[16]

3

Charisma and Modernity: The Use and Abuse of a Concept

JOSEPH BENSMAN
and MICHAEL GIVANT

From time to time a relatively esoteric academic field and/or its concepts becomes highly popular among lay audiences, and its vocabulary enters the common language. Thus the concepts of physics associated with the atom bomb, at least at the level of vocabulary—for example, fission, fusion—are part of the ordinary speech of millions of people. Psychology, especially Freudian psychology, has enriched or, according to some, helped to debase everyday language. Sociology has produced or reintroduced such terms as serendipity, alienation, anomie, and a wide variety of other terms usually deemed barbaric by defenders of literate English. In this essay we are concerned with the term charisma, which by now is not only the name of a perfume and the title of a pop tune, the name of a laundry, and a shirt brand, but also widely applied to virtually every situation in which the popularity of a political or any public personality is involved. Edward Shils makes a similar point about the vulgarization of the term charisma in his now famous article, "Charisma, Order, and Status": ". . . charisma has come to be widely used in current high and middle-brow speech, in sociological and political analyses, and in the superior ladies' magazines."[1] However, it is the contention in part of this essay that Shils in his own way contributes to the contemporary shift in the meaning of the term.

The transformation or migration of meaning of such terms is always of interest; for as a term gains currency, some of the specific original meaning may be lost and new meanings added. In addition, once the new meanings are added, readers who take the new meanings as given, read into the earlier discussions meanings that were not intended and do violence to the original literature and to the historical context to which they refer. The term charisma is such a term; but since it was originally a coined term, it is possible to trace the migration of meaning in specific documents. The term was originally coined by Rudolf Sohm in his *Kirchenrecht* and referred to the gift of grace, the possession of pneuma by a religiously inspired individual.

WEBER'S CONCEPT OF CHARISMA

Sohm's term was adopted by Max Weber and became an important part of his sociology of religion and of his political sociology. In adopting the term, Weber placed great emphasis not on the possession of grace itself (as in Sohm) but on the *belief* by the followers of such a religious leader and by the leader himself of such possession. The belief in possession of divine inspiration (or mana in the case of military charisma) was critical for Weber:

> The term *charisma* will be applied to a certain quality of an individual personality by virtue of which he is considered extraordinary and treated as endowed with supernatural, superhuman, or at least specifically exceptional powers or qualities. These are such as are not accessible to the ordinary person, but are regarded as of divine origin or as exemplary, and on the basis of them the individual concerned is treated as a "leader." In primitive circumstances this peculiar kind of quality is thought of as resting on magical powers, whether of prophets, persons with a reputation for therapeutic or legal wisdom, leaders in the hunt, or heroes in war. . . . What is alone important is how the individual is actually regarded by those subject to charismatic authority, by his "followers" or "disciples."[2]

The link between the charismatic hero and his followers is direct; it is not mediated by established institutions, organizations, doctrines, or rituals. The charismatic hero occupies no office within established religions or military organizations.[3] If he occupies an office, the attribution of charisma is not based upon his office:

> The charismatic hero does not deduce his authority from codes and statutes, as is the case with the jurisdiction of office; nor does he deduce his authority from traditional custom or feudal vows of faith, as is the case of patrimonial power.
>
> The charismatic leader gains and maintains authority solely by proving his strength in life. If he wants to be a prophet, he must perform miracles; if he wants to be a war lord, he must perform heroic deeds.[4]

He invokes his claim to leadership not on the basis of office but rather upon belief in the direct and unmediated possession of the gift of grace:

> The prophet, unlike ordinary pathologically ecstatic men, had no vision, dreamed no dreams, and heard no mysterious voices. Rather he attained clarity and assurance through a corporeal divine voice of what Yahwe had meant by these day-dreams, or

the vision, or the ecstatic excitement, and what Yahwe had commanded him to say in communicable words . . . Always . . . the prophet's calling came directly from Yahwe, and the classical prophets among them told us of their visionary or auditory "call." None of them used any intoxicants, the use of which they cursed on every occasion as idolatry.[5]

Weber makes the same point with reference to Jesus's charisma:

It must not be forgotten for an instant that the entire basis of Jesus' own legitimation, as well as his claim that he and only he knew the Father and that the way to God led through faith in him alone, was the magical charisma he felt within himself. It was doubtless this consciousness of power, more than anything else, that enabled him to traverse the road of the prophets.[6]

The nature and conditions of a society or group governing the assumption of charisma establishes much of the subsequent characteristics of charisma. First, charismatic leadership, according to Weber, usually arises in times of crisis in which the basic values, institutions, and legitimacy of the society are at least in question. War, revolution, military defeat, foreign domination, natural disaster, or unexplained natural phenomena all shake the faith in the legimacy of the established order and established belief systems. The religious, political, and social hierarchies that sustain and are identified with these belief systems are similarly questioned.

This crisis in faith, and thus in the legitimacy of previously accepted leaders and leadership groups, provides opportunities for unmediated claims for power by would-be charismatic leaders. In some cases of primitive military charisma, the charismatic leader arises periodically even in the absence of crises of the social order. Charismatic leadership is the normal but intermittent way by which a warrior assumes, at least temporarily, the leadership of a band. The potential leader (military or religious) often isolates himself from his peers and from all others, undergoes rites of purification and mortification in the attempt to induce possession by mystical, psychic states, visions, dreams, and signs that he has been visited, possessed, or seized by mana, a god or the powers of god. If, after he returns to tribe and peers, he can provide evidence of such possession and power, he may recruit a band of followers who believe that his possession of powers will grant success to their joint enterprise. The continuance of his leadership depends on his demonstrating charismatic qualities as evidenced by success in raids, warfare, and the hunt:

Where war and the big hunt are absent, the charismatic chieftain—the "war lord" as we wish to call him, in contrast to the chieftain of peace—is absent as well. In peacetime, especially if elemental calamities, particularly drought and diseases, are frequent, a charismatic sorcerer may have an essentially similar power in his hands. He is a priestly lord. The charisma of the war lord may or may not be unstable in nature according to whether or not he proves himself and whether or not there is any need for a war lord. He becomes a permanent figure when warfare becomes a chronic state of affairs.[7]

Failure in such activities is evidence to his followers that he no longer possesses charisma. Thus while primitive societies institutionalize charisma, charismatic leaders appear intermittently. Such leadership is of uncertain duration, and reappears only after the failure of earlier institutional charismatic leadership:

> Even the old Germanic kings were sometimes rejected with scorn. Similar phenomena are very common among so-called primitive peoples. In China the charismatic quality of the monarch, which was transmitted unchanged by heredity, was upheld so rigidly that any misfortune whatever, not only defeats in war, but drought, floods, or astronomical phenomena which were considered unlucky, forced him to do public penance and might even force his abdication. If such things occurred, it was a sign that he did not possess the requisite charismatic virtue and was thus not a legitimate "Son of Heaven."[8]

Moreover, the charismatic military leader is drawn from no particular hereditary leadership group, nor is he elected by any regularly and routinely operative machinery of election or co-optation. Rather the charismatic military leader "selects" himself, and achieves "selection" if he can evoke and direct an immediate belief among a band of followers that he possesses divine power or mana.

In all these cases, the evocation of charisma and charismatic leadership always leads away from the world of everyday life. It rejects the routine life of traditional societies, the purely hierocratic elements of religions, the bureaucratic and machine operation of political organizations; and it rejects as undignified the methodical, rational pursuit of money or wealth. It occurs in times of crises.

Thus pure charisma not only claims extraordinary powers but occurs in extraordinary situations and leads, at least temporarily, to actions, movements, events, and organizations which are extraordinary, not routine, and outside the sphere of everyday life.

It is important to note—and, as we shall see, it is almost always overlooked—that pure charismatic leadership (with the exception of primitive military charisma) is revolutionary. It is a means by which established institutions and organizations become fully delegitimated. It thus conflicts with the established order. The concept of pure charisma is also a means, in Weber's overall philosophy of history, by which traditional and rationally organized power structures and their bases of legitimacy become replaced by new and discontinuous forms of order, which are subsequently justified with new bases of legitimacy.

Weber may well have overemphasized the importance of charismatic leadership in introducing indeterminacy to the historical process. Equally important, if not more important, according to Weber, is the intellectual process of rationalizing the world. Ideas, driven by the dynamic of interest, determine the course of history.[9] Thus Luther's and Calvin's ideas, leading to the Protestant ethic, arose primarily from an autonomous intellectual development, the process of rationalizing existing ideas to make them more consistent and accurate. But in the process, *new* ideas emerged, which were selected and reinterpreted by existing and emerging classes and status groups to meet their economic, political, religious, and ideological needs (real and ideal interests). Once harnessed to these interests, the ideas helped to transform the world, in virtually all dimensions of human existence.

While pure or genuine charisma is personal, direct, radical, revolutionary, and extraordinary, when the charismatic *movement* is successful charisma becomes ordinary; its leadership becomes routinized, depersonalized, and deradicalized. Thus Weber writes: "Every charisma is on the road from a turbulently emotional life that knows no economic rationality to a slow death by suffocation under the weight of material interests: every hour of its existence brings it nearer to this end."[10] Charisma may become attached to an office,[11] that is, the gift of grace becomes attached to whomever occupies the office. In so becoming, it is depersonalized; but more important, in being attached to an office in an established political, religious, or military order, it is no longer radical. In such circumstances the magic or grace of charisma can become the basis for the legitimacy of the order itself. Thus Weber develops subtypes of routinized,[12] depersonalized, and "legitimate" charisma. These include charisma of office (as defined above); lineage charisma,[13] where a whole clan or kin group may claim unusual power and privileges on the basis of descent from a charismatic hero; and hereditary charisma,[14] in which a prince, king, or emperor may justify his rule by descent from a charismatic hero.

A special form of the concept of charisma of office is used by Weber in the attribution of magical qualities to Chinese emperors and mandarins. The emperors (and offices) are invested with a special magic despite the fact that their accession to office is routinized (and in the case of officials is the result of passing examinations). But the emperor (or the governor of a province) receives the divine grace of heaven in the exercise of his function. If war, natural calamity, or disaster occurs, it is because heaven has withdrawn its grace. The emperor, or official, loses his charisma and can be removed.

But all of these cases are the opposite of pure charisma. The pure charismatic leader most often opposes or attacks the various kinds of routinized, established, or depersonalized regimes which often descend from earlier pure charismatic leaders.

In these later contexts Weber uses the term charisma almost as a synonym for legitimacy, as the basis for faith or belief in an established order, institutional leader, or leadership group. In almost all other contexts, Weber differentiates between pure charisma (which is revolutionary, direct and unmediated, and outside all institutional organization) and the charisma of office, which is, while legitimate, the opposite of pure charisma in each aforementioned respect and different from primitive military charisma which is not revolutionary, that is, which is institutionally permitted but not prescribed or routinized.

In pure charisma the claim to obedience is personal. It is based on the ability of the charismatic cult leader to evoke the sense of faith, loyalty, and obedience of a group of personal followers to the message that the charismatic leader has derived from his unmediated communication with supernatural power:

> . . . the personal call is the decisive element distinguishing the prophet from the priest. The latter lays claim to authority by virtue of his service in a sacred tradition, while the prophet's claim is based on personal revelation and charisma. It is no accident that almost no prophets have emerged from the priestly class. . . .
>
> But the prophet, like the magician, exerts his power simply by virtue of his personal gifts. Unlike the magician, however, the prophet claims definite revelations, and the core of his mission is doctrine or commandment, not magic.[15]

However, the charismatic man becomes a leader only if there are followers:

> Charisma is self-determined and sets its own limits. Its bearer seizes the task for which he is destined and demands that others obey and follow him by virtue of his mission. If those to whom he feels sent do not recognize him, his claim collapses; if they recognize it, he is their master as long as he "proves himself."[16]

Thus Weber uses the prophetic phrase, "It is written but I say unto you." The legitimacy of charismatic leadership in the sociological sense, as Weber uses it then, is an attribute of the *belief of the followers* and not of the quality of the leader. The leader is important because he can evoke this sense of belief and thereby can demand obedience. "However, he does not derive his claims from the will of his followers, in the manner of an election; rather, it is their *duty* to recognize his charisma."[17] Potential charismatic leaders do not passively await recognition by their followers:

> The genuine prophet, like the genuine military leader and every true leader in this sense, preaches, creates, or demands *new* obligations—most typically, by virtue of revelation, oracle, inspiration, or of his own will, which are recognized by the members of the religious, military, or party group because they come from such a source. Recognition is a duty.[18]

Finally, charismatic leadership is not rational in the sense that it is based on rational argumentation, presentation, and defense. It is based primarily on the faith of the followers and the leader that the leader has access to the divine and therefore has unquestionable authority. The charismatic leader thus does not attempt in principle to argue logically the validity of his message, though he does attempt to claim for his message the authenticity of its divine source. He validates his claim by success or, rather, the faith in the success of his possession of charisma based upon the results of his prophecy or action. Thus rationality in the sense that it implies a formal logic is not relevant to charismatic leadership:

> Since it is "extra-ordinary," charismatic authority is sharply opposed to rational, and particularly bureaucratic, authority, and to traditional authority, whether in its patriarchal, patrimonial, or estate variants, all of which are everyday forms of domination; while the charismatic type is the direct antithesis of this. Bureaucratic authority is specifically rational in the sense of being bound to intellectually analysable rules; while charismatic authority is specifically irrational in the sense of being foreign to all rules. Traditional authority is bound to the precedents handed down from the past and to this extent is also oriented to rules.[19]

Weber points, in addition, to the conflict between charisma and rational-legal norms: "Hence, its attitude is revolutionary and transvalues everything; it makes a sovereign break with all traditional or rational norms: 'It is written, but I say unto you.' "[20] He stresses the contrast between bureaucratic rationalism with respect to modes of "proving" their claims to legitimacy:

> . . . the power of charisma rests upon the belief in revelation and heroes, upon the conviction that certain manifestations—whether they be of religious, ethical, artistic, scientific, political or other kind—are important and valuable; it rests upon "heroism" of an ascetic, military, judicial, magical or whichever kind. Charismatic belief revolutionizes men "from within" and shapes material and social conditions according to its revolutionary will.[21]

However, to the extent that validity or authenticity is measured by "success," there is an experiential test of charisma. The unsuccessful leader loses his charisma:

> By its very nature, the existence of charismatic authority is specifically unstable. The holder may forego his charisma: he may feel "forsaken by his God," as Jesus did on the cross; he may prove to his followers that "virtue is gone out of him." It is then that his mission is extinguished, and hope waits and searches for a new holder of charisma. The charismatic holder is deserted by his following, however, (only) because pure charisma does not know any "legitimacy" other than that flowing from personal strength, that is, one which is constantly being proved.[22]

Proof of success, to some extent, lies in the hands of the followers of the charismatic man:

If proof and success elude the leader for long, if he appears deserted by his god or his magical or heroic powers, above all, if his leadership fails to benefit his followers, it is likely that his charismatic authority will disappear.[23]

In almost all the historical cases of pure charisma, the routinization of charisma did not occur within the lifetime of the charismatic leader. Therefore the radical nature of the religious rejection of the existential world was maintained during the lifetime of the leader. As previously noted, when a charismatically led movement is successful, the nature of charisma becomes modified in the process of routinization, and charisma is attributed to office, lineage, or clan. Charisma is no longer pure charisma in the original sense as discussed above; but the routinization of charisma provides the basis and the legitimacy for newly established traditional or rational-legal hierarchies and systems of domination, which, in the process of routinization, become conservative. The radical nature of charisma disappears with routinization.

CURRENT REVISIONS OF THE WEBERIAN CONCEPT

In the above discussion, we have argued that Weber used the concept of charisma in precise ways. When he referred to a specific aspect of charisma he tended to qualify the term, indicating the specific aspect of the meaning he intended. Thus "pure" charisma, charisma of the office and/or "genuine," lineage, and hereditary charisma are all precise and differentiated specifications of meaning. We have also noted that in some cases Weber used the term in an undifferentiated way, suggesting in these cases a meaning that comes close to that meant by the term legitimacy. However, in these cases, primarily in ancient China, the legitimacy so indicated is the legitimacy of princely power. Apart from these latter contradictions, Weber's delimitation of the various subtypes of charisma indicates that each subtype may have opposite and contradictory social consequences and functions: some types of charisma are revolutionary, innovative, and delegitimizing while other types are "institutionalizing," conservative, and legitimating of established regimes and societal orders. Thus an unspecified or unqualified concept of charisma would overlook the specific social functions of charisma and would ignore the specific meanings and theoretical problems posed by Weber with his use of the term.

The new and popular usage of charisma among lay audiences contains such unspecified or unqualified usages. It selects only one aspect of all the various meanings of the term and treats that aspect as its only (or major) meaning. The selected and emphasized quality is the quality of the extraordinary character of the charismatic hero. Extraordinariness is treated in two senses. One sense is the unusual psychological qualities and "presence." The other is an unusual ability to embody the central values of society.

The focus of these aspects of charisma leads one to ignore what is central to Weber's analysis: the revolutionary qualities, the irrationality and the discontinuity in social structures accounted for by the emergence of pure charisma and by the subsequent institutionalization of charisma. In short, Weber is interested in charisma as a process accounting for changes in fundamental social structures.

Edward Shils attempts to refocus the discussion of charisma, claiming, in part, that Weber's concept needs such refocusing.[24] In so doing, Shils emphasizes the elements in charisma that link it to established orders. Thus charisma becomes, for all intents and purposes, legitimacy. The major qualities that to Shils are relevant for these legitimacy-conferring aspects of charisma are the "awe and reverence" evoked by charisma. The charismatic hero is the extraordinary man. The qualities that are extraordinary beyond personal presence are the fact that the charismatic hero personifies and embodies the central or core values of man's existence, man's life, and the cosmos, together with an intensity of presence which makes it extraordinary: "The centrality is constituted by its formative power in initiating, creating, governing, transforming, maintaining, or destroying what is vital in man's life."[25]

Charisma, as thus related to man's existence, man's life, and the cosmos, is difficult to define, since such centralities have different meanings in different societies and at different times and social locations within a society. Its destroying, formative, initiating, creative, or transforming powers can only be known empirically after the fact of its specific creations, institutions, etc., are known.

Charisma's "maintaining and governing" powers can be posited by definition or metaphysically as referring to man's ultimate life and existence and the cosmos, but known only as related to a given existing social order, society, or set of legitimating values and are therefore historically specific.

The idea of centrality can and does refer either to the central values of an ongoing society or to the "essential" values of that society. Referring to central value systems, Shils defines charisma as follows:

> That central power has often, in the course of man's existence, been conceived of as God, the ruling power or creator of the universe, or some divine or other transcendent power controlling or markedly influencing human life and the cosmos within which it exists.[26]

But charisma, according to Shils, is also related to specific social orders, in addition to being the creator of a generic order:

> The generator or author of order arouses the charismatic responsiveness. Whether it be God's law or natural law or scientific law or positive law or the society as a whole, or even a particular corporate body or institution like an army, whatever embodies, expresses or symbolizes the essence of an ordered cosmos or any significant sector thereof awakens the disposition of awe and reverence, the charismatic disposition.[27]

It is anything in the order of society that produces a sense of awe and wonder among the populace. It includes transcendental values and the order conferring powers of corporate and political bodies and the wielders of power, the older and dominant classes, status groups, elites, and occupational groups.

In the original Weberian sense of the term, neither set of meanings of centrality is relevant. The charismatic hero, in the sense of pure charisma, is a deviant, radical, or revolutionary figure. The values that he espouses are not necessarily central to the ongoing central order—except when the charismatic hero can refer to values which have been discarded by the established political, economic, legal, or religious orders. To the extent that the pure charismatic hero bases his prophecy on values that have been central to the past, those values in order to be radical or revolutionary must be deviant or, at least, not central to ongoing established institutions. To the extent that its values become central to a society, they become central—that is, established—after charisma loses its radical and revolutionary quality and becomes a specialized form of charisma different from and opposed to pure charisma. It is this latter, specialized form of charisma that Shils treats as the generalized quality of charisma. Shils thus is manifestly concerned with the diffusion of charisma throughout a society; its embodiment not in a charismatic hero, nor in the charisma of an office, but in the entire institutional structure of a society, in the society itself, in its elites, in its central values, in its population and in groups that have high prestige.[28]

In these illustrations and in all other references to charisma except those that directly summarize Weber's work, Shils' use of the concept does not, in contrast to Weber, refer to a charismatic hero, prophet, officeholder, lineage, or king. Rather it refers to the general quality, an inherent element, that evokes awe and reverence, wherever that quality may appear. It thus has no specific institutional base, nor any specific attributes. It is a free-floating attribute that can attach itself to anything, including individuals. It is, so far as we can see, a metaphysical entity.

However, charisma is, according to Shils, included as a component in every act of voluntary obedience to established authority.[29] Thus charisma is legitimacy, as that concept is usually defined.

It is difficult to argue against such a broad definition of charisma, since it includes the legitimation of everything that is established. The very broadness of Shils' usage inhibits the making of specific distinctions, and does not allow the principle of falsifiability to operate. Thus Shils is concerned with the diffusion of charisma throughout an established order and its adhesion to all established institutions, classes, and elites in a social order. Shils attempts to ground this generalized adhesion of charisma to established orders by locating it in what he conceives to be a metaphysical need for order. It is a metaphysic in the sense that the need for order is taken as a given, beyond explanation or beyond reduction to simpler elements. Thus Shils states:

> I do not know why this need for order exists. It is not simply a need for an instrumentally manageable environment, though that is a part of it. It is more like the need for a rationally intelligible cognitive map, but it obviously is more than cognitive. There is a need for moral order—for things to be fit into a pattern which is just as well as predictable.[30]

The individuals in a society need to have conceptions of the social world, or cosmologies, and relationships to others that are meaningful. The quality of providing meaning can be conceived of as rendering intellectual, theological, emotional, and psychological order.[31] The function of the charismatic hero in the past and charisma in the present—that is, in less personified terms—according to Shils is to provide systems of meaning and systems of order:

> The central power might be a fundamental principle or principles, a law or laws governing the universe, the underlying and driving force of the universe. It might be thought to reside in the ultimate principles of law which should govern man's conduct, arising from or derived from the nature of the universe and essential to human existence, discerned or elucidated by the exercise of man's most fundamental rational and expressive powers. Scientific discovery, ethical promulgation, artistic creativity, political and organizational authority (auctoritatem, auctor, authorship), and in fact all forms of genius, in the original sense of the word as permeation by the "spirit," are as much instances of the category of charismatic things as is religious prophecy.[32]

Shils explains the individual's metaphysical *need* for charisma and charismatic "others" as follows:

> Most human beings, because their endowment is inferior or because they lack opportunities to develop relevant capacities, do not attain that intensity of contact. But most of those who are unable to attain it themselves are, at least intermittently, responsive to its manifestations in the words, actions and products of others who have done so. They are capable of such appreciation and occasionally feel a need for it. Through the culture they acquire and through their interaction with and perception of those more "closely connected" with the cosmically and socially central, their own weaker responsiveness is fortified and heightened.[33]

Thus in embodying central values, as Shils defines the term, charisma makes systems of meaning and order available to society. He gives to the concept of charisma all the qualities that Weber attributes to the process of intellectual rationalization and to rational systems for the diffusion of intellectually rationalized thought; these are not and never before have been thought of as charismatic. All of these, according to Shils, are charismatic functions. In this sense any institution may have charisma if it also has power even though there were no charismatic elements in that institution's past:

The charisma of an institution or of a corporate body does not depend on its foundation by a charismatic person (although it might well be true that only charismatic persons can command the authority and resources to create a new and very powerful institution or corporate body). Corporate bodies—secular, economic, governmental, military, and political—come to possess charismatic qualities simply by virtue of the *tremendous* power concentrated in them.[34]

To the extent that a system of thought or the promise or claims of a charismatic hero may have order and coherence (and that coherence may exist at a logical, psychological, emotional or aesthetic plane), any system of thought, of course, has order. But one can *not*, as Shils apparently does, equate the order of a system of thought with an "order" of society. For Shils, charisma produces this linkage. Thus Shils states:

The disposition to attribute charisma is intimately related to the need for order. The attribution of charismatic qualities occurs in the presence of order-creating, order-disclosing, order-discovering power as such; it is a response to great ordering power. The effectiveness or successful exercise of power on a large scale, on a macro-social scale, evokes a legitimating attitude. Every legitimation of effective large scale power contains a charismatic element.[35]

Pure charisma, in the Weberian sense, may have order to the extent that it has coherence, but pure charisma inevitably and by definition attacks the "order" of a society. Therefore pure charisma is always opposed to the existing social order until it is institutionalized in the newly established and ongoing order. It is important to note that political or social order as embodied in the structure of society need not be logical or coherent. To prove that political orders are also logical or meaningful is, in any empirical situation, a major task. Shils attempts to reconcile the various meanings of the term order by indicating the order-conferring functions of power: simply because power is centralized, the institutions and groups that have power in a society evoke charismatic attachment. They accomplish this because they are salient and because they confer intellectual order on the society as a whole:

This is "institutional" charisma; it is not a charisma deduced from the creativity of the charismatic individual. It is inherent in the massive organization of authority. The institutional charismatic legitimation of a command emanating from an incumbent of a role in a corporate body derives from *membership in the body as such, apart from any allocated, specific powers.*[36]

Because these institutions "order" and organize the society as a whole, they evoke the awe and reverence of the populace. They answer the metaphysical need for order that is apparently necessary to social man.

Again Shils proves too much. Pure charisma, according to Weber, arises in opposition to centralized power, the order embodied in and provided by powerful institutions. If awe and reverence are functions of centralized power, then new forms of charisma, pure charisma, could not come into existence. One can rescue Shils' position, however, by arguing with some degree of plausibility that new forms of charisma, pure charisma, come into existence with the failure of a political order to provide or sustain its power. This, of course, appears to be tautological in the sense that Shils is arguing that when a system of power loses authority it loses its authority. It does so because legitimacy is equated solely with authority in Shils' sense of that term; and if charisma means legitimacy and legitimacy means the acceptance of authority, then the failure of legitimacy is the failure of authority; or, substituting terms, the failure of authority is the failure of authority.

In addition, the equating of power with charisma does not explain the fact that some relatively powerful groups or institutions in a society do not appear to have much charisma: some gigantic corporations are relatively unknown and thus appear to have relatively little charisma. On the other hand, some relatively powerless individuals who have "presence," personality, and appeal appear to have much more charisma. Thus one of the most persistent problems in the fields of advertising and public relations is how to make the corporation known to a wider public. The economic and institutional power that a corporation has does not by itself confer charisma and legitimacy. Special techniques and processes of diffusion are required. The personalities that we and Shils have identified with the vulgarization of the term charisma are not necessarily powerful persons.

Shils, however, reverses himself and argues that tremendous centralized power, the awe and reverence inspired by powerful institutions, are not enough to confer legitimacy on a society, its government institutions, other central institutions, its class and status system, elites, occupational groups, and on the society itself. The power, and the awe and reverence caused by power and the need for order, *must* be moralized, that is, equated with moral order.[37] Thus priests, religions, intellectuals, scientists, as well as symbolic leaders, create symbolic systems, ideologies, that confer moral order and consistency on the political power which by itself confers legitimacy—that is, charisma—to the system.

But society is stratified with respect to distance from the central sources of power and hence charisma. Distant groups and emergent groups do not have as much charisma as those close to the centralized power and institutions in society. Older ideologists are closer to the moral order of the society.[38] These newer groups, ascendent groups, and distant groups attempt to appropriate charisma for their own purposes by denying deference to charisma-monopolizing groups, by developing ambivalence to established definitions of charisma, to its exponents, and to the political order itself. In extreme cases those distant groups can reject the established order and its established forms of charisma.[39]

But if charisma is power, is legitimacy, is awe and wonder, and resides in the central values, institutions, and collectivities of the society itself, then the above summary of Shils' argument states that charisma also resides in the opposition to each of the major central dimensions that contain it. A theory or concept that explains equally a phenomenon and its opposite explains nothing.

Shils makes the concept of charisma general and diffuse in equating it with centralized power and with legitimacy. In equating charisma with legitimacy, he apparently follows Parsons, who says, in *The Structure of Social Action*:

> The distinction between legitimacy and charisma can be stated, in general terms, as follows: Legitimacy is the narrower concept in that it is a quality imputed only to the norms of an order, not to persons, things or "imaginary" entities, and its reference is to the regulation of action, predominantly in its intrinsic aspects. Legitimacy is thus the *institutional* application or embodiment of charisma.[40]

If, however, legitimacy is, by definition, institutionalized charisma, then all voluntary obedience is by definition charismatic. Given the definition, there is no need to prove one is related to the other, or to use both terms. By using both terms and the definition, Parsons, like Shils, is simply being tautological.

Shils also destroys whatever specific utility the concept may originally have had. In defining the concept specifically, in limiting it, and in specifying subtypes of charisma, Weber was able to apply specific concepts of charisma to particular historical and organizational contexts. He was thus able to treat the various concepts of charisma as independent factors to be counterpoised in analysis against concepts of power and authority in relationship to revolutionary and conservative movements in history. The concepts he used permitted a resolution of the problems he posed in historical and empirical research. The problems were not resolved by definition, nor were their solutions contained in his statement of the problems.

Finally Shils, in his argument, suggests the diffusion of charisma throughout the society and through all of a society's major components; but he does not articulate the specific mechanisms by which such a diffusion takes place. One can conclude only that, given the metaphysical need for intellectual order and the availability of political order, the supply generates its own demand by unknown metaphysical processes and that the demand in time elicits the supply. But since individuals and groups are differentially placed socially, economically, politically, and with reference to the available supply of transcendental and institutional charisma, these individuals and groups modify and manufacture their own charisma. But Shils does not specify these institutional processes.[41] Charisma appears to be a universal phenomenon, metaphysically available at all times and places, but which adheres to all established, central, and powerful institutions of society, as well as to those individuals and movements that ultimately become powerful.

CHARISMA AS A PSYCHOLOGICAL CONCEPT

The psychologizing of the concept of charisma is self-consciously attempted and carried through most thoroughly and brilliantly by Donald McIntosh in his article, "Weber and Freud: On the Nature and Sources of Authority."[42] McIntosh is aware of the divergencies between a sociological and psychological point of view, is aware of Weber's rejection of the psychological point of view, and is further aware of those aspects of Weber's work, especially in his treatment of charisma, which are amenable to psychoanalytic development. Yet he, in violation of Weber's caveats, chooses quite explicitly to make such extensions. In principle, one cannot be opposed to such extensions of an idea into another field, if such work helps to promote clarification. There is danger, however, that the stretching of the concept, in this case of charisma, obscures the problem which evoked the original concept and obfuscates the central issues which are the focus of analysis in the original field.

McIntosh emphasizes the idea of the extraordinary quality of charisma and locates this extraordinariness in magic, the belief in the power of magic as embodied in primitive religions. He emphasizes that attitudes toward the supernatural are the source of all charisma, whether magical or prophetic, and states—incorrectly, we believe, but somewhat like Shils—the idea that "the legitimacy of all authority rests on attitudes toward the supernatural."[43] In doing so, he does not, however, discuss Weber's concepts of warrior charisma, primitive military charisma, or political charisma as exhibited in ancient China. He does not mention hereditary or lineage charisma, nor does he mention the charisma of office. The revolutionary nature of charisma is briefly mentioned but then dropped. Charisma thus becomes virtually a pure psychological state. Thus McIntosh states: "The outstanding quality of charisma is its enormous power, resting on the intensity and strength of the forces which lie unconscious in every human psyche," and "charisma is an unconscious force which has been displaced outward."[44] The bulk of McIntosh's work is thus an effort to demonstrate the basic psychological components and dimensions of charisma.

Again, if one is to accept the notion that charisma is purely a psychological state, the definition of its components would be perfectly acceptable. McIntosh, however, goes beyond this construction of a psychological phenomenology of charisma. He finds, like Shils, charismatic components in traditional and rational forms of domination, and in each form he finds the psychological correspondences of charisma in that form of domination.

Since he does not distinguish between the various types and subtypes of charisma, he does not distinguish between the differing functions and forms of charisma for each system of domination. Nor does he deal with the tensions between the forms of charisma and the various forms of order. Thus he argues like Shils that charisma "for Weber is the legitimating principle behind all authority."[45] We find no evidence for this statement in the corpus of Weber's work. Such a notion would invalidate Weber's entire work on bureaucracy and on the rational-legal form of legitimacy. To be sure, traditionalism may have charismatic components—that is, the traditional leader may be a descendant of a charismatic hero whose charisma has become routinized. However, the basis for the legitimacy of traditionalism is not charisma but the sanctification of usage. Legal authority is a major basis of legitimacy and produces a charismatic element—the charisma of office. Legal authority, according to Weber, is not, however, based upon charisma. But the converse is true: charisma of office is possible only because it rests on legal and traditional authority. McIntosh thus makes essentially the same error as Shils: he treats charisma as an undifferentiated trait (for McIntosh, a psychological trait), universalizes it by ignoring its specific forms, and then posits the generic psychological form as the basis for completely different kinds of institutions, potential orders, and forms of legitimacy. Thus McIntosh says, not unlike Shils, that "charisma is a universal human experience,"[46] an idea that we find nowhere in Weber. Such a statement, whether or not found in Weber, would lead us to expect all social actions, institutions, social movements, and forms of legitimacy to be deeply imbued with charisma. Such an argument would force us to ignore all noncharismatic types of action. Moreover, it would conclusively prove that the extraordinariness of charisma is ordinary. Because of this remarkable inversion, the universalization of the extraordinary, all elements in society must be imbued with the extraordinary. This again is similar to Shils' equating of legitimacy with charisma, and to his contention that all forms of authority, elites, dominant institutions, upper-level prestige groups, the nation, the state, and the "people" are charismatic.

Yet the foregoing arguments are only preliminary to McIntosh's major argument. That contention is:

> On Weber's account, when authority has a religious justification, the leader himself may or may not possess charisma. What is crucial is that his authority is backed or validated by a divinity. Secularization must thus involve more than a change in vocabulary and imagery through which the charisma of the leader is described and understood. In addition, the secular equivalent of a legitimating divinity must appear.[47]

and:

But once it is grasped that the modern state is legitimated by a secular charisma fully as powerful and effective as the previous religious charisma, and entirely compatible with the new institutional forms, the Weberian opposition between charisma and reason appears to disappear.[48]

To us it would not seem difficult to accept the notion that secularization would require a different, nonreligious kind of charisma. Weber himself was aware that secular, political charisma could exist in the modern, secular state:

. . . in times of great public excitement, charismatic leaders may emerge even in solidly bureaucratized parties, as was demonstrated by Roosevelt's campaign in 1912. If there is a "hero," he will endeavor to break the technician's hold over the party by imposing plebiscitary designation and possibly by changing the whole machinery of nomination. Such an eruption of charisma, of course, always faces the resistance of the normally predominant pros, especially of the bosses who control and finance the party and maintain its routine operations, whose tools the candidates usually are.[49]

Weber discusses the necessity of monetary contributors and sponsors. He then states:

The regular manager and political professional, the boss or the party secretary, can expect their financial support only if he firmly controls the party machine. Hence every eruption of charisma is also a financial threat to the regular organization. It happens quite frequently that the warring bosses or other managers of the competing parties combine in defense of their common economic interests to prevent the rise of charismatic leaders, who would be independent of the regular party apparatus. As a rule, the party organization easily succeeds in this castration of charisma. This will also remain true of the United States, even in the face of the plebiscitary presidential primaries, since in the long run the continuity of professional operations is tactically superior to emotional worship. Only extraordinary conditions can bring about the triumph of charisma over the organization.[50]

In addition, Weber attributed charisma to Gladstone,[51] a special form to Kurt Eisner,[52] and to modern business Maecenases.[53]

Carl Friedrich has objected to the application of the term charisma to any phenomenon other than a religious one. He bases his objection on the first use of the term charisma in the New Testament. He argues that to broaden the term would be to combine such "genuine" leaders as Jesus, Calvin, Buddha, and Luther with such profane leaders as Lenin, Mussolini, and Hitler.[54]

While such a combination might be grotesque to a religious person, Weber recognized the possibility. He argued that his use of the term did not imply a metaphysical validity in the attribution of charisma, nor his approval or disapproval of such attribution. All that mattered was that followers accepted the claim of unusual powers, gifts, mana, of a charismatic leader.

THE APPLICATION OF THE CONCEPT TO MODERN POLITICS

A number of scholars, using this Weberian notion of acceptance of charismatic claims, have found it easy to find modern charismatic leaders.[55] We are less willing to make such designations without first attempting to reformulate the concept of charisma as it applies to the modern world.

Certainly modern "charismatic" leaders have claimed universal power because they have allegedly embodied the genius of the "race," have concentrated in themselves the spirit or essence of an earlier, more glorious period in a nation's history, or have claimed to be uniquely qualified to understand the dialectic or the laws of history and thus to bring the future into being. But secular charisma as an abstract, generalized, universal quality has exactly the same conceptual weaknesses as the conception of an undifferentiated religious charisma. Some secular charisma is revolutionary, some is conservative. Some secular charisma can be based upon personal qualities, and some on particular roles in organizations. Some may appear to be irrational, others while appearing to be irrational are based upon rational calculation, bureaucratic organization, and organized staff work. But McIntosh, in his article, deals, somewhat like Shils, only with those forms of charisma that are attached to the state, corporate bodies, and established institutions or highly organized social movements. While the whole burden of his essay suggests the "irrational" psychological bases of the attribution of charisma by followers, he does not examine, though he implies through his illustrations, that charisma is evoked by rational bureaucracies and the staffs of political and economic elites. While the charismatic followers may see substitutes for personal relationships (paternal or maternal ego identification), the surrogate personal relationships are offered on an impersonal basis by centralized, bureaucratic, rational staffs and elites.

McIntosh makes an important criticism of the application of Weber's sociology of religion to the modern world. He argues, as we have noted, that the secularization of religion means that religious charisma is no longer important in a world that is no longer religious and that a secular charisma replaces the older religious charisma.[56]

Weber was at least partly aware of these phenomena. He argued in all his late works[57] that the process of intellectual and formal rationalization and the "disenchantment of the world" increasingly made the world seem senseless, and this senselessness led to a quest for the irrational, for "experience," and for sterile excitation. However, Weber did not argue, except in the previously cited references, that such senselessness led to charisma.

In making this criticism, McIntosh neglects to make a more serious criticism of the applicability of charisma to the modern world. That criticism rests upon the manipulation of charisma by rational, impersonal, established groups. McIntosh seems partially aware of this point when he argues:

> This point may also be made with respect to other institutions besides the modern state. The business corporation has reached the most advanced form of rational organization in the United States. Precisely those firms in the forefront of this process have sought, more or less successfully, to legitimate their role among the members of the firm by fostering ties of identification and loyalty similar to those which legitimate the nation-state. We seem to be dealing here also with a secularized charisma.[58]

One can agree that modern corporations attempt to legitimate themselves in the eyes of their employees and foster ties of identification and loyalty. Whether this is charisma or not is a separate question. Modern corporations may or may not claim extraordinary powers in the specific sense denoted by the term charisma. Very few are radical in the sense of pure charisma, and the evocation of charisma is rational, planned, and due to the operation of a bureaucratic staff.

Ultimately, McIntosh sees secular charisma in social groups as "ego identifications among the members and superego identifications of the members with a leader . . . or, we would add, a personalized institution."[59] Given this definition, one could argue then, as he does, that all successful group socialization is charisma. He concludes:

> This formulation suggests the position adopted here: that in general a stable order within a social group must depend on sentiments of legitimacy springing from superego identifications. On this view, a stable non-legitimate order would be possible only when imposed coercively by one group over another, or for a group which operates inside the framework of a larger legitimate order. If the possibilities of identification with an institution are taken into account, nonlegitimate domination may be rarer than Weber thought.[60]

Thus McIntosh, unlike Shils, concludes that legitimacy is achieved when an elite group or would-be elite group succeeds in causing a subordinate group to identify with and accept its dominators. Whether this type of legitimacy is charisma or not is the crucial question. McIntosh appears to be using Weber's definition of legitimacy, but he like Shils seems to equate all legitimacy with all charisma.

The only process of legitimation specified by McIntosh, apart from "fostering," is that of identification. The psychological process of identification with the master by the subordinate is, of course, important in understanding the psychology and sociology of secular charisma; but processes of identification, as social processes, are equally important when organized, ordered, conceived and planned by noncharismatic leadership. Thus the processes of identification are broader than the processes of charisma or of the routinization of charisma.

In a specifically secular, modern world composed of large-scale states, business organizations, political parties, mass media, all operating over vast social and psychological distances, the processes leading to identification, to legitimacy, and to charisma are somewhat more differentiated, specific, and complicated than can be subsumed in any one term or concept, whether that term be charisma, legitimacy, or identification. The broadening of each term, as done by Shils and McIntosh, so that it subsumes the other, leads neither to clarity nor to understanding of the modern world. Rather, the breakdown of conceptual distinctions leads only to a theoretical circularity wherein each term dissolves into each other, with little reference to what occurs in the empirical world.

MODERN CHARISMA

Of all the recent popular definitions of charisma perhaps the best one is *political presence.*[61] Some political leaders seem to have the ability to project themselves directly, clearly, immediately through the mass media in images that seem larger than life. They can dramatize issues, project sincerity, induce suspension of disbelief, attract personal followers and distant suporters. They can become the objects of intense admiration.

In the theater, cinema, and television such qualities have been called stage presence or star quality. At various times the embodiment of these qualities in an individual has been called sex appeal or personal magnetism. Such personal qualities refer not only to the ability to project oneself over larger distances than are usually encompassed by the physical presence of the actor but, in so doing, to project a larger, more powerful image than mere physical presence suggests.[62]

Professional athletes, too, due to the massive televising of sports, can become "charismatic" heroes in the warrior image—especially with the aid of movie, television, or commercial merchandising exposure.

Such presence has been an object of self-rationalization in the development of "personal magnetism" in salesmanship, in institutional leadership, and in interpersonal relationships. But it is not charisma, as we hope to demonstrate in the following pages.

The concept of charisma as used by Weber appears to be historically limited, and far removed from popular or political stage presence. It appears to be limited primarily, but not exclusively, to discussions of ancient civilizations.

The broadening and generalization of the concept of charisma in modern society is not inaccurate, in and of itself, since language derives its meaning by usage and convention, and terms and concepts change meaning over time. However, the changes in meaning sometimes obscure specific theoretical problems, the answers to which might be useful in the analysis of the worlds referred to by such language and concepts. The dimensions of the concept of charisma that are obscured by the broadening of the concept are fundamental. These, as we have noted perhaps too often, are: (1) the personal nature of charisma; (2) its radical (or revolutionary) nature; (3) and its irrationality. Ultimately the modern usage of the term charisma refers to an ability to project an image of a direct, warm, or exciting, sincere, engaging, personal or unofficial and "human" persona. The very term project implies, in the modern world, that these qualities are presented from a distance. The personality projected is a personality that can be projected despite the existence of the vast social, physical, and psychological distances that prevail in modern mass and bureaucratic societies. Modern mass communication uses charisma to overcome these distances. Modern charisma entails the ability, whether planned or unplanned, to use or be used by the mass media in such a way as to convey a sense of immediacy that appears to negate the very media that require its uses.

Karl Loewenstein and Reinhard Bendix have specifically recognized the importance of the mass media in modern "charismatic" politics. Bendix writes:

> Modern means of publicity can give such leadership all the appearance of charisma: the singular gifts of the leader and the unquestioning devotion of his followers. But such appearances can be misleading.[63]

Loewenstein states:

> In a closed and authority-directed society, in which the organs of propaganda are controlled by the supposed holder of charisma and his subservient following, the mass media can produce a reinforcement and deepening of an originally spurious but artifically promoted charisma attributed to the ruler.[64]

Loewenstein thus argues that "in earlier times" charisma had to be genuine to have lasting effects, and in modern times it is spurious and artificial. He argues, as does Bendix, that genuine charisma in modern times may be a rare event.

We would agree entirely with Loewenstein that the "genuine" charisma of the ancient (pre-Cartesian) world rarely exists in the modern era. We also have indicated that Weber was aware of the existence of spurious or, in his words, demagogic charisma (in the case of Kurt Eisner). Because of changes in the mass media, changes in social and political structures covered by politics, the distinctly modern form of charisma is spurious charisma.

While we call this modern form pseudocharisma, we recognize that genuine charisma may be possible in the modern world, but that the most frequent form of modern charisma is not charisma in the original Weberian sense of the term. When Bendix uses the phrase "the appearance of charisma," he properly suggests that much of modern charisma is not genuine.[65] Karl Loewenstein makes this point even more strongly:

> No one familiar with the mechanism of his [De Gaulle's] plebiscites will have much doubt that what zealous legend-builders may represent as charisma is actually the result of extremely skillful manipulation of propaganda techniques.[66]

Loewenstein goes on to argue that radio intensified the personal magnetism of Franklin D. Roosevelt because of the special quality of his voice and oratory. However, he argues that daily presentation of the would-be charismatic leader via mass media in an open society discenchants the public.[67]

Modern charisma imparts to social relations, to use Merton's term, a form of pseudo-*Gemeinschaft*[68] which, by the very nature of the media and the social order that frame it, makes genuine *Gemeinschaft* impossible. Charismatic leadership in the classic sense of the term meant direct, immediate social relations; it was not conveyed by indirect, mediating, or intervening agencies.

Thus charisma as used in the modern, undifferentiated sense of the term takes for granted the existence of a large-scale mass society and psychological distances that are both created and appear to be overcome by highly organized networks of communication and by social and economic organizations which themselves are part of the very structure of mass bureaucratic societies.

David Apter, in his study of political leadership in Ghana,[69] attempts to retain the notion of personal leadership by suggesting a two-stage process of leadership. Thus Nkrumah as a political leader had a small personal cult of followers, who, Apter, claims, stood between him and a mass following. The entire study suggests the use of conscious cultivation of an image of personality by Nkrumah and his staff. Stuart Schram[70] similarly suggests the conscious manipulation of a cult of personality in the creation of Mao as a charismatic leader.

Robert Tucker[71] presents a convincing image of Lenin as a powerful personality, but does not inquire into the mechanics or techniques by which Lenin achieved his effects. Richard Fagan[72] advances Fidel Castro as a charismatic hero, but again does not inquire into the mechanics, the media and stage effects by which such results are achieved. Ann Ruth and Dorothy Willner[73] detail some of the psychological and personal methods used by modern charismatic political figures, but do not emphasize the organizational and media devices.

Charisma adds a veneer of personality to the impersonal relations that govern urban, market, bureaucratic and mass technological societies. To the extent that such a veneer is the result of planned, rationally calculated programs, and to the extent that such a veneer is what is vulgarly referred to as charisma, the personal elements projected in modern charisma may be viewed as fraudulent. The concept of genuine charisma, as used by Weber, referred to actual personal relationships between a leader and his followers. The mass media substitute symbolic social relationships for actual ones.[74] To the extent that the evocation of charisma is the result of rational calculation, and that planning may create the image of a warm, sincere, emotional or "genuine" personality, it violates the original criterion that charisma is irrational or nonrational.

Every study of modern charisma but two suggests the rational planning and calculation of the appearance of charisma. These two exceptions are Fagan's and Tucker's, which, as we have indicated, do not inquire into the central issue. The case of Nkrumah is especially enlightening. Some theorists (e.g., Apter) argue that Nkrumah was a charismatic leader who lost his charisma when he tried to shift to parliamentary tactics. Others argue that Nkrumah was a genuine charismatic leader who simply lost his charisma, and still others (like Runciman[75]) claim that Nkrumah never had genuine charisma. Charisma would seem, according to Runciman, to reside in Nkrumah's political party, not in Nkrumah.

Apter, as we have indicated, provides sufficient data in his own study to demonstrate the rationality, impersonality, and institutionalized aspects of Nkrumah's regime. He also provides evidence that Nkrumah was personally appealing and popular, and that some followers might have regarded him with the awe and reverence that might have led to his characterization as a charismatic leader. Once it is clear that modern charisma is not necessarily genuine or pure charisma, in Weber's sense of the term, then these contradictions disappear. Nkrumah achieved the *effects* of charisma partly by rationally calculated means. He succeeded in some cases in creating a charismatic response, while simultaneously achieving mere popularity and negative responses. The fact that he was not successful in maintaining his charisma may be due less to the failure of charisma than to the failure of his policies, his strategy, and his planning.

Modern charismatic leaders may rationally select irrational themes, motifs, and values to personify those themes and values and a sense of pseudo-*Gemeinschaft* to distant publics. The managers of large-scale political parties, bureaucracies, advertising and media agencies will often select an individual who seems peculiarly able to project the desirable qualities to a "target population." The selection of a leader who embodies these desired qualities is thus the result of rational decision making by formally rational bureaucratic or political staffs whose very existence precludes the spontaneous self-selective nature and self-discovery of charisma. In addition, the development of the qualities that project personality images through the mass media is a result of product planning, of rational and systematic media strategies, of political market research, and of the training of voice, gestures, drama, and make-up.[76]

The development of modern "scientific" politics includes the rational, planned search for a star, that is, a "charismatic" leader. Public-opinion research, audience testing, pretesting of issues, themes, symbols, and slogans for their salience and valence, and the ability of various potential charismatic leaders to embody or project the selected themes are by now standard political methodology.

Thus, to a large extent, the modern "charismatic" leader is given speech and dramatic lessons, is surrounded by elaborately planned ceremonies and rites. Parades are presented in settings that are likely to induce the sense of excitement or warmth, and emphasize personality. A sense of awe and mystery is evoked by the use of emblems and symbols—the swastika, the fasces, the red star, the hammer and sickle, the enlarged portrait. Some "charismatic" leaders will, after achieving a degree of prominence, demonstrate their larger-than-life humanity by showing themselves in carefully arranged situations to be human and personable. Others will emphasize the awe and mystery by maintaining distance and an attitude of formality toward their followers. Lighting, camera angles, makeup, distance, and camera focus as well as, at times, face-lifting and other cosmetic and illusion-producing stagecraft help to produce "charisma."

The procedures employed are no different from those used in the creation of movie, theatrical, or television stars. The image of the movie star is enhanced by public relations, press releases, planted personal anecdotes, managed television interviews, photographic posters. But a central characteristic of all these techniques is that they are planned and thus represent formal rationality. For our purpose, it matters little whether the modern charismatic leader makes himself over and thus uses himself as the medium for image projection, or that political planners select and use a leader for such purposes. The important element, as related to the concept of pure charisma, is that rational planning is involved rather than the direct imputation of supernatural power or the divine gift of grace by followers without the planned intervention of rational political managers and staff. In the Weberian sense, the pure charismatic leader does not worry about his image, for his image is, to him, his reality; and that reality is an attribute of God or of a power beyond himself. He need not calculate the effect of his imagery on his actions because the outcome of his actions is not the result of his own efforts but rather the effect of the power that possesses him. Failure is not the result of his conscious decision-making but of the effect of his failure to retain the power that possesses him.

Modern charisma, in addition, rests upon the conscious selection of themes, appeals, slogans, and imagery that is based upon the systematic study of audiences, target populations, constituencies, and strategic publics. Such planning of appeals may be a result of a political outlook which convinces a leader or leadership group that they possess knowledge of the secrets of political practice or the techniques of measuring the importance and range of political appeals. Theoretical rationality in the practice of political arts is a distinctly modern phenomenon, emerging with Machiavelli and achieving full application with the French Revolution and the study of the Revolution by Marx, early Marxists, and Lenin. American public relations and advertising based upon Freudian and behaviorist psychology give scientific rigor to such efforts, as does the science of public-opinion polling.[77]

This, of course, does not mean that charismatic leadership is equivalent to popularity. Even pseudocharisma attempts to produce an attitude of awe and wonder or extraordinariness. Some modern fascist political leaders, basing much of their theory on Marxian teaching, carried out the rational exploration of irrationality to previously unheard-of limits. But by now the principles of the employment of personality and pseudo-*Gemeinschaft* in politics are so general that it is extremely difficult to conceive of a modern political or social movement, democratic or totalitarian, without a "charismatic leader" to personify it.

Not all political leaders are charismatic or even attempt to present charismatic images (excluding, of course, the charisma of office). The decision to attempt to project a charismatic image by a political leader may rest on his or his staff's estimate of the leader's personal resources, his potential following, other resources, his milieu, or the political situation.

In the underdeveloped world, highly sophisticated, European-trained political leaders adopt the masks of charismatic leadership in order to create a national consciousness among a populace that under colonial administration had been fragmented by localism, tribalism, and the absence of a tradition of citizenship and a viable public opinion or of a national political or moral community. Such charisma becomes a device by which the charismatic leader attempts not only to construct the idea of a nation for his followers but also a national bureaucracy and state machinery as well as the foundations for a political tradition and a nationwide public opinion. Thus the appearance of charisma is often a screen for the construction of national political forms used by leaders who often have to create the appearance of irrationality in societies where personal, irrational forms and symbols are the only meaningful styles of communication.[78]

This, however, is not too different from what takes place in advanced Western societies in which, from time to time, the response to impersonality, rationality, incomprehensibility, and crises force national political leaders to adopt various styles of irrationality as a screen behind which highly sophisticated, rational political programs are presented.

In modern bureaucratic government and politics, an image of charisma may be evoked—using all the aforementioned techniques—in which the images of bureaucratic impersonality, dehumanization, economic exploitation, political corruption, etc., are raised as counterimages to justify a claim to power by a reformer or aspirant to power. In such cases, the reformer may project all the characteristics of personality, of anti-institutionalism or radicalism; but the reformer aspires to a position in the establishment, and usually seeks it by using the established machinery of election or selection. He does so with a political or elective apparatus that is part of the on-going institutional machinery of the society. Beyond this, such evocations of charisma are usually rationally planned and calculated, despite the appearance of spontaneity and personality that is projected as the manifest content of the political message.

Finally, such reformers usually do not seek to reconstitute radically the political order or even the bases for legitimacy of a political order. They usually seek to restore, reform, or implement the original institutional or normative forms of an established order.

Nevertheless, many, if not most, reform movements attempt to use charismatic leaders, persons who symbolize youth, honesty, energy, and incorruptibility as counterimages to the political machines they seek to destroy, reform, or replace.

The employment of such charismatic leadership by political and bureaucratic organizations implies another contradiction between the concept of pure charisma and the reality of modern charismatic leadership. As indicated, pure charisma is revolutionary in its political stance. Modern rational charisma becomes a set of techniques and devices used by rational leaders and planners to both transcend and to veil the use of rationality in political action. Charisma in such a context means the use of selected techniques regardless of ultimate goals or political values. Modern charismatic leadership can be revolutionary or nonrevolutionary. It can be instrumental to liberal, conservative, or reactionary traditions and goals. Modern charisma is no longer connected to the original radical, deinstitutionalizing forces attributed to it by Weber.

Another key issue, in the contemporary application of the concept of charisma to modern society, is the conditions under which charisma may arise. Blau has argued that Weber did not adequately specify the conditions under which charisma occurs. He states that Weber's theory of charisma

> . . . encompasses only the historical processes that lead from charismatic movements to increasing rationalization and does not include an analysis of the historical conditions that give rise to charismatic eruptions in the social structure.[79]

This argument has been repeated by a number of scholars. David Apter cites the following conditions under which charisma develops:

> It is likely to arise where there exists an attenuated normative situation which, although it may not challenge pre-existing norms directly, allows new combinations, where behavioral situations show a more random basis for the selection of normative alternatives than is presupposed by an institutionalized acceptance of any one particular set, traditional or modern.[80]

Weber made essentially the same point when he argued that charisma arises in times of crisis:

> . . . the "natural" leaders—in times of psychic, physical, economic, ethical, religious, political distress—have been neither office holders nor incumbents of an "occupation" in the present sense of the word, that is, men who have acquired expert knowledge and who serve for remuneration. The natural leaders in distress have been holders of specific gifts of the body and spirit; and these gifts have been believed to be supernatural, not accessible to everybody. The concept of the "charisma" is here used in a completely "value-neutral" sense.[81]

CONCLUSIONS

We have sought to demonstrate that the concept of charismatic leadership as developed by Weber is of little use to the analysis of modern political and social movements. This is not because the modern movements are secular and the older ones were religious. The Weberian concept was originally applied to highly personal social movements that were not only personal but were revolutionary and irrational. The modern world, at least at the political level, is based upon political machinery that is geared to mass-scale operation. Impersonality, formal rationality, and bureaucracy are central to the very operation of contemporary society. The scale of mass politics involves the participation in politics by millions. These millions are not always socialized to stable political traditions and to institutions which have become routinized and legalized. The very size, impersonality, and fragility of mass society produces crises and stresses that can be exploited on a mass scale by means of the rational use of the forms and styles of irrationality by leaders who are rational, at least in their decision to employ such devices of irrationality. This is a possibility that Weber did not fully foresee. Weber saw mass democracy only as related to the occasional irrationality of coffeehouse intellectuals and the quest for irrational experience by youth who could not cope with the extremes of rationality, impersonality, and disenchantment that a fully rationalized image of the world entailed. He also saw, as indicated above, the use of pseudocharisma by reformers of caesaropapists and machine demagogues in mass-political democracies.[82]

But he did not foresee the systematic use of the appearances of charisma as a continuous, rationally calculated strategy by the staffs and agencies of bureaucratic and political machines and elites in large-scale mass bureaucratic societies.

In short, he failed to foresee the "rational" political movements based on the systematic exploitation of irrationality. He did, however, see that the quest for a deeper, meaningful, irrational, emotional and spiritual existence could lead to new forms of totalitarianism.

While Weber's original concept of pure charisma may not be applicable to most modern political movements, the recent correction of this deficiency in Weber's work may be even more inadequate, for treating charisma as a free-floating universal element or as purely personal or psychological attribute—almost as a form of dramatic presence—beclouds or minimizes the very contradictions between pure charisma and the modern world which make the original concept inadequate to the modern world.

It is the contradiction between the impersonality of social relations in the modern world and the use of images of personality that is central to the political processes of the modern world. Similarly, it is the rational exploitation of irrationality that has been a major theme in political and social movements in the modern world since the French Revolution and possibly even the earlier Counter-Reformation. Finally, it is increasingly true that modern establishments, regardless of their political orientation—right, center, or left, conservative, liberal, or radical—use revolutionary symbolism, slogans, and appeals whether or not the employment of such devices is aimed at radical social change. Thus a concept that focuses attention upon the tension between political means and ends, motives and practices is of particular usefulness in the analysis of modern political and social movements.

If the concept of pure charisma is irrelevant to the exploration of these tensions, the use of charisma as a personality trait avoids focusing on critical modern political processes. It also avoids focusing attention on those substantive issues, interests, ideologies, and interest and ideological groups, classes, and elites which are hidden or hide behind the personality screens of charisma. Treating charisma as a universal, and thus abstracting it from its particular historical, social, and economic context, diverts attention from the use of charisma as a screen for specific ideological or material interests by relevant interest groups. In addition, the reduction of particular historic forms to their alleged metaphysical essence automatically bestows a kind of universalism to those forms. Thus the fraudulent becomes the real, and the use of the concept can help to bestow legitimacy on groups that would claim power on the basis of their rational manipulation of symbols of charisma.

To avoid these reifications, we propose the term pseudocharisma in much the same manner that Merton has used pseudo-*Gemeinschaft*.[83] Pseudocharisma simply means the employment of the means, the imagery, the appearance of charismatic leadership as a rational device by which rationally calculating leadership groups attempt to achieve or maintain power. A major strategy is the selection or creation of a leader who appears to possess the forms and styles of an extraordinary man. Such selection and assumptions, however, are rationally induced. Appeals are made to ultimate and irrational values which the leader purportedly symbolizes. But the leader, in addition, conveys or is made to appear to convey a direct, personal contact that transcends the distance between himself and his followers. The concept of pseudocharisma suggests that charisma is a series of devices that serve other goals, purposes, and interests. In pointing out the manufactured appearances in pseudocharisma, the concept focuses upon the motives, the interests, the rationality or irrationality that may lie behind these devices and underscores the extent to which the symbols and images are consciously fabricated. It would focus then on the means of fabrication as well as the ends for which they are fabricated.

The focus on the fabrication of charisma as a means of concealing or obscuring other, hidden ends by an interest group would lead to—in fact, force—the analyst to consider the nature of the underlying interests, goals and ends that are the latent content of the pseudocharismatic message. It would necessitate the probing into the relationship between various levels of meanings, latent and manifest, and motivations contained in modern pseudocharismatic leadership. It would entail the analysis of the policy implications of messages that apparently have little direct relevance to policy.

Such a program would not necessarily preclude the possibility that pure charisma might exist. But one can only establish whether in fact pure charisma does exist by inquiring into the means and the intentions that govern the attribution of charisma by followers, leaders, sponsors, and supporters. Beyond this, the explanation of the indicated ends and means would allow one to ascertain the specific content of pseudocharismatic leadership movements at specific times and places and their relationships to ongoing historical social structures.

Nor would such a program preclude the possibility that genuine or spurious charismatic leaders are capable of inducing a sense of awe and reverence in a given population. But when this occurs, the research would focus upon more than the aforementioned techniques of evocation of charisma. It would focus upon what are the qualities of followers who attribute charisma to a real or pseudocharismatic leader; what are their class and status positions; what sense of crises, tensions, alienation do they respond to; what specific social, economic, or political conditions give rise to charisma both as leadership and response? What aspects of a charismatic message are salient and attractive? Finally, what specific needs does charisma meet among those who accept specific charismatic leadership?

All of these questions are, of course, traditional Weberian questions, as they are traditional questions in political sociology and political science.[84]

4

Charisma and Illegitimate Authority

RICHARD S. BELL

During the last decade the "problem of authority" or "crisis of authority" has reemerged as one of the major preoccupations among intellectuals in this country. There are at least two aspects to this preoccupation which are striking. First, it is occurring during a period of relative quiescence. Second, it appears to be inclusive of virtually the entire political spectrum. Traditionally, it was thought that concern for the authoritative status of the received verities was the special dispensation of conservative thinkers. Today this dispensation is shared by intellectuals of both the right and the left.[1]

Richard Sennett, a sociologist avowedly of the left, argues that though it is necessary, in the interest of preserving our sanity, to reject "the childish collages of strength and compassion which the authorities present as pictures of themselves," it is nonetheless at least as equally necessary to devise alternative conceptions of authority not predicated upon fantasies of wish-fulfillment and guilt.[2] Sennett argues that because Weber "identifies authority with legitimacy," however, the Weberian perspective is incapable of comprehending the phenomenon of "illegitimate authority" as a salient feature of contemporary institutional life, and opts for Freudianism instead.

I will argue, rather, that Weber's discussion of charisma alone can be seen as a fairly elaborate presentation of illegitimate authority, and one that has the singular advantage of not requiring nearly as many assumptions concerning human psychology as are required by following Sennett in adopting a modified Freudian approach.

It would seem, upon immediate inspection, that nothing could be easier than establishing a link between charisma and illegitimate authority in Weberian terms. As Bensman and Givant have pointed out, the notion of delegitimation forms the very cornerstone of Weber's discussion of "pure" charisma. This does not entirely meet Sennett's challenge, however, because revolutionary, pure charisma stands outside of established institutional life. The type of authority structure we are concerned with, by contrast, is one which derives its authority from its lack of legitimacy and its assault upon it while *simultaneously* being thoroughly embedded within established institutional boundaries.

Yet, as Bensman and Givant also note, Weber did not confine himself to one type of charisma. There were, for example, heroic ecstasy, warrior charisma, the charisma of the hunt, office charisma, and the charisma of the political hero.[3] I wish to focus upon this last type. Just as Weber distinguishes between pure charisma and its attenuated version in the form of political heroism, so we may distinguish between the revolutionary illegitimacy of pure charisma and what I term the institutionalized, or extra-legal, illegitimacy of the the late twentieth-century political hero.

CLASSICAL CHARISMA AND REVOLUTIONARY ILLEGITIMACY

It is doubtless the case that it is in pure or "classical" charismatic authority that we see authority *de facto* most clearly exemplified in the strict sense.[4] It would be an undue simplification of Weber's treatment of classical delegitimizing charismatic authority, however, to confine charisma to this one personalistic dimension. This would, indeed, be more appropriate for a consideration of modern charismatic heroism. In dealing with classical charisma, we must employ an expanded version of authority *de facto*, which can be derived from Weber's notion of substantive value rationality.[5] Before addressing ourselves to this problem, it is necessary to list some of the salient features of classical charisma.[6]

1. The charismatic leader, in absolute opposition to bureaucratic leadership, which is typically delegated, is self-ordained and "self-styled." This type of leader defines his or her destiny, and demands of others that such a destiny be acknowledged.
2. The authority of classical charisma is derived from the *duty* of the followers to recognize the leader, once such a destiny is acknowledged.
3. The self-determined nature of pure charisma precludes any form of rationally methodical economic acquisition. Weber observes that "pure charisma is opposed to all economic activities; in fact, it is *the* strongest anti-economic force, even when it is after material possessions, as in the case of the 'charismatic warrior.' "
4. Corresponding to this anti-economic bias, the very nature of charismatic authority is inherently unstable, because the leader is in a continuous process of self-proof.

It is clear that this very serious meaning of genuine charisma is radically different from the convenient pretensions of the present "divine right of kings," which harks back to the "inscrutable" will of the Lord, "to whom alone the monarch is responsible." The very opposite is true of the genuinely charismatic ruler who is responsible to the ruled—responsible, that is, to prove that he himself is indeed the master willed by God.

This does not, of course, render such rulership democratic. According to Weber, democracy refers to a set of external arrangements, usually an array of procedures, whereas classical charismatic authority is "qualitatively delimited from within."

5. Because pure charisma involves more than merely acknowledgment, but rather complete surrender on the part of the disciple, it must by its very nature be revolutionary or, at the very least, potentially subversive. This is due to the fact that pure charisma cannot recognize any competing claim, including that of the state, as legitimate.

Such a revolutionary or subversive monopoly on legitimacy follows from the very logic of this type of authority. Obviously, if competing claims are acknowledged by the followers, then a state of surrender has not been attained, and it is therefore doubtful that one could speak of this type of authority as being thoroughly charismatic. "Because of this mode of legitimation genuine charismatic domination knows no abstract laws and regulations and no formal adjudication."

It is easy to see why this extraordinary personalistic foundation to charismatic authority must, practically by definition, constitute a threat to the state or any pre-existing legal structure, no matter how sublime, gentle, or pacific the doctrine taught by the master may be. "Genuine charismatic justice does not refer to rules; in its pure type it is the most extreme contrast to formal and traditional prescription and maintains its autonomy toward the sacredness of tradition as much as toward rationalist deductions from abstract norms."

6. It follows that the nature of the charismatic revolution is always characterized by great pathos. Bureaucratic rationalization revolutionizes human beings by transforming their external conditions. "Charismatic belief revolutionizes men 'from within' and shapes material and social conditions to its revolutionary will."

7. On the basis of points 5 and 6, we can state that a—if not *the*—defining characteristic of classical charismatic leadership is that the followers constitute a genuine discipleship in which submission is inspired by the extraordinary qualities of a specific individual. This discipleship is subsequently transformed once charismatic authority undergoes routinization and its revolution is externalized. "The ruler's disciples, apostles, and followers become priests, feudal vassals, and, above all, officials."[7]

8. Of particular importance for our concerns is that the charismatic leader points to some "outside or beyond." This reference to the outside is at once delegitimizing and at the same time suggests either the emergence of a new constellation of values or a drastic reformulation of a preexisting one.

"The bearer of charisma enjoys loyalty and authority by virtue of a mission believed to be embodied in him; this mission has not necessarily and not always been revolutionary, but in its most characteristic forms it has inverted all value hierarchies and overthrown custom, law, and tradition."

Even bearers of charisma must somehow render themselves comprehensible to real people, and they must do so in terms already in use by people. Charismatic authority can be seen as a "Divine mission," as Weber points out, only where "the idea of God has already been established." Regardless of how self-determined classical charisma may be, that self-determination is invariably modified through the limits imposed by the specific group to which the leader's mission is directed. It would seem, therefore, that the demands of the mission and the requirements of comprehensibility alone place the bearer of charisma in the context of some pre-established valuational system.

When considering these eight features of classical charisma—particularly 3, 6, 7, and 8—it becomes readily understandable why this type of authority is largely pre-modern. Unmediated, personal rule and submission in the form of a discipleship are phenomena we normally associate with ancient and traditional cultures.

This type of rulership also constitutes a striking example of how authority *de facto* can operate. On the one hand, classical charismatic authority is overwhelmingly personalistic. There is no question regarding the location of its "author." On the other hand, charismatic leadership, once it is fully developed, reflects or embodies some theory of power and of the world—a theory which may or may not be radically innovative.

In other words, charismatic authority in its pure form involves an unusually successful intermingling of subjectivistic and objectivistic dimensions. Although this is not made explicit by Weber, it is reasonable to hypothesize that both dimensions are linked by a conception of the leader's mission. It is this that provides the foundation for the belief that one has a duty to acknowledge the leader's charisma. The important point to underscore here is that classical charisma is fundamentally complex, much more so than modern variants.

THE LEGITIMIZING POLITICAL HERO

Due to certain elective affinities between the "two basically antagonistic forces" of classical charismatic authority and traditional authority, it is understandable that once the routinization of charisma set in it did so along traditionalist lines.[8] Thus, with the irony so common to Weber's sociology, that which was once synonymous with revolution becomes transformed into the very essence of legitimacy itself.[9]

Within the rationalizing context of market economies and democratic suffrage, however, there emerged a new form of charismatic legitimation, albeit one that is much weaker, whose origins were not initially revolutionary —that of the "political hero." In his insightful discussion of George Washington and "the whig conception of heroic leadership," Barry Schwartz defines heroic leadership as "a form of domination which evokes strong reverential sentiment in the context of fateful enterprises, campaigns, and movements."[10] The hero "is not any leader who is revered because of the authority or the personal qualities he possesses, but one who uses these attributes to mobilize people for strenuous efforts to change or maintain existing cultural values and institutional structures." Again dual aspects of authority *de facto* are displayed. The leader employs personal attributes in an effort to "change or maintain existing cultural values and institutional structures," and is thus linked to a preexisting constellation of values which forms a part of the "strong reverential sentiment" so evoked.

There is, nevertheless, one very important provision which qualitatively separates the political hero from the classical charismatic leader. After reflecting upon the almost excruciatingly *un*charismatic quality of George Washington's personal attributes and the fact that he was an object of veneration in the anti-authoritarian culture of eighteenth-century America, Schwartz offers the following observation: "Hero worship entails not the recognition of greatness but the transformation, by social definition, of the ordinary into the heroic. If we are to understand this transformation, we must place it in proper context." Thus statements about the hero "must be matched by statements about the central needs and concerns of his society."

An important distinguishing characteristic of these two authority types, classical charisma and political heroism, then, is that with the former, authority is a matter of recognition, but with the latter, of transformation—*from without*. The personalistic dimension of political heroism is much more decidedly dependent upon general public perceptions and general public needs (or upon those who organize and articulate them) than is that of the pure charismatic leader for the very obvious reason that the personal qualities of the hero are, in and of themselves, "ordinary." We shall return to this point when we deal with the problem of pseudocharisma and manufactured charisma.

Schwartz contends, in a manner unfortunately reminiscent of Sennett, that Weber's discusison of charisma offers little or no utility for an understanding of modern political heroism. He is able to argue this by making the common mistake of thinking that Weber collapsed all forms of charisma under the rubric of pure charisma: "Max Weber's conception of charismatic leadership deals with only one type of heroic leadership—the great men whom Weber considers are dedicated exclusively to radical change. . . ." If this is so, one wonders why Weber insisted upon using the qualifying words "pure" or "revolutionary."

Schwartz also contends that although Weber did not ignore the social context, nonetheless "the personal virtuosity of the leader is the central and prior element in Weber's formulation. Emerging in the midst of structural conflict and psychological ambiguity, the charismatic leader satisfies the need for a new order by exercising extraordinary personal power." This is true, but once again it is true only of pure or revolutionary charisma.

Finally, Schwartz maintains that because "Weber's leader is also an authoritarian leader," his theory can contribute nothing to an understanding of "the American struggle for independence"—the inference being that "Weber's leader" contributes nothing to understanding democratic struggles in general. Yet Weber was able to write that "charisma is not alien to all modern, including all democratic, forms of election. Certainly the democratic system of so-called plebiscitarian rulership—the official theory of French Caesarism—has essentially charismatic features, and the arguments of its proponents all emphasize this very quality.[11]

Indeed, it is this observation that forms the basis for Weber's conception of the political hero. Central to this conception is the antagonism between the hero as plebiscitary leader and the party organization. Weber writes: "All attempts at subordinating the representative to the will of the voters have in the long run only one effect: they reinforce the ascendancy of the party organization over him which alone can mobilize the people."[12]

I would argue, contrary to Schwartz, that Weber definitely possessed a conception of political heroism and that, though it is not an intrinsically democratic force, it plays a prominent role in democratic politics. Second, I would argue that Weber was obviously very aware of the social context within which political heroism emerged and by which it was limited. Weber was able to do this because he was never confined to a single type or subtype of charismatic authority to begin with.

The following features of modern legitimizing political heroism form the necessary contrast to that of classical charisma:[13]

1. Far from being self-ordained, the political hero is almost exclusively the product of party politics, i.e., of candidate selection and "electoral agitation through personal influence and appeal to material and ideal interests." This agitation requires extensive organizational and financial backing. It is this backing which, more than likely, does the ordaining.

2. If the hero is to prevail in the politics of mass society, it is mandatory that the hero's support organization engage in some form of methodical acquisition. Hence the ongoing tension between the political hero and the party organization which, left on its own, tends toward greater and greater bureaucratization. "The more bureaucratization advances and the more substantial the interests in benefices and other opportunities become, the more surely does the party organization fall into the hands of experts, whether these appear immediately as party officials or at first as independent entrepreneurs—witness the American boss."

3 and 4. As in the case of pre-modern charisma, political heroism must prove itself on a fairly regular basis. One might therefore suppose that a

claim can be made that success implies a duty to follow. This claim, however, simply may not be acknowledged by the electorate. An instructive example of this can be found in Churchill's defeat during the British general election of 1945.[14] Clearly we are dealing here with notions of "duty" and "mastery" that are considerably less riveting than those associated with pre-modern charisma.

5. Perhaps nothing less characterizes political heroism, at least in the liberal democracies, than the notion of complete surrender on the part of a followership. Indeed, for Weber the *struggle* between the hero and the ever intransigent party organization was central to his conception of political heroism:

> Since all emotional mass appeals have certain charismatic features, the bureaucratization of the parties and of electioneering may at its very height suddenly be forced into the service of charismatic hero worship. In this case a conflict arises between the charismatic hero principle and the mundane power of the party organization, as Roosevelt's [1912] campaign demonstrated.

Elsewhere, Weber continues to underscore this conflict, again citing Theodore Roosevelt's campaign of 1912:

> If there is a "hero," he will endeavor to break the technician's hold over the party by imposing plebiscitary designation and possibly by changing the whole machinery of nomination. Such an eruption of charisma, of course, always faces the resistance of the normally predominant pros, especially of the bosses who control and finance the party and maintain its routine operations, whose tools the candidates usually are.

If Weber is correct and this struggle is a central and logically defining characteristic of political heroism, then it is unlikely, if not impossible, that acknowledgment of the hero's status will be accompanied by a corresponding relinquishment of competing claims required for a revolutionary followership. We might add that this would be the case *regardless* of whether the rhetoric adopted by the hero were revolutionary or not.

6. Correspondingly, the changes effected by the political hero cannot be "qualitatively delimited from within" except in the most transitory sense. This is a function of the organizational requirements for political pre-eminence, the externalities of democratic procedures, and the process of candidate selection. "For not only the material interests of the job hunters depend on the selection of the party's candidates, but very much also those of the party sponsors—banks, contractors, and trusts."

7. On the basis of features 5 and 6, it is extremely unlikely to suppose that the political hero could generate a true discipleship, although a following which resembles it may surface. Schwartz notes, for example, that Washington was the object of cult worship, and Weber himself spoke of "hero worship" as an aspect of party struggle.[15] A cult, however, is a sig-

nificantly less structured type of organized veneration than is a discipleship. Perhaps we may hypothesize that the best a political hero can aspire to is to become an object of cult adoration.

8. Like the classical charismatic leader, the legitimizing political hero traditionally had to personify some substantive value system, some legitimizing theory of power and of the world. The hero had to be seen as linked to intensely felt normative claims about the integral nature of social life in order to be the recipient of genuine veneration. This was the case regardless of the fact that the hero's personifications were virtual rather than actual.

Yet Weber suggests that under distinctively modern conditions, the "charisma of rhetoric" becomes almost co-equal with the "power of money" in gaining decisive influence over the mass politics of "democratic electioneering." In other words, once a certain point is reached in the rationalization of political life, the hero is no longer obliged to embody anything of substance or to be linked to a set of normative claims that is even remotely coherent:

> The more mass effects are intended and the tighter the bureaucratic organization of the parties becomes, the less significant is the content of the rhetoric. For its effect is purely emotional, insofar as simple class situations and other economic interests do not prevail which may be rationally calculated and manipulated. The rhetoric has the same meaning as the street parades and festivals: to imbue the masses with the notion of the party's power and confidence in victory and, above all, to convince them of the leader's charismatic qualification.

The charisma of rhetoric thus displaces completely the "mission" of the classical charismatic leader and those remnants which still hold together a more complex style of leadership are thereby dissolved. In this fashion we move insensibly from the legitimizing charisma of political heroism to the emotivist politics of extra-legal charisma.

DELEGITIMIZING POLITICAL HEROISM

We may state that there are two quite fundamental and defining characteristics of the political hero. First, the political hero possesses attributes that are pedestrian, and in order for the hero to become an object of veneration these attributes must be transformed. Second, the political hero operates *within* the prevailing institutional and power arrangements.

Thus far we have been considering the political hero whose created attributes are perceived to embody a legitimizing theory of power and authority. In this section we consider the obverse—the political hero operating within the prevailing institutional boundaries whose transformed charismatic attributes are delegitimizing or are perceived to be illegitimate.

I have adopted the term "extra-legal" to designate this type of charismatic hero simply as an endeavor to avoid confusion. Both extra-legal charismatic heroism and classical charismatic leadership are delegitimizing. However, in the case of classical charisma the delegitimation is revolutionary, and the extraordinary attributes which personify the revolutionary mission of the master are his own. In the case of extra-legal charisma the delegitimation involved is never revolutionary nor is it particularly radical. This type of heroism, rather, derives its authority from a charisma of rhetoric which is overtly hostile to the legal structures of the administrative state but has neither the intention nor the capacity to displace them.

Extra-legal charismatic authority therefore designates a species of nonrevolutionary delegitimation and nothing more. It is the type of delegitimation that is most congenial to the emotivist politics of bureaucratic individualism.

There are at least two senses in which we may speak of this authority type as illegitimate. First, it is—strictly speaking—fraudulent. The claim made for a leader's charismatic status is, in the last analysis, predicated upon fabrication. These fabrications are often designed to conceal the real interests of dominating elites. The personal characteristics alleged to be those of the leader are employed in much the same way as is the legitmizing phraseology of emotivist interaction. This is simply another dimension of bureaucratic individualism. Second, this type of charismatic heroism can be seen as illegitimate because it derives its authority from having successfully conveyed the impression that it is unencumbered by substantive claims or any theoretic criteria of authority and by the understanding that such criteria are utilized solely for other-than-stated purposes. This may be extended to produce an atmosphere of latent danger which often proves for many to be an all but irresistible source of attraction. It is in this second sense of illegitimacy that bureaucratic individualism comes to understand and appreciate itself.

As Glassman notes, charisma ought to be seen as nontransferable only in a technical sense. As the size of political dominion was enlarged and succession struggles became ever more virulent, hereditary charisma became, correspondingly, a matter of stage management in which every conceivable prop was used. The entire process appears to be cyclical: a crisis or series of crises precipitates the reemergence of a natural charismatic rebellion that "dereifies" the established manufactured charisma. Once this has occurred, the new charisma is ultimately hollowed out and reduced to a set of dramaturgical techniques. Subsequent would-be charismatic movements then become objects of repression, and the cycle begins anew.

The important question here centers around belief: To what degree was it necessary for the traditional elites who engineered the manufacture of charisma to adopt a fundamentally Machiavellian conception of their own behavior? It was Machiavelli, after all, who underscored the importance of irrationalist components to legitimacy as well as the subsidiary importance of manipulating appearance. Glassman suggests that this level of sophisticated, or perhaps disillusioned, self-consciousness was required only to a very limited degree.

This leads to another, related question: Is this lack of self-consciousness available to the leadership class and to the political heroes they create in the era of the modern administrative state where the process of manufacturing charisma has become thoroughly rationalized? This is another way of asking whether the charismatic authority of the *modern* political hero can possess legitimacy in the eyes of its fabricators.

The most reasonable answer to this question is that, given the intrinsically disenchanting nature of rationalizing techniques, we may suppose that the perception of legitimacy must be quite weak as compared to that of the premodern elites discussed by Glassman. Indeed we may posit this as perhaps the central dilemma confronting the late twentieth-century political hero: How can an enchanted species of authority, charisma, be regarded as legitimate when it is manufactured by processes that are overtly disenchanting? Given the ubiquity of these processes in the realm of mass communication, it is hardly surprising that illegitimate authority has become a salient feature of contemporary institutional life; nor should it be surprising that it has become so for largely Weberian reasons, as Bensman and Givant elaborate in their discussion of *pseudocharisma.*

This argument parallels Weber's discussion of the dilution of the objectivistic dimension of charismatic authority. For Weber, once the preoccupation with mass manipulation and the organizational control of the party reaches a certain point, the classic mission of the leader degenerates into the charisma of rhetoric. This rhetoric is largely contentless, dissembling, and avowedly emotivist. Correspondingly, the subjectivistic or personalistic dimension of charisma is displaced by second and third order mediating agencies which transform the absolute self-assuredness of the classical leader into the painfully self-conscious "imagery" of the modern hero.

In both instances charismatic authority is profoundly simplified, but only at the expense of having rather drastically undermined these two legitimizing dimensions. This is virtually the inevitable consequence of manufacturing charisma through the instrumentalities of rational calculation.

That the type of charisma in question *must* be manufactured is a direct function of the fact that the hero's initial attributes are, by and large, ordinary. These attributes are transformed "from without." Yet in mass industrialized societies this transformation can only be devised and successfully projected with the aid of rational planning and extensive bureaucratic organization. Thus if charismatic delegitimation is the all but inevitable consequence of rational calculation, this calculation is, in turn, the all but inescapable requirement for the successful attainment of heroic status in the era of the administrative state.

Thus far we have been dealing with illegitimate charismatic heroism in terms of the manner in which it is generated. We can conclude by reconsidering illegitimate authority in terms of what it actually conveys, only now as delegitimizing heroism.

Max Weber regarded the charisma of rhetoric as conveying little or nothing. Bensman and Givant argue, in effect, that this is not quite the case. They suggest that there is an elective affinity between pseudocharisma and anti-institutional reformism. Although such counterimages as bureaucratic impersonality, dehumanization, economic exploitation, or political corruption make up a goodly portion of the political hero's rhetorical charisma in modern bureaucratic politics, this style of charisma is not, in the last analysis, anti-establishmentarian. The political hero continues to operate within the ongoing political or electoral system of the society.

Hence the extra-legal character of this authority type is manifested. Extra-legality, furthermore, as a technique in the hero's repertoire is by no means confined to the politics of the left; rather, it cuts horizontally across the entire political spectrum. Indeed, an excellent case can be made that extra-legal charismatic authority has recently received its most accomplished expression in the politics of the right.

In the case of the delegitimizing charisma of extra-legal heroism, the anti-institutionalist counterimagery is not confined merely to slogans concerning end-states or goals. It also includes, though often only by implication, much the same orientation toward institutionalized means as well. It is for this reason that extra-legal authority conveys the aura of dangerousness, of serious—even desperate—risk-taking. One could indeed make the case that it is this aspect of extra-legal authority which accounts for its almost unfailing appeal from the Kennedy era up to the present.

This development has served as an object of some anxious concern on the part of a number of analysts of the American political scene. Sheldon Wolin, for example, worries that the American political system will eventually produce elites who have completely unburdened themselves of the need to acquire even so much as a semblance of accountability. Wolin explains this in terms of the emergence of a special kind of dependence and with it a special kind of demoralization.

> Dependence signifies the existence, first of a surplus population that must be managed, and, second, of a type of population that can be, as it were, expanded or contracted, depending upon the requirements of a relatively volatile and somewhat unmanageable economy. . . . Demoralization stands for living continuously and hopelessly in circumstances where one is assailed endlessly by forces one cannot understand, much less control, but that others seemingly do know about and do control.[16]

Illegitimacy and extra-legal charisma are, therefore, to be seen as the logical consequences attendant upon the creation of a vast hostage population. For such a population the very notion of accountability and its twin concept legitimacy must seem increasingly irrelevant, if not actually bizarre.

Samuel P. Huntington offers a fundamentally neoconservative construction upon the growing dominance of illegitimate authority. For Huntington, American political history consists of long stretches of complacency and hypocrisy informed by drab interest-group politics. These stretches are disrupted roughly once every sixty years by outbursts of enthusiasm which he designates "creedal passion periods." All such periods involve assaults upon authority in the name of an unsparing and purist interpretation of the "American Creed." The last such assault, referred to by Huntington as the "years of sixes and sevens," left the American authority structure, particularly the foreign policy establishment, seriously debilitated. This then paved the way for the election of one of the most pronounced anti-Washingtonians, Ronald Reagan.[17] We are being told, in other words, that the youth movements of the 1960s and 1970s are to blame for the victorious New Right of the 1980s. In contrast to the position being offered here, however, Huntington does not see the breakdown of authority as the loss of evaluative criteria upon which a rationally autonomous life may be predicated. Instead, he sees it as a generalized failure to sustain the long-term imperatives required by a superpower in carrying out its world affairs.

A very different commentary is provided by both Robert Bellah and John Diggins, who tend to see the emergence of delegitimizing political heroism in terms of the extirpation of the Puritan heritage. For Bellah this receives its quintessential expression in Watergate and its immediate aftermath. In describing the political atmosphere of that period, Bellah touches upon the secret appeal of extra-legal charisma: "A sense that the basic institutions of society are unjust and serve the interests of a few at the expense of the many, is used to justify the inapplicability of moral obligations to one's self." There is "an admiration of the few who have manipulated the system in their own favor, and a desire to emulate them, if not in actuality, then in fantasy. . . ."[18] For Diggins delegitimation is the end consequence of the historic triumph of Madisonian egoism over Puritanical communitarianism in American political culture. "The doctrine of total depravity was effectively harnessed to the Enlightenment conception of harmony as the mutual cancellation of egoistic drives to produce an ethic overwhelmingly hostile to the collective demands of any commonwealth."[19] It is also an ethic that is profoundly conducive to a conception of the political hero as a master of anti-institutionalist and even anti-social counterimagery.

Each of these approaches can account for delegitimizing charismatic heroism in a manner that is more or less compatible with a Weberian framework. With the exception of Huntington's, each of these approaches can also be made congruent with Alasdair MacIntyre's discussion of "emotivist" culture and its ethos of bureaucratic individualism.[20] MacIntyre's formulations, however, have the advantage of being applicable to the modern administrative state in general and not just to the American political scene. We can now sketch the relationship between bureaucratic individualism and the anti-institutionalist message of contemporary rhetorical charisma.

The source of bureaucratic expertise and of technocratic rationality in general is to be found in the drive for power. This irrationalist foundation to modern bureaucratic management induces crises of authority because it divests this species of domination of its legitimacy. Why, after all, should a drive for power which is expressed in the prevailing political, cultural, and economic arrangements be accorded greater moral precedence than a corresponding drive to displace those arrangements?

Because this question cannot be answered and because this is generally sensed by a periodically disaffected populace, modern organizations will continue to experience occasional challenges to their always doubtful authority. MacIntyre contends, in effect, that questions concerning moral precedence or authority cannot be answered in a culture such as ours in which bureaucratic individualism attains its final consequence by reducing all evaluative utterance to the status of mere means for the purpose of manipulating the emotions and prejudices of others.

Given the ubiquity of the organizational context, it is not, therefore, surprising that the most effective species of evaluative manipulation is at once anti-institutionalist *and* establishmentarian. In an emotivist culture one is never required to forgo access to the instrumentalities of power that establishments provide simply because these very establishments are felt to be and are believed to be utterly arbitrary.

CONCLUSION

Central to the notion of delegitimation is the concept of atheoretic authority in which substantive claims about the nature of the world are systematically displaced by the emotivist conception of evaluative discourse and by the attendant array of techniques designed to engineer feelings of acceptance and acquiescence. It is this engineering that has become the fully operationalized definition of contemporary authority. Indeed, so compatible is Weberian sociology for an understanding of this process that a case can be made that illegitimate authority ought to be seen as one consequence of the domination of formal rationality.

With respect to charismatic authority a distinction has to be made between revolutionary delegitimation and nonrevolutionary delegitimation, between that anti-institutionalist authority figure who challenges the established power arrangements or seeks to overthrow them and the institutionalist who seeks only to acquire them. This distinction is valid in Weberian terms because Weber distinguishes between the classical charismatic leader of the pre-modern world and the political hero who is largely the product of modern party struggles. The difficulty lies, on the one hand, in the fact that Weber was not nearly as clear as he could have been in drawing this distinction, while on the other hand, one must confront the persistent tendency on the part of some social scientists to assume that Weber confined his thinking to just one type of charismatic leadership.

A further difficulty centers around the problematic conception of an authority type whose core characteristic rests upon the influence of enchantment being manufactured through the rationalizing techniques of mass communications, techniques that are popularly acknowledged to be disenchanting. Such an anomaly can be at least partially resolved if this type of charismatic authority is taken out of the categorical realm and conceptualized in largely processualist terms. First, if one follows Schwartz's discussion, the features of any would-be political hero must be transformed, and then second, if this occurs for structural reasons through the rationalization process, this too is simply a part of delegitimation.

Finally, it should be reiterated that the entire issue of illegitimate authority carries with it certain normative implications with respect to the health of a polity. This is because legitimacy is janus-faced. It is employed on the one hand by ruling elites to universalize, and thus render obscure, their power and its exercise. Yet on the other hand, legitimacy can be seen as a kind of non-elitist critical theory that is not confined to academics but is available to an entire citizenry. The mere propagating of legitimizing rationales on the part of ruling elites helps ensure that this untoward aspect of legitimacy remains readily available to the majority of a citizenry. Yet legitimacy in the era of the modern administrative state has become exceedingly thin. It appears that it is sufficiently strong to provide a rationale for the prevailing distribution of wealth and power, while at the same time being wholly inadequate in providing a foundation either for genuine democratizing change or for self-reflective personal liberation. It is in this context that illegitimate authority must be assessed.[21]

PART II

Charisma and Religion

5

Charismatic Calvinism: Forging a Missing Link

WILLIAM H. SWATOS, JR.

Regardless of its overall effect on our understanding of Max Weber's work, there can be little doubt that the bulk of scholarly interest and criticism of his thought has focused on the essay collection known as *The Protestant Ethic and the Spirit of Capitalism.*[1] Recent scholarship has sought to bring increasing integrity to this topic and the debate that surrounds it. Gianfranco Poggi, in particular, has noted that the causal argument that Weber spins is foreshortened: the first step in the chain, Calvinist doctrine, is slighted. Weber begins from "the intervening term rather than with the religious ideas 'upstream' of it," from the ethic to the capitalist spirit without a thorough discussion of the underlying ideational context in which the ethic develops—perhaps assuming more mutual understanding between himself and his readers than time has borne out.[2] With respect to doctrinal points themselves, David Little provides careful documentation of Puritan ethics in Calvin's theology, and we can hope that confused and confusing challenges here have once and for all been put to rest.[3] S. N. Eisenstadt, furthermore, has recognized the importance of the Protestant Ethic as a charismatizing force in the breakthrough to modernity.[4]

Yet none of these, nor Weber's other critics or advocates, nor even Weber himself has made explicit a simple but essential point to the whole argument: *John Calvin exercised charismatic leadership.*[5] Perhaps because Calvinism as a theological system is so seemingly logical, cold, and humanly heartless—as emotionally fulfilling as double-entry bookkeeping—this elementary historical experience has avoided clear articulation. If Calvin is seen as a charismatic leader, however, and Calvinism in practice in his own time as a form of charismatic domination, then not only is a cloud of unknowing lifted with respect to *why* the Protestant Ethic had such impact upon Western social life, but in addition Weber's argument on the relationship of protestantism to capitalism becomes clearly integrated into his larger corpus.

I do not intend in these few pages to provide a detailed description of Calvin's life or work. Instead I wish to focus on a few elements of his time that lend credibility to my thesis. In particular, whereas charismatic domination constitutes a specific type of relationship between leader and followers, I want to contrast Calvinism and Lutheranism in their earliest years with respect to their religiosocial anthropology as it is reflected in Weber's essays. I also intend to draw source material primarily from a group of nineteenth-century essays written in America prior to Weber's work.[6]

We can begin with Weber's assertion that Lutheranism was "traditionalistic," while Calvinism paved the way toward modernity.[7] In this observation Weber grasps a whole series of biographical and theological statements. Luther was a priest who had served faithfully for a decade prior to the posting of the 95 Theses and continued for some time thereafter in a relatively filial relationship to the Church. Calvin was never priested. Luther began his "reformation" by proposing a series of arguments that primarily addressed specific practices within the Church. Calvin had a "divine call" to leave the Church. Regardless of the outcome, Luther's intent was to perfect the Catholic Church by removing specific objectionable accretions. Thus Luther told his sympathizer Justus Jonas, who much disliked having to teach canon law at Wittenburg, to help the students "unlearn what it taught."[8] Luther retained essential sacramental theology as well: Baptism conveying divine grace; Christ present "in, with and under" the Eucharistic elements; penance to mediate God's forgiveness to the sinner. His life exemplifies *virtuoso religiosity* which *contrasts with charisma.*[9] His ideal was to restore to the Church its biblical foundations and renew it as an instrument of God's grace freely given.

At one point, for example, Luther came across the work of Johan Wessel. He found the resemblance in their analyses striking and wrote: "Had I read Wessel's works before [putting forth my own ideas] my opponents would have said 'Luther has borrowed his ideas from Wessel,' so great is his resemblance. This greatly encourages and comforts me. . . . He agrees with me so perfectly in his feelings, in his views and even in his expressions."[10] The major disagreement between Luther and Erasmus for sociological attention is not their debate on the freedom of the will, but on whether more good could be accomplished by working within or without the church structure of the time. Erasmus the Catholic repeatedly had to defend himself from the label "Lutheran," a problem he never had with "Calvinist."[11] R. D. C. Robbins writes of the reformed churches prior to Calvinism:

> The Reformed Church established in Switzerland by Zuingle [Zwingli], was little known beyond that country. The Swiss, hemmed in by their own mountains, did not

seem anxious to disseminate their own views in other lands, and but for John Calvin, centuries might have glided away ere the little leaven that was at work there, had pervaded the surrounding countries. The first great battle of the Reformation had been fought, but a new leader and a new mode of attack were necessary. Luther's call was to pull down, to demolish, another must build up. The German Reformer by dwelling upon one article of the Christian scheme in opposition to the abuses of Rome, was well fitted to rouse attention, to influence the masses, but he left them without any sure guide.[12]

The circumstances of the times, Luther's "traditionalism" that broke down Romish additions to "pure Christianity" but left no structure of authority in its place, called for a new leader and a new system. Calvin, in spite of his biblicalism, was actually proclaiming an entirely new system of faith and order. He began his rise while still studying the law at Orleans, where Beza says Calvin was "already chosen as a special instrument for the work of the Lord"; thus during this early period Calvin

so united wisdom with zeal for the kingdom of God, that he advanced it astonishingly in many families, not with formal language, which he always avoided, but with so great depth and so much dignity of speech, that even at that time no man could hear him without astonishment. . . . Among others the Seigneur of the little town of Lignieres who with his wife was accustomed to hear him, said of him: "This man teaches us at least something *entirely new*."[13]

Calvin jettisoned the sacramental system. Not the purveying of grace, but the enforcing of law, was the Church's essential function. Baptism was a sign of obedience, not a vehicle for salvation. At the altar Calvin *offered nothing*: God could not be influenced in his eternal decrees by the Mass, nor could the recipient's eternal status be altered by participation. Although Luther rejected mere tactile succession of the ministry, he endorsed the principle of apostolic succession as *historical* succession of faith. For Calvin historicity itself was a meaningless category. Indeed, what makes Calvin so preeminently the apostle of modernity is his utter rejection of any "saving" value to tradition. The radical significance of this attitude may be measured in its contrast with the oft-invoked sociological truism that religion as a "conservative" force is the bearer of sociocultural tradition. It is part of the genius of Weber's sociology, by contrast, that he recognized in both the Protestant Ethic essays and his work on charisma the role of religion as an agent for change.

Luther and Calvin also contrast in their understanding of civil authority. Luther's critics have often pointed to his almost fawning attitude toward the princes in his own time and the possible complicity of Lutheranism in Nazism. A less biased analysis would recognize that as a traditionalist Luther affirmed the divine institution of the state and secular magistrates. Luther's doctrine of the "two kingdoms" was not only an endorsement of the rights of the rulers of this world, but also a critique of papal involvement in temporal politics. While "Luther and Melanchthon confined themselves to a reformation of faith and doctrine," the great church historian Philip Schaff wrote in 1857, "Calvinism is, to this day, the most powerful element in the religious and ecclesiastical life of the Western world," for Calvin overthrew established leaders and substituted his own "ruling elders" as magistrates—an office he himself never held.[14] In Geneva specifically these constituted Weber's typical "charismatic band." The same process can be observed, though at some remove, in Knox's Scotland and Puritan Massachusetts. That Calvin's new administrators may also have represented different class interests from those already in power in no way detracts from the charismatic base upon which they stood. As Poggi states, "the *whole* story shows how a certain body of religious ideas . . . typically leads the believer to adopt a certain ethical posture. . . . This posture in turn—within certain groups, *already involved in the practice of business*—engenders a certain occupational ethic."[15] When Lutheran reforms and Calvinist reforms are compared from society to society, there is a clear sense of adaptability, even in church government, in the former system (Swedish and Finnish bishops, for example), in contrast to an intolerant shaking of the foundations in the latter.[16]

Calvin did far more than challenge papal hegemony. He attacked the fundamental conception of authority upon which it was based. Whereas Luther attempted to spiritualize the Church anew, Calvin moved to secularize spiritual authority into restraint of the reprobate, aggrandizing to himself the magesterium. The entirety of Calvin's system rises or falls on whether or not he personally is elect. *The unique primal dispensation of God's grace to John Calvin must be accepted* before any of his theology can be, and if his personal claim be accepted, then one is duty-bound to follow his teaching. Lutheranism, rather, rests on whether Luther's reading of Scripture is more accurate than that of the Roman Church, and if so, whether the corruption is so great as to justify schism.[17] John Calvin stands in a line of visionaries whose radical claim to authority depends not on argument but upon a personal relationship between themselves and the believers who assent to their unique gifts of grace. "I would rather ten thousand times, be swallowed up," he wrote, "than not to obey what the Spirit of God commands me to do through the mouth of his prophets."[18] As Calvin's charisma was subsequently routinized, the ministers obtained interpretation of the Word, a charisma of office, not in the context of tradition (the Roman model), but by direct inspiration.

In England—where Weber picks up the Protestant Ethic saga for his own argument—David Little has shown clearly that the crux of the Anglican-Puritan confrontation was the law-and-order question. The seat of authority and the locus of power were the critical issues around which all others revolved. Although English Puritanism clearly was a routinization of

Calvin's own life and band well after he had died and Geneva much changed—the *impersonalization* of charisma, as Schluchter and Roth would have it—at its heart was a totally new political agenda.[19] It was for this reason that the Puritans were never satisfied with Anglican concessions in church ceremonies and why ultimately both James and Charles could not come to terms with the Puritan party.[20] Nothing short of revolution filled the Puritan bill, because Calvinism was imbued with the specifically revolutionary force of charisma which could not be restrained by technical concessions. That Puritanism in England developed differently from Scotland or Geneva yet finally had far larger ramifications is to be explained sociologically precisely in the specific historical conditions in which it took its stand, conditions which by their very adversity encouraged systemic routinization to a greater extent than elsewhere. In short, the swiftness of Calvin and Knox's successes actually deterred the pervasiveness of their effect, because this was more closely tied to specific personalities. The "theocentric dualism" of Calvinism, its non-magico-mythical worldview, enabled the Calvinist mission to be separated from Calvin's personality and thus "stabilized against" personalistic attacks.[21] Thus William Haller can define Puritans as "Calvinists with a difference."[22] That difference was the impersonalization of charisma that makes "not Calvin, but Calvinism," as Gerth and Mills note, Weber's interest. Time, place, and circumstance encouraged the systematizing and consolidating of the "wonder" of the charismatic relationship into a body of principles and offices, a "mission," that existed independently of personalities and seeped into far more layers of society.

Ernst Troeltsch has, admittedly, characterized Calvin as a medievalist, and this view continues to have its sympathizers. To the extent that it refers to a cosmological worldview—God, earth, heaven, hell—it is accurate.[23] There is a great deal of truth, for example, to the assertion that Calvinism would not have had its appeal if people had not been primed for it by the late medieval teaching on hell. Clearly, the psychological appeal of so thoroughly negative a system as Calvinism was that it freed people from the constant fear that a wrong move might damn them eternally or cost their heirs dearly. Predestination gave people the freedom to act creatively and capitalized upon the "practical atheism" of the Renaissance.[24]

As a sociological anthropology, however, Calvinism stood at complete odds with the medieval view. Instead of institutional mediation of grace imparted to traditional authorities, Calvin substituted the unique standing of the individual in an existential relationship to the total environment, with only a negative system of rules as a check on pure anarchy.

> The predestination dogma, by engendering the faithful's "need for proof of election", *cranks up the tension* in him . . . to this tensed-up individual the doctrine of God's transcendence *opens up the world* as a thoroughly objectified, profaned, manipulable field for purposeful action. . . . A world to which no sacred signifi-

cance and valences are attached is by the same token (from a religious point of view) a manipulable world.[25]

Wherever Calvinism has taken root, furthermore, revolution has followed in its wake. "Individual salvation" notwithstanding, Calvinism is an authority structure with fundamentally social consequences. The same cannot at all be said of Lutheranism.[26]

It is significant, also, to Calvin's charismatic authority structure that his reformation occurred not in his home or in the ferment of Paris, but in Geneva. He was called there because the fiery Farel, who had aroused the populace, "was by no means fitted" to the task of total social change that the demand for religious and political liberty in Geneva called forth. Beza recounts the scene:

In the evening Farel hasted to the inn at which Calvin [who had become something of a peripatetic preacher-teacher] had taken a lodging for the night. He explained to him the situation of the Church and besought him to tarry and assist him. Calvin, startled by this unexpected appeal, adduced, in opposition, his plans, his desires, his tastes. The more Farel insisted, the more did his [Calvin's] apprehension increase at the prospect which suddenly opened before him. Then Farel, trembling with a holy anger rose to his feet. "And I," cried he, with a voice of thunder, "declare it to you in the name of Almighty God. You adduce your studies as a pretext. If you refuse to devote yourself along with us to the work of the Lord, God will punish you, for you seek your own interest rather than that of Christ."

Calvin himself remarks that "This adjuration so terrified and shook me that I desisted from the journey I had undertaken . . . as if God from on high had laid his hand on me to arrest me."[27]

Yet Calvin's charismatic authority was not immediately accepted. Conflicts with anabaptists, who promised and appeared to deliver more freedom than he, led to a sentence of banishment from the city. With the apostolic protest that "It is better to obey God than men," the minister left the city.[28] But here was what later came to be thought of as the perfect test, and the final proof of Calvin's election:

Disorder reigned both in the Church and in the State. But God in kindness sent chastisements upon them [the Genevans]. Those who had been most forward in opposing the restraints of their guides [i.e., those who would not abide by Calvinist decrees], received the just reward of their misdeeds. Within two years, one of the four syndics who were leaders of the faction in 1538, was executed for murder, a second convicted of sedition, in attempting to escape by a window, fell and was instantly killed; the other two, on account of their treasonable conduct while absent from the city, were prohibited from returning. These *disorders and changes* prepared the way for the recall of the exiles.[29]

In 1541 the council of Two Hundred called for Calvin. Jacob Bernard, one of two ministers left in Geneva, wrote to Calvin,

The cry was unanimous for Calvin, that good and learned man, "Christ's minister." Come then, venerable father in Christ. Ours you are, for *the Lord God has given you to us.* All sigh for you. Worthy is our church of your aid, and God will require her blood at your hands if you do not come, for he has made you a watchman of the house of Israel among us.

Calvin's return thus "was looked upon as a special token of the favor of God."[30]

At this point, then, Calvin set up his famed Court of Morals and married church and state. If Calvin's authority constituted a complete break with tradition, however, might it not also be the inception of modern bureaucracy, itself in Weber's work a revolutionary force and an ultimate product of the Protestant Ethic? Clearly, it could be, but it was not. It was "government according to the Word":

The people of Geneva are regarded as the people of God and shall be ruled as the people of Israel were in accordance with His declared will. Calvin adopts the part of the Old Testament legislator and prophet, speaking in the name of God, as well as the New Testament apostle and evangelist. . . . Both Government and people are bound to accept his interpretation of the law and the Gospel and act in accordance with it. He therefore frequently appears in the Council to remind the members of their responsibility to God, on whom the Government of the city depends, and exhort them to humble themselves before Him, to confess their sins, and to have regard to His honour in the repression of all vice.[31]

The relationship of Calvin to the government of Geneva was one of personal authority, "impersonalized" by reference to the Word. Once his authority was accepted, recognized by the people, disagreement was tantamount to damnation. Although Calvin regularly encouraged study of the Scriptures, it was not for individual enlightenment, but only to see that he was right. Genevan life was life "under the domination of Christian insight," and that meant Calvinism's charismatic authority.[32]

Two aspects of Calvin's domination are of particular significance from a Weberian standpoint. The first is the extent to which Calvin's authority was not an act of his independent creation, but born in the needs of Geneva. He did not go to Geneva to solve its problems, rather Genevan circumstances called forth Calvin's leadership. The second charismatic quality is the way Calvin at one and the same time ran the government yet did not involve himself in day-to-day routine, profane, mundane affairs. This apparent withholding of self from routine while knowing what's going on and keeping a handle on it is an essential element in Weber's charismatic type. Whenever a leader becomes too involved in the everyday, a diminution of charisma is likely to follow. It should be clear that this occurs specifically because followers' perceptions of the leader change. "Images of kings topple before their thrones do."[33]

At this point we may again compare Calvin and Luther with respect to their degree of self-revelation and in the degree to which their followers encouraged this behavior. Luther is depicted regularly as paterfamilias, a traditional father-figure sitting at table holding forth to an extended family. This traditionalist image is epitomized in the volume of his works entitled *Table Talk*. Throughout his writings and those of his closest associates and admirers, however, we hear the most intimate details of everyday life. Luther's most elemental urges have provided material for both scatological drama and serious psychoanalysis.[34]

In Calvin's biography, by contrast, his personal life is largely an unknown.

> In his private life, Calvin was exceedingly plain, self-denying, and ascetic. [As a childless widower most of his life,] for years he took but one meal a day. He refused a high salary and presents of every description. . . . He was averse to all earthly enjoyments. We look in vain, in his writings, for even an incidental expression of sympathy with the wonders of the visible world. He is not one of those men who encourage familiarity and take hold of one's feelings and affections, like the open, straight-forward, warm-hearted, humorous Luther. . . .[35]

In short, little of Calvin's "human side" is revealed, which may in turn lead to the possibility of wondering whether he had one. But if not that, then what? While his family background may have given him a "refinement of manner" which Luther lacked, it remains true that his intimates did not chose to portray him in mundane terms.[36]

Calvin forbade the erection of any marker on his grave, and this wish was enforced by his followers.[37] While *in actu* the decision probably signals nothing more than the personal effect of friendship, the result was to strengthen further the charisma of Calvinism as an authority structure. The unknown grave became almost as powerful a symbol as the empty tomb. This "positive dehumanization" of charismatic leaders by their disciples is a recurring characteristic, and perhaps a necessity to a mission being extended through impersonalization rather than either dying or being routinized into traditonal or rational-legal channels.[38] Not their routine lives, but their special natures, are what charismatics' followers want to remember. That we may now know something more of the routine lives of some charismatic leaders both past and present is due more to contemporary historiography on the one hand, or a fall from grace on the other. Ironically, what makes Luther a far more interesting personality today is a result of his *ordinariness* in his own day, while Calvin's "specialness" makes him now seem dull.

In terms of Weber's causal chain, then, my argument is this: I concur with Weber in the thrust of his theory and with Poggi that its statement is enthymemic, specifically with respect to the first premise of the basic triad. What I wish to add, however, is that the "certain body of religious ideas," which was Calvinist doctrine itself, gained in importance *because* it was connected to a particular type of authority structure, namely charisma. Luther, in spite of his immense popularity as a virtuoso, never exercised charismatic authority—i.e., Lutheran*ism* was not a charismatic system of domination. His accusation against the Roman Church was that it had violated Christian *tradition*, and he saw his "vocation" as its *restoration*. This is true in spite of the fact that in claiming fidelity to tradition Luther was at some level redefining tradition, that the doctrine of the "priesthood of all believers" had a democratizing effect, and that the concept of "calling" was an apparent precondition to the powerful effect of Calvin's teaching on predestination.

What made Calvinism fundamentally different (while superficially the same) was precisely the difference between the two in operative systems of dominance.[39] Because Calvinist doctrine was attached to an authority structure, it became a worldview, rather than simply a theology. Because Lutheranism specifically eschewed a "kingdom of this world" for the Church, it fit nicely into any tradition of political dominance with which it came into contact. Calvinist doctrines could be transformed into the Protestant Ethic, because in charismatic Calvinism—i.e., Calvin's rulership of Geneva—a new structure of dominance appeared "*in statu nascendi*."[40] The specific content of this system ultimately segued into a bureaucratic rather than a traditional routinization, moving from impersonalization to depersonalization, because it held tradition to be totally null and utterly void as a basis for meaningful action. This is the unique social-structural precondition for the breakthrough to modernity—complementing the social-psychological effects of the predestination dogma upon the motivations of the believer—signaled by the Weberian concept, "the Protestant Ethic."[41]

6

Hasidism and Moonism: Charisma in the Counterculture

ALAN L. BERGER

This essay seeks to elucidate the nature of charismatic authority by analyzing its relationship to a traditional norm which may function as a check on charismatic excess. Weber's typology of legitimate authority—rational-legal, traditional, and charismatic—classifies the latter, in its "pure" sense, as being specifically outside the ordinary and profane spheres. Yet there is the possibility that charisma may be regulated by a higher, traditional law which maintains both behavioral and theological boundaries. In contemporary culture, furthermore, charisma has become infantilized, like many other symbols of sacrality. Infantilization means conceptual impoverishment, the debasement of a symbol. Symbols are subjected to a process of rationalization or degeneration as they are "interpreted on increasingly lower planes."[1] Reified charisma results in idolatry; in the Western religious tradition, imprecise ascription of ultimacy to the penultimate. The charismatic leader is viewed by his followers as an agent who shapes destiny independent of a transcendental order. There are, in short, no clear external theological checks and balances which serve to limit or define charismatic claims. The relationship between charismatic authority and fixed norms which are shaped, mediated, and modified by dynamic interaction with tradition, has become ambiguous.

Two contemporary religious groups in America, Hasidism and the Unification Church, represent two genres of charismatic religion. The origins of the Jewish and neo-Christian examples are similar. Both embody a response to world disenchantment and a reaction to the assault on personal inner freedom. Moreover, Hasidism and the Unification Church share a concern for the experiential, an emphasis on commitment and community, elaborate educational and indoctrination techniques, clearly articulated social organization based upon charismatic leadership, and effective fund-raising efforts. Theologically, both movements evince a messianic concern. Sociologically, both originated in times of widespread anomie and institutional weakness. Although neither group is indigenous to America, Hasidism and the Unification Church have devised strategems which enable them to grow in their new surroundings. Both groups are active on college campuses and in urban areas, although members retain their insulation from mainstream groups by distinctive dress and speech, and their isolation by having specified locations for living as well as designated types of work.

However, I suggest that a fundamental difference exists between the two groups in their conception of what constitutes *la vie serieuse*. Hasidism, a two-hundred-year-old Jewish pietistic mystical revival movement, began as a protest against a spiritually moribund Rabbinism. Hasidic attitudes toward the world include both enthusiastic and quietistic phases. However, in all its phases, Hasidism emphasizes world enchantment and a transcendent ethical source. The Holy Spirit Association for the Unification of World Christianity (Moonies) is still in the generation of the founder. Essentially a world-transforming movement, the Unification Church appears to have an equivocal relationship to transcendence. Consequently, and perhaps unwittingly, the movement has succumbed to scientism, the dominant, if largely unarticulated, ideology of the twentieth century. Scientism is "the conversion of science into a revelation of ultimate reality."[2] Epistemologically, scientism asserts that the scientific method is the only reliable means to truth. Ontologically, scientism contends that only the items which emerge from this method can be believed to exist. These assumptions disenchant the universe.

Specifically, I compare the authority of *zaddik*, the hasidic communal leader and holy man/mystic, with the authority of the Reverend Sun Myung Moon, leader of the Unification Church. I also ask the question: To what extent are the actions and activities of the charismatic leader chained by traditional prescriptions? Normative Judaism, *halakha*, while admitting a variety of charismatics, has not permitted what it judged antinomian behavior (seventeenth-century Sabbatianism and various actions of zaddikim, personified by the nineteenth-century Menachem Mendl of Kotske). On the other hand, Moonism has displayed great ambiguity in the relationship of its secular force to its religious teachings. My study focuses upon guidelines for charismatic claims, the role of ritual life in charismatic movements, and the relationship between charismatic authority and transcendence.

LOSS OF TRANSCENDENCE

A sea change in the spiritual life of the Western world crystalized in the twentieth century. Transcendence, which customarily is associated with tradition, was relegated to the historical scrapheap. This concluded a process initiated some three centuries earlier. The concept of *homo religiosus*, it can be argued, came under increasing assault with the advent of modernity. Seventeenth-century science and the Enlightenment of the following century sought to free humanity from the grip of that which was beyond demonstration. Religion was viewed as a parochial impediment, a surmountable obstacle on the road to inevitable human progress. Transcendence was lost as a norm against which human values and actions could be judged, and this resulted in the self-aggrandizement of humanity. Man now inhabits a desacralized world, a place where he "regards himself solely as the subject and agent of history," accepting "no model for humanity outside the human condition as it can be seen in the various historical situations."[3] Far from liberating humanity, the Enlightenment inheritance ended by constraining man and desacralizing existence.

Man increasingly became the measure of all things. Human behavior, unrestrained by reference to transcendence, displayed unprecedented arbitrariness. Humility, a hallmark of traditional religion in the West, was discarded. Man could not achieve freedom "until he had killed the last god."[4] Monstrous evil, such as Nazi Germany's Holocaust, was unleashed in the world. The corrosive effects of the loss of transcendence in history have recently been chronicled in a succinct and provocative fashion by Richard Rubenstein, yet without calling for a return to or reappropriation of transcendence. Instead, this chronicler embraces neo-paganism by critically reappraising the three myths of the origin of civilization—Judeo-Christianity, Freud, and Hegel.[5] Nonetheless, the search for absolutes continues. The new panaceas are political and psychological.

CHARISMATIC LEADERS—THEIR TASK

The search for certainty spawned countless gurus, messiahs, "panaceamongers," swamis, and others whose messages suggested order amidst an increasingly chaotic world. Cults and new religions, which began in the counterculture and flourished throughout the sixties and the seventies, grew in America at a pace more rapid than at any time in the last two hundred years. It is no exaggeration to claim that America in the last two decades has undergone a third (or fourth) "Great Awakening." However, this most recent awakening differs from its predecessors by stressing Eastern forms of piety, and often by ascribing unrestrained power to its leaders, who are perceived as possessed with supernatural endowments—or charismatic. The charismatic leader articulates and embodies a cosmos. Amidst an unstable environment, the charismatic advances a plan of action and a vision which will yield permanence, a transformed order, meaning, and the defeat of evil, however the latter may be defined. Although charismatic leaders may appear at any time, they seem especially prominent during periods of widespread anomie, and indeed, Durkheim indicated that one characteristic of an anomic situation is a turn toward the bizarre and novel.

This charismatic outbreak in the midst of an advanced technological and bureaucratic setting illustrates both a need, or longing, for the sacred, and a dissatisfaction with the routinized messages of the Judeo-Christian tradition in America. Moreover, charisma in its American context bears out the contention that "in advanced Western society, it appears that claims to real charisma, if they are to succeed, must be supported by exotic provenance."[6] One has only to think of contemporary claimants to divine inspiration, for example, A. C. Bhaktivedanta Swami Prabhupada, Maharishi Mahesh Yogi, among others.

Charismatic domination consists of a reciprocal relationship between leader and followers. Charisma denotes a social relationship which involves the acknowledgment on the part of a charismatic audience that their leader possesses extraordianry power. Members of the charismatic audience experience anxiety, or distress, which they believe their leader can alleviate because of supernatural endowments.[7] Followers receive answers and assurances for the crisis arising from their realization that the world is frequently incoherent. The charismatic audience of the last two decades is distinguished by its relatively high level of education and its origin in a stable socioeconomic class.

Weber's study of charisma stressed its revolutionary role in religion and politics. The charismatic leader is "always in some sense a revolutionary, setting himself in conscious opposition to some established aspects of the society in which he works."[8] Such a leader is both an innovator who specifically announces a way, and one who provides a model for emancipation from the routine. While it is accurate to stress the point that charisma constitutes a break from the ordinary and profane, too sharp a distinction between this phenomenon and traditional authority may obscure continuing charismatic elements in mixed structures of domination as they occur in practice. Charismatic leadership may become institutionalized without ceasing to be charismatic. Charisma may be chained or at least moderated by tradition.

Charismatic leaders are further hedged by having to place their authority and their teaching within guidelines elaborated by the past. They must provide signs that their message will in the future lead to salvation, and these can be interpreted only through some meaningful relationship to past and present experience. Charisma never operates in a cultural vacuum.

MYSTERY AND FAITH IN THE RELIGIOUS LIFE

The distinction between religion and idolatry in Western religions rests largely upon the role of mystery in religious life. Mystery implies a limitation on the merely rational. Without advocating the overthrow of reason, religion upholds the possibility of divine eruptions in human existence. For example, Martin Buber spoke of the religious perception of the world in terms of astonishment. The scientific revolution, for its part, attempted to enlarge man's scope of knowledge. As such, there is no irreconcilable difference between religious mystery and science. By the second half of the twentieth century, however, our understanding of science had deteriorated into scientism, which has grave implications for leadership and religion. In distinction to science, scientism is a severely limiting concept. "It goes beyond the actual findings of science to deny that other approaches to knowledge are valid and other truths are true . . . in doing so it deserts science in favor of metaphysics—bad metaphysics. . . . [Scientism] also carries marks of a religion—a secular religion, resulting from overextrapolation from science."[9]

Scientism attempts to explain life and the universe without recourse to the possibilities of mystery and astonishment. In fairness, it should be observed that some individuals are willing to acknowledge the existence of that which to them is inconceivable. But they proceed to undermine their acknowledgment by the claim that, if the inconceivable does exist, it is irrelevant.[10] Scientism errs in assuming that science exhausts all modes of reality. Science infantilized becomes scientism. The essential difference between enchantment and secularized existence, with its reliance upon scientism, is that "Man does not live by explanation alone, but by the sense of wonder and mystery. Without it there is neither religion nor morality, neither sacrifice nor creativity."[11] This observation constitutes nothing less than a warning against the temptation of idolatry or dogmatic attempts to explain away the sense of mystery, to divinize the merely human. The charismatic leader of the Unification Church is one who may well have blurred the crucial distinction between divine and human.

Nowhere has the perspective of scientism undermined and transformed Western religion more than in the perception of faith. The certitude of faith is not a once and for all certitude as understood in most religious traditions. Faith means struggle. New challenges, disasters, and catastrophic occurrences must always be measured against the meaning system provided by one's faith. For just as surely as one can gain faith, it can equally be lost. Attainment of faith cannot be equated with its permanent possession. Will Herberg has thus delineated the essential nature of the faith problematic: "Faith is a never-ending battle against self-absolutization and idolatry; it is a battle which has to be refought every moment of life because it is a battle in which the victory can never be final. But although never final, victory is always possible."[12]

Scientism's absolutizing of its findings have conceptually banished the possibility of achieving faith, in the religious usage of the term. The Unification Church appears, perhaps again unwittingly, to have utilized scientism's presuppositions in suggesting its own understanding of faith. For example, the Church's faith in the Reverend Moon proposes to overcome all doubt, explain away all conflict, and reduce what remains to the realm of Satan.

HASIDISM

Although by definition new religions announce the advent of a New Age of Aquarius, of New Consciousness, the Age of the Lord of the Second Advent, and so forth, there is nothing new about the *conditions* which produce such claims. The decline in real power of Jewish self-governing institutions in Eastern Europe in the early eighteenth century and the undermining of the moral caliber of the rabbinical leaders were antecedent conditions of Hasidism's emergence.[13] Parallels between that time and contemporary America have been noted by Martin Buber and Elie Wiesel, among others. It has been widely suggested that the religious orientation, if not the ritual, embraced by the Hasidic revival is a remedy for contemporary man's anomie.[14]

The perimeters of charismatic authority for Judaism in modernity and in tradition have been clearly outlined.[15] But modernity advocated a new type of charisma, the charisma of reason. Both modern rationalist reform (Western) and Hasidic reform (Eastern) sought to overcome the fetters which shackled existence. However, there is one significant difference which has a bearing on this discussion. Rationalist reform "seeks to free the life of the human intellect."[16] In Western Europe, the French Revolution signaled the end of religious domination and the emergence of a secular order. Beginning with *haskallah*, or Enlightenment, Jewry of the West yielded a new ideal, the *maskil*, the man of reason. Unlike the scholar, the *talmid hakham*, who studied, strove to understand, interpret, and transmit the Torah, the *maskil* challenged, undermined, and finally ignored the authority of orthodoxy (i.e., traditional authority). The *maskil* followed the charisma of reason. On the other hand, Hasidism sought to open channels between man and God. The Hasidic revolution was not against traditional authority, but rather against its abuse and decadence.

The Problem of Authority

In the generation of the founder, Hasidism was locked in fierce struggle with its opponents (*mitnaggdim*). The latters' most serious accusation was that the zaddikim were guilty of the sin of refusing to study Torah and of mocking the scholars. The conflict was between traditional authority (ethical prophecy as represented by the rabbis with their stress on a transcendent deity), and charismatic authority (based upon intimate and intense religious experience of exemplary prophets in the zaddikim who emphasized divine immanence). However, transcendence and immanence are aspects of the same deity, so the conflict was not irreconcilable.[17]

The role of zaddik was ascribed by definition to one who had achieved *devekuth*, communion with, or adherence to, the divine. Zaddikim attract a following based upon their vivid personal religious experiences. But these experiences are in themselves insufficient. The movement's founder, Israel ben Eliezer, the Ba'al Shem Tov, or Besht (d. 1760), was also a healer, magician and miracle worker. Significantly, Besht merely as magician was unacceptable as a religious leader to extant groups of Hasidim. It was only after he proved himself adept at *halakha* in a nonscholarly manner that his pronouncements and interpretations were accepted as authoritative.[18]

Zaddik as Chained Charismatic

The zaddik is a mystic. But even here, in the most intimate attachment of man to the divine, a sense of distance remains between Creator and creature. The so-called Jewish ideology of traditionalism demanded that the zaddik be humble. Humility is the "qualification for the *Shechinah's* [Divine Presence] resting upon a man."[19] Yet, the zaddik is seen by his followers as the embodiment of all 613 *mitzvoth* (commandments). As a spiritual superman, the zaddik's success in achieving *devekuth* served to widen the gap between himself and his followers. Commentators who claim that Hasidism "democratized" mysticism simply have not accurately understood the role of zaddik. Yet, the zaddik's submission before God through the demands of *halakha* was the criterion of authenticity.

In spite of theological constraints, something akin to saint cults developed around certain of the zaddikim. This compares to a similar development in Islam, where the intense devotional practices of sufis frequently culminated in the divinization of their shaykh. The remarkable feature of zaddikism is not its abuse and deterioration into charlatanism, but rather the infrequency of these occurrences. The zaddik's actions were seldom perceived as arbitrary or capricious. Individual pronouncements and deeds were testable against *halakha* to which both the zaddik and his followers subordinated themselves.

Zaddikim function as social engineers within the frequently elastic boundaries of *halakha*. However, if the zaddik deviates in such a manner as to clash with traditional authority, his followers may abandon him and seek a different leader. An example is provided in the account of the life of Menachem Mendl of Kotsk (d. 1859). According to traditional sources, the Kotsker deliberately extinguished the Sabbath candles, left the room, and retreated into solitude. A faithful disciple brought meals to the zaddik who remained secluded in his room until his death. Most of the Kotsker's followers were alarmed by their leader's antinomian behavior in desecrating the Sabbath, a religious prohibition, and they looked elsewhere for leadership. While the authenticity of this tale is problematic, its meaning is clear: Charismatic authority may not deteriorate into charismatic license—particularly as this also involved the withdrawal of the leader from leadership. There is a fixed norm from traditional authority by which all charismatic activity is evaluated.[20]

Disciples of the zaddik, hasidim, grant their leader absolute authority. This attitude is one of "religious masochism." As the hasidim achieve *hitbatlut* (self-extinction) before the charismatic leader, so the zaddik is, ideally, humble before the Creator. The zaddik's role is both social and cosmic. He exists to serve his community. Yet the zaddik is also charged with the task of *tikkum ha-olam*, repair or restoration of the world. All the zaddik's skills and wisdom are believed to be derived from God, a traditional source. However, these talents also belong to the zaddik's followers, "since they [the talents] exist only for their [the followers'] sake, for whatever he possesses, he possesses *on their account*."[21]

Not all zaddikim pursued a social role. Some preferred meditation to counseling, depending upon the temperament of the leader rather than the office of zaddik. Zaddikim are those able to articulate a meaningful pattern in the seemingly random and chaotic events of Jewish existence. Prior to the twentieth century, this meant accounting for the existence of forces which attempted to harm or bring chaos to Jews, for example, demons, evil, and gentile society. Currently the zaddik is still concerned with theodicy.

Ritual Life

Hasidic ritual life is lived in both the public and private realms. The individual hasid may seek a private audience with his zaddik to receive advice or blessings or both. The discussion may include secular as well as sacred matters. When the zaddik speaks, his followers insist that it is the voice of the divine presence which they hear speaking through their leader. Public rituals are centered at the residence or "court" of the zaddik. Here activities include meals, singing, dancing, and a gathering—*farbrengen*—a type of brotherhood, a ritual moment of "collective effervescence." At this time the zaddik is approachable in a communalistic sense. Prayer and worship in corporeality are two central moments in hasidic ritual life. One worships in corporeality by transforming the apparently profane into an occasion for worshipping the divine. Hasidic mysticism does not divinize but attempts to elevate the world. Those unable to achieve *devekuth* alone may do so by clinging to the zaddik and to the community. There is no mediator between the zaddik and the hasid. Hasidic ritual life envisions a transcendent or cosmic purpose assisting the coming of the messiah. Rituals are performed for cosmic rather than merely personal reasons. Sociologically, this develops a bond between members of the "community of Israel."

Hasidim have a financial obligation to support their zaddik. This duty stems only partly from the traditional emphasis upon *tsedakah* (charity). Economic assistance to scholars and preachers was a normative component of Judaism. The zaddik had many expenses for his personal staff and had to maintain the quarters where his followers were frequently housed and fed. Elimelech of Lizensk (d. 1786), founder of "practical zaddikism," stressed the hasidim's financial responsibility toward their zaddik. The innovative nature of the zaddik's support—here Weber's observation that the charismatic shuns all rational types of economic activity by relying on contributions is most helpful—resides in the fact that the zaddik, unlike the scholar or preacher, was to rely entirely upon the beneficence of his disciples.

Reconciliation with Traditional Authority

Two significant events made Hasidism a vital force in helping to shape the contours of subsequent Judaic expression. Dov Haer, the Great Maggid (preacher) of Mezyritch, successor to Besht, sent out emissaries to establish their own Hasidic enclaves which later became dynasties. Decentralization provided for accommodation to various local customs. Shneur Zalman of Lyady, a third generation leader, founded HaBaD Hasidism (*Hokomah* = wisdom, *Binah* = understanding, and *Daat* = knowledge), which represents the rationalizing branch of Hasidism, and was the forerunner of the contemporary Lubavitch Hasidism. Shneur Zalman was also a great halakhic master, and author of the *Tanya*, a mystical interpretation of the Torah. The zaddik, in HaBaD, was one who helped guide his Hasidim to a deeper, spiritual knowledge of Torah. Early on, the role of zaddik became hereditary.

Historically, there was a reconciliation between zaddikism and rabbinism. Hasidism's fervor was aimed at renewing rather than invalidating the tradition. Hasidism upheld the halakhic framework of Judaism and never opposed study of Torah. Rather, hasidic opposition was in the nature of an *ecclesiola in ecclesia*. Far from forming a seceding sect, zaddikim frequently served to strengthen Jewish society by providing access to salvation through a variety of practices following the dissolution of Jewish central governing bodies such as the Council of Four Lands in 1764.

The newness of the institution of zaddikism rests in the intensity and enthusiasm which it brings to religious life, and not in the teaching of theological innovations. Zaddikim are guides who interpret biblical and halakhic Judaism, while realizing that varying interpretations exist. In submitting to a given norm, the zaddik at the same time indulges in a self-conscious scholarly effort. His "revelation" concerns a dimension of sacred writing, such as the Bible, Midrash, or Talmud, which has contemporary relevance. The audience sees what their guide leads them to see. However, they must discover or interiorize the truth of his interpretation by themselves. By definition, the zaddik and his followers are bound to Torah in its multivalent interpretations.

The contemporary appeal of Hasidism or neo-Hasidism has been attributed to its "intimate connection with types of emotion and patterns of thought generated in a modern technological society."[22] This appeal is based on ideological, psychological, and existential grounds. Against the technological and secularized environment, neo-Hasidism asserts the value of intimacy, personal freedom, and the authenticity of the individual. This is accomplished, paradoxically, by a return to tradition. Menachem Mendl Schneerson, who is current zaddik of the Lubavitch Hasidim and was trained as an engineer at the Sorbonne, commented on the zaddik's power. "As a believer," he testified, "I am convinced that it can only be given to a 'keeper of Torah and *mitzvot.*' "[23] Observance of traditional authority enriches and guides subjective religious experience. Today the term *hasid* is synonymous with orthodoxy. Hasidim are among the most fervent and animated observers of Judaic rituals and halakhic standards.

UNIFICATION CHURCH

The Unification Church is one of the most controversial of the new religions. Unlike many of its counterparts, the church advocates world change rather than abandonment of, or indifference to, the world. There are many often contradictory interpretations of the Reverend Sun Myung Moon and his church. In no small measure, the confusion results from the teachings of the Reverend Moon himself. Eclecticism and triumphalism characterize the movement's theology. Evangelical and messianic Christianity combine with Korean Shamanism, biblicism, scientism, and a markedly dispensationalist view of history, with its karmic-type explanation of evil. The whole of the Unification Church is vastly different from the sum of its parts. Moreover, despite the many extant studies on the Unification Church, there is a dearth of scholarly study on charismatic leadership in the movement. Interested observers must rely on documents by and about the group—frequently written with competing purposes in mind—and on interviews with members and former members for hints and clues on charismatic leadership in the church.

Sun Myung Moon was born in 1920 in North Korea. Exposed early in life to Presbyterian evangelists, Moon allegedly became sensitive, while still young, to the sufferings of humanity and was early concerned with religious experience. After studying engineering in Japan, he was jailed by the North Koreans. Church literature testifies to the founder's prodigious feats of spiritual concern and care for his fellow inmates. Moon is portrayed as giving his food to others and physically carrying those weaker than he. Adherents are told that "pains of the members are minor compared to those once suffered'' by their leader.[24] As is typically the case, a veritable hagiography of the founder appears to be developing which conforms closely to what Martin Dibelius termed ''the law of biographical analogy'' in sacred biography.[25] Moon is clairvoyant, clairaudient, and purportedly has had visionary experiences of the Buddha, Moses, and Jesus, among others.

The Problem of Authority

Authority in the Unification Church appears to reside, penultimately, in the *Divine Principle*, which is a sacred text based upon the revelations that Moon has professed to have received from God over a multi-year period. The first English translation from the original Korean appeared in 1960. The work is basic to the group's proselytizing mission and to its devotional life. *Divine Principle* examines and resolves all theological issues (theodicy, redemption, and the second advent—complete with charts and tables). Some sections consist of the repetition of numbers and phrases which, like their counterparts in other sacred texts, have the effect of semi-hypnosis upon auditors when read properly. *Divine Principle* aims at providing a set of unerring guidelines for behavior. No aspect of life is excluded from guidance.

According to *Divine Principle*, humanity inherits and suffers from original sin. Eve's impetuousness postponed harmony within the triad God-Adam-Eve, so that producing perfect children became impossible. Central to Moon's teaching is the ''base of four positions,'' which includes God-Adam-Eve-Perfect Children. In order to restore the harmonious relationship between God and Adam's descendants against Satan's power, God provided the mechanism of Indemnity. Good acts may indemnify evil. The conditions of indemnity may be either vertical, as in the historically accumulated conditions of indemnity which all predecessors such as Abraham, Noah, Moses, and Jesus had failed to alter, or there may occur ''horizontal restoration through indemnity.'' This horizontal condition is achieved by ''indemnity centering on one who has a specific mission.''

The text combines theology and politics. Politically the world is perceived through Manichean lenses. Nations of the world are either Cain or Abel types. Apocalypticism—predictions of the impending collapse of the social order in the final struggle of God with Satan—mingles with predictions and assertions that twentieth-century history is leading to unification in religion, politics, and culture. According to Moon, the Second Advent is in the process of realization: Allied victory in World War I signaled the defeat of satanic forces responsible for Adam's sin. Victory in World War II symbolized defeat of the satanic forces which prevented Christ from fulfilling his mission, and the expected defeat of Russia's aim of world communism is to signify the establishment on earth of good and freedom by the Lord of the

Second Advent. However, this message is ambiguous both with respect to signs of the impending New Age and the identity of the Messiah—although followers know that the Reverend Moon is the Messiah. Moon refers to his wife at disciple gatherings, for example, as the "Mother of the Universe" and the "Bride of Christ."

Moon as Unchained Charismatic

Ultimate authority for the Unification Church apparently resides in the Reverend Moon. His followers believe that he has a divine mission to complete the "cumulative indemnity of the past 2,000 years by 'discovering' the dynamic of God's plan to restore mankind to perfection and by forming the ideal 'base of four positions' with God in 1960 at the time of his second marriage."[26] Christ's mission failed because he never married and was thus only able to achieve spiritual but not physical perfection. Moon's followers believe that he has combined spiritual and physical wholeness.

Moon is exalted by his followers as redeemer of mankind, resolver of all conflicts concerning life and the universe, and the ultimate exegete of *Divine Principle.* Thus, the sacred text of the Unification Church is not authoritative like those of Western traditions. Moon is the absolute authority for the faithful. A disciple testifies that:

> It certainly is the case that there is a kind of primacy to the Rev. Moon's person, and to his words or to his speeches that I suppose we wouldn't give to the other writings. [Here the respondent lists the Old Testament, New Testament, Koran, *and Divine Principle*, among others.] If there was a question which required us to give precedence to one source of truth over another, then we would probably give that precedence to Rev. Moon because he is a living being and can therefore give a particular response to a particular question in a particular context.[27]

On the macrocosmic level, Moon represents "the coming of the kingdom," the central figure around whom adherents perform their rituals. The Lord of the Second Advent is to achieve restoration through indemnity.

Moon is a charismatic leader who exhibits mastery of fate and incorporates the ideals of the faithful. He speaks in Korean, and at great length, yet attracts non-Korean-speaking audiences. A translator is always present, but the auditors come to see, hear, and be near the Reverend Moon. Weber and others emphasize, however, that charisma means more than personal endowment. The term is used in three ways: (1) supernatural ability and endowment of the leader, (2) sacred or awe-inspiring property of roles, objects, or groups, and (3) secular or political charisma which is based on personality rather than a "gift of grace." The Unification Church embraces all three of these modes.

Ritual Life

The ritual life of the Unified Family is bonded to expressions of obedient discipleship to Moon. An ability to follow the Master is the chief criterion of the faithful. Independence in achieving religious experience is to come only with the Second Advent. *Divine Principle* is clear on this matter:

> There is no one among fallen men who can really stand . . . all by himself. Therefore, we must understand all these things through the Lord of the Second Advent, who is to come as the completion of the providence of restoration. By believing in him and becoming one body with him, we must be in the position to set up, horizontally, all the vertical conditions of indemnity in the history of the providence of restoration.[28]

Moon is present through a variety of specially designated places and objects.[29] Each church center reserves a "Father's Room" for Moon. In addition to complete furnishings, the room is well supplied with pictures of Moon and his family. Two full water goblets in front of Moon's picture symbolize purity. A place setting, "Father's Plate," is part of the meal ritual held in the kitchen. "Holy salt," blessed by the Reverend Moon, is used to: (1) purify funds which have been collected, (2) banish evil spirits, and (3) overcome evil thoughts or influences on individual followers (who in this case sprinkle the salt on themselves). New York, Amsterdam, and Jerusalem have a "holy ground" which Moon has personally blessed and where special meetings and prayer sessions are held. It can, of course, be argued that these "charismatic symbols," far from bringing Moon closer to his followers, serve instead to reinforce the sense of the leader's distant omnipotence. An elaborate theology may isolate the charismatic leader from his followers. Private audiences with the master seem to be a privilege granted only to his personal staff.

The Church's ritual life appears to center on fund-raising, also called witnessing or donationing. Witnessing is frequently accomplished by special units, MFTs, or mobile fund-raising teams. Status in the organization seems to depend upon success in fund-raising as much as it does upon adherence to Moon and to the *Divine Principle*.[30] Each church center is required to send specified amounts of money to Moon every month.

Fund-raising is accomplished mainly through the sale of ginseng tea, flowers, and candles. However, Moon's position concerning the nonrational accumulation of money is ambiguous. On the one hand, he is the recipient of donations from his numerous church centers. Yet, the Unification Church appears to be in the process of routinizing its financial activities. The Church owns considerable property and sponsors a $100,000 World Tuna Tournament in Gloucester, Massachusetts. Fund-raising is ostensibly to assist various charitable organizations, but it is unclear whether funds have ever gone for purposes other than support of the Church and Moon himself.[31]

DIFFERENCES BETWEEN HASIDISM AND MOONISM

Crucial differences between the Hasidic movement and the Unification Church exist in the areas of humility and mystery. The source of charismatic authority in Hasidism is intense personal religious experience, the attainment of *devekuth*. But the zaddik's virtue resides in his ability to exemplify one or more traditional values, for example piety, mercy, or charity. Allegiance to the zaddik is based on the belief that he is both an effective intercessor with the divine and a channel through which an abundance of divine grace flows. The zaddik's prayers are thought to be more powerful than those of his followers. His exegesis of Bible, Talmud, and midrashic literature is believed by followers to be divinely inspired. His charisma coincides with, and is dependent upon, his access to the transcendent. Moreover, the religious experience of the zaddik is expected to be transformed into actions beneficial to the community as a whole. A relatively unelaborate theology may account for communal access to the zaddik.

On the other hand, Sun Myung Moon is a charismatic whose source of authority is based upon his stated mission as God's messenger who is called to establish the kingdom of heaven. Resolver of all conflicts, Moon is a religious leader, the general of the army warring against Satan, and as "True Parent" he symbolizes victory over evil. The faithful assist by maintaining their commitment to Moon, reading the *Divine Principle*, and by communal living with other church members.

For Hasidism life and the universe can be explained, but they cannot be explained away. Meaning can never be exhausted by human effort. Life remains for Hasidism, in Weber's felicitous phrase, an "enchanted garden." One attempts not to explain mystery, but to live with it. The zaddik's charisma is derived from a twofold source: contact with transcendence and embodiment of tradition; that is, he has "become Torah." Hasidism attempts to maintain the vitality of religious life by infusing rituals with pristine vigor and intensity, not by abandoning either the rituals themselves or the halakhic (normative) basis of the tradition. On the other hand, the Unification Church asserts a rational explanation of the world and of human relationships. The Reverend Moon's claims obviate tradition, heralding a New Age. His explanations seemingly restrict the fullness, individuality, and variety of traditional religious life.

Moon, the *Divine Principle*, and the Unification Church seem to portray religion primarily in terms of scientism. What emerges is the ornamentation of a secular religion which confuses rationalism, or the desire to live in a world of laws and explanations, and dogmatism, in which the world is composed only of laws and explanations. For example, rational theology never excluded the possibility of mystical experience. Moon rejects mysticism ostensibly because perfection is attainable within a transformed secular order. However, there seems to be ambivalence concerning the source of his authority. Mystics who have had a "peak" experience may no longer require any sacramental assistance, whether it be mediated by the *Divine Principle* or the person of Moon. In fairness, it should be added that the Unification Church reflects the frequent uncertainty expressed by many traditions concerning the relationship of mysticism to religious authority. But this uncertainty here seems exaggerated by the church's lack of clarity in treating its relationship to transcendence.

Moon's charisma is both theological—he is God's messenger bringing salvation—and sociological—the contemporary situation has yielded people whose rootlessness and anxiety lead them to seek stability amidst an imperfect, changing, and threatening environment. Consequently, the disconfirmation of many of Moon's predictions concerning the time of victory over Satan has not yielded any mass defections from the church. This would appear to modify Weber's assertion that "the charismatic leader gains and maintains authority solely by proving his strength in life. Above all . . . his divine mission must 'prove' itself in that those who faithfully surrender to him must fare well. If they do not fare well, he is obviously not the master sent by the gods."[32] The centrality of community in the Unification Church suggests, however, that some converts are less interested in theology than they are in feelings of security. To the extent that these remain in spite of failed predictions, the "charisma" may still be working.[33]

The difference between the charismatic role of zaddik and that of Moon appears finally to reside in the distinction between religion and scientism (contemporary idolatry). Humility, mystery, elevation of life in adherence to the ethics of traditional authority based upon a transcendent source, and the function of faith serve to distinguish the charismatic role of the zaddik. Typologically, the zaddik appears to function in much the same manner as did Jesus. Both act to revitalize tradition, by at once challenging it and reaffirming "living" sacrality. On the other hand, the Unification Church, in attempting to transform the world, also desacralizes it. The Reverend Moon's concern for secular matters threatens to overwhelm the religious message of the underlying traditions upon which it draws for inspiration. Here one sees the ambiguity in movements whose primary allegiance is to an individual subject to purely personal motivations, rather than to fixed norms which have been hammered on the anvil of history.

Charisma and Continuity

Charismatic movements which have had historical impact and duration typically provide for transfer of authority. Another is sought whose insight or model provides a more meaningful revelation of the fixed or traditional authority. Hasidic examples abound in which disciples have turned away from their masters either to become masters themselves or to learn, study, and observe in the vicinity of one whose teachings and mode of being would be more beneficial. Nor is this unique to Hasidism: Biblical references, for example, indicate a multiplicity of leader-follower relationships in the Judaism of Jesus' time.[34] On the other hand, leadership in the Unification Church seems only partially to depend upon enriched religious experience or deeper commitment to and understanding of the fixed norm. Moreover, the Reverend Moon apparently recognizes no other prophet's interpretations as authoritative. Moon, like Mohammed, is the seal of all prophecy. Unlike Mohammed, however, Moon's teachings are unclear as to whether a transcendent source is the judge of his actions. Moon's theological position appears to be that he is required neither to submit nor to subordinate himself to sacred text or fixed norm. Rather, one is confronted with the singular nature of his claims and decisions.

The death of the founder always marks a crisis for charismatic groups. Hasidism solved the "crisis of continuity" by making the role of zaddik hereditary. Charisma became inherited (*erbscharisma*). In Weber's terminology, the routinization of charisma in zaddikism is "incomplete." At this time it is unclear what the fate of the Unification Church will be. Will Moon or the *Divine Principle* be authoritative? Will the sacred text emerge as a traditional authority, augmented by the sayings and deeds of the founder? Will one of Moon's children or one of his disciples head the church?

Significance of the Unification Church

Moon's movement has underscored the deficiencies of an impersonal society having an ambiguous relationship to transcendence. The Moon phenomenon functions as a challenge and a warning to liberal Judeo-Christian churches. The messages of the Moonies seem to be multiple: (1) to return to the textual sources of tradition, (2) to take seriously the desire on the part of many youths to improve the world, (3) that evil is a reality against which people wish to struggle, (4) that religion must treat seriously the problems of meaning and morality in the last quarter of the twentieth century, and (5) that charisma, commitment, and community are cohesive forces in a fragmented world. But what is being offered in return may be a further shrinking of the possibilities of existence. For example, it is quite likely that the Unification Church, lacking any clear-cut commitment to the transcendent, will become, after the founder's death, merely a lost current in the American spiritual sea. A similar fate befell Father Divine's Peace and Light Movement after the founder's death.

CONCLUSION

"Charismatic leadership" is a prominent feature of the world which arose out of the "shattered theological framework" of the post-World War

II period. The crisis of the old religious order, precipitated by the failure of the Judeo-Christian legitimation of the world, led to a widespread quest for "meaning," centered primarily on non-Western traditions. Scientism coupled with infantilization has resulted in a pseudomastery of the universe (including pseudocharisma).

Two forms of charisma emerged with great clarity in the postwar period: religious charisma and the charisma of scientism. The degradation of charisma occurs when transcendence ceases to be its sole legitimating force. Sun Myung Moon appears to be the object of worship for his church. Moreover, the origin of Moon's charisma is unclear. Does it stem, for example, from a transcendent order, or from a demonstration of mastery over the empirical world? The Reverend Moon's charisma has the trappings of infantilization. The zaddik, by contrast, is a charismatic whose deeds and prayers point beyond himself, just as Jesus constantly referenced his works to "the Father." Yet the zaddik is accessible and accountable to the community. His charisma is constrained both by transcendence and a fixed norm, and by community—perhaps the central theological category in Judaism. Both Hasidism and Moonism are types of charismatic religiosity which attempt to respond to assaults on the human spirit, though their reference points appear to be quite different.

Charismatic leadership in its idolatrous context appears to restrict life's possibilities. For example, Unification is a synonym for conformity. However, charisma remains a potent force for the revitalization of religious life. While it is possible that a lessening of social and existential tensions may occur, thereby alleviating conditions of distress, it is more likely that the unholy alliance between technology and its bureaucratic overseers will further frustrate humanity's attempts at contact with the transcendent. The age of scientism has yielded a vulgarized form of *homo religiosus* and produced extreme "charismatic" outbreaks. Recovery of transcendence may prove the greatest discovery in our disenchanted world, legitimizing the utilization of the term *charisma*.

7

Against Satan: Charisma and Tradition in Iran

MICHAEL S. KIMMEL
and RAHMAT TAVAKOL

The Iranian Revolution has presented a puzzle to many analysts since it erupted in the streets of Tehran early in 1979. While it appeared to be anti-imperialist and anti-American, it has remained equally hostile to the Soviet Union in particular and socialist economic and political strategies in general. While it appeared to be a mass-mobilized, populist revolution involving perhaps the largest protest demonstrations ever seen in human history (over two million participants on various occasions in Tehran and millions more in other cities), the mobilization has come entirely from urban areas. The countryside has been relatively quiet, contradicting the general pattern of Third World revolutions as rural, peasant insurrections.[1] Furthermore, although an anti-imperialist, "leftist" revolution on one level, the Islamic revolution also seems to augur historical "regression" with respect to the role of women and to ethnic and national minorities. At once revolutionary and reactionary, it contains seemingly unresolvable paradoxes.

These are compounded by the presence of the Ayatollah Khomeini, the revolutionary leader who exerts a powerful, decisive force on the scope and direction of post-revolutionary Iran. Khomeini's bearded visage, angrily sneering at Western infidels, has been imprinted on the American mind in much the same way as Hitler's haughtily arrogant stance at Nuremberg, arm raised, surveying the gathered masses who had come to acclaim him. Yet Khomeini, very much unlike Hitler, appears relatively unaffected by the international spotlight he has come to occupy. Concerned not with personal aggrandizement and the acquisition of wealth through his office, he remains modestly self-denying. No wonder, then, that the Iranian Revolution has baffled Western scholars: anti-American yet anti-Soviet, led by an absolutist leader who appears indifferent to totalitarian temptations, a mass movement of urban followers, revolutionary yet reactionary.

We believe that a Weberian analysis of the Iranian revolution can resolve many of these apparent paradoxes. Specifically, by unpacking Weber's notion of charismatic authority, we can use charisma as a lens through which to view both pre-revolutionary Iranian development and the process and outcomes of the revolution. Through this lens, we can see the Iranian Revolution as a reaction against modernity, thus the reassertion of traditional authority, accomplished through religious revivalism and charismatic symbolism. The charismatic breakthrough engineered for the Ayatollah thus accomplishes a reversal of rational economic development.

To make such an argument, we shall examine certain themes with which Weber was preoccupied throughout his life: the comparative sociology of religion and the relationship between religious ethics and secular politics and law; the relationship between city and countryside, state and society, leader and followers; types of authority; and above all, *the tragic irony of modernity*—that the search for meaning facilitates social changes that, over time, facilitate the loss of meaning.

After a brief discussion of Weber's concept of charisma, we shall examine empirically the dynamics of development in pre-revolutionary Iran. We observe how the modernization strategies of the Shah led to both remarkable economic progress and agonizing social dislocation for a variety of social groups. Dependent development yielded the bitter fruits of domestic discontent and political opposition. We shall then turn to a discussion of Khomeini's "charismatic" character, his ability to break through the rationalizing cycle of development, and alter irrevocably the course of Iranian history. Here we shall also ask on what social foundations Khomeini's charismatic authority was built—his relationship to his followers. We shall argue that the Iranian Revolution was inspired by an anti-modernist vision of traditional community, of intimate emotional relationships among members of the same organic totality, and that Khomeini's charismatic authority was the vehicle by which this vision could be realized in a rapidly industrializing and modernizing society. Finally, we will speculate about the direction of Iranian development in a post-revolutionary anti-modernist society.

WEBER ON CHARISMA

Society is ultimately held together, Weber argues, by relationships of domination that are legitimated by reference to a variety of normative and ethical systems. Their forms, however, vary historically. Both traditional and rational-legal authority are stable, self-perpetuating forms of authority of the classic Weberian typology, in which authority—the justification to rule—inheres in the normative and ethical systems themselves. Charismatic authority is qualitatively different from either traditional or rational-legal authority.[2] Charisma is historical, whereas they are transhistorical. Charisma is temporal, whereas they are, potentially at least, eternal. Its legitimacy derives from the perceptions of others, rather than inhering in the system itself.[3]

Historically, charisma does not arise without social preparations. It is the "product of crisis and enthusiasm," Bendix writes,[4] a conception echoed by Gramsci's discussion of Caesarism, in which the charismatic leader allows temporary unity of political and economic interests—a revolutionary coalition. Gramsci goes on to argue that charisma cannot, by itself, produce fundamental change because of its transient nature; lasting change requires a political party, the active expression of the general collective will of the political community. Charisma achieves "powerful results without power."[5]

Like all forms of authority, charisma relies on a relationship between the dominator and the dominated. As personalized power, Bendix argues, "the charismatic leader derives his authority solely from the demonstration of his power and from his disciples' faith in that power."[6] Weber writes that the leader's "power position depends on his . . . followers," while charismatic justice "does not refer to rules," but to the "legitimation of personal heroism or personal revelation."[7]

Charismatic authority, vested in the extraordinary characteristics of an individual, is, Weber notes, "sharply opposed to rational, and particularly bureaucratic, authority, and to traditional authority. . . ."[8] As such, whenever it appears, it is revolutionary in its implications. The charismatic leader is "always a radical who challenges established practice by going 'to the root of the matter,' " Bendix adds.[9] The leader "repudiates the past," Weber writes, and charisma is "in this sense a specifically revolutionary force." This is true, in part, because charisma does not seek pecuniary gain or aggrandizement as normally understood, but remains estranged from most economic activity. Charisma, Weber argues, "rejects all rational conduct" and is "specifically foreign to economic considerations." The leader does not seek wealth but "repudiates economic exploitation of the gifts of grace as a source of income," and charisma is "never a source of private gain for its holders."[10]

By definition, charisma is unstable. Human life is temporal, and an authority that finds its legitimacy in a human being will inevitably face a crisis of succession, a crisis of maintaining the authority of the leader after death or other removal. By definition, then, charisma, vested in the individual, is a transitional form of authority, which sociologists have most frequently understood as the vehicle by which the move from traditional authority to rational-legal authority may be accomplished.[11] By the charismatic breakthrough, they argue, the eternal cycle of self-referential traditionalism is severed, and the solution to the problem of succession rationalizes charismatic authority into a set of coherent normative expectations, i.e., formal organizations. Charisma dissolves in a sea of rationality as its original compelling power is institutionalized in the very mechanisms that were designed to preserve it. When charisma is not a vehicle by which the passage from traditional to rational-legal authority may be accomplished, it may break through traditional authority only to dissolve itself into a new traditionalism. Thus, Weber writes, charisma "cannot remain stable, but becomes either traditionalized or rationalized or a combination of both."[12]

Yet social scientists have rarely explored a third route for charisma hinted at by Weber, one particularly suited to deconstruct the dynamics of revolution in many Third World nations. In the final paragraphs of *The Protestant Ethic and the Spirit of Capitalism*, Weber despairs that the economic order of modernity has become an "iron cage," a mechanical housing, rationalizing everyday life, disenchanting the world, and voiding it of meaning. In one particularly haunting line, he suggests that the only potential sources of challenge to this rational order may be that "at the end of this tremendous development entirely new prophets will arise, or there will be a great rebirth of old ideas and ideals, or, if neither, mechanized petrification embellished with a sort of convulsive self-importance."[13] While these last phrases constitute a most eloquent exposition of the "culture of narcissism," there is an implicit theoretical assertion here that only charismatic or traditional authority can break the chains of rationalization that have led to this predicament. Perhaps, as we will explore, charismatic authority is the vehicle by which the challenge against legal-rational authority is launched, the means by which the anti-rational, anti-modernist vision may be implemented in a concrete historical situation.

In the remainder of this essay, we want to examine this suggestion in light of the evidence provided by the Iranian Revolution of 1979. In order to do this, we will outline the dynamics of pre-revolutionary Iranian development to indicate the impulse toward rationalization, and suggest some of the sources of discontent caused by this industrial surge. Then we will discuss the structure of Khomeini's authority itself, paying particular attention to the anti-modernist vision expressed by his pronouncements. Finally, we shall conclude with a discussion of the dilemmas and contradictions of "traditional" development since the revolution.

MODERNIZATION UNDER THE SHAH

The Shah undertook an ambitious program of industrialization and economic development that was designed to bring Iran into an elite circle of the five most prosperous nations in the world, to make it, as he said, "the Japan of the Middle East."[14] His plan roughly paralleled the plans of other "bureaucratic-authoritarian" nations in Latin America. Based on the triple alliance of local capital, foreign capital, and the state, economic development would involve investment in heavy industry and import substitution of consumer durables: Import Substitution Industrialization (ISI) is the mode of industrialization in Brazil, Chile, Argentina, and Mexico. The Shah's state attempted to direct the course of Iranian development to maintain the leadership of this triple alliance, but he was ultimately subject to the political and economic pressures of foreign capital.

The overwhelming presence of foreign capital concentrated in one industry—oil—significantly skewed the development trajectory of Iran, as compared with other dependent developers. From the beginning of his industrialization plans, oil revenues were literally the fuel for Iranian industrialization. Oil revenues provided a unique historical opportunity, a flood of money in state coffers rather than the perpetually empty state accounts typical of Third World nations. For example, oil revenues in 1953 totaled 34 million dollars; 20 years later, oil revenues had reached five billion; by 1977, they topped 20 billion.[15] The Shah placed all his hopes on the oil boom, gearing his entire development strategy to rises in prices. In 1963-68, the Third Development Plan was dependent on oil revenues for 62 percent of its program; a decade later, the Fifth Development Plan was to be 80 percent financed by oil revenues.[16]

Reliance on oil revenues put the Iranian economy almost entirely in the hands of foreign, multinational capital. By 1974, 183 firms had invested in Iran. While many other nations maintained corporate outposts in Iran, clearly the United States was the dominant country maintaining corporate linkages there. In 1975, the United States controlled 28 percent of Iran's capital goods market, and by 1978, United States investment in Iran exceeded 682 million dollars. The employment of highly technical, highly capital-intensive technology in the production of oil required skilled operatives; by 1978, there were *50,000* Americans living in Iran.[17]

Thus the Shah embarked on an ambitious program of industrialization and agricultural transformation, fueled by oil revenues. The state invested directly in industry through the various development plans, as well as building an industrial infrastructure. It was the state that undertook power and water projects, road construction, and the development of telecommunications systems. The result was a "rentier state," used by the Shah to create a dependent capitalist class through generous tax exemptions, industrial subsidies, credit and licensing policies, and high tariff walls which were designed to keep foreign competition low. Large industrial units proliferated under such ideal conditions: in 1956, there were 694 large industrial corporations; by 1961, there were 1191, 3661 in 1966, and by 1972,

5671. Overall, industry's share of the gross national product jumped from 13.6 percent in 1960 to 20 percent in 1972, while agriculture's share was almost halved from 30 percent in 1959 to 16 percent in 1972.[18]

Accompanying the Shah's program of ISI was a comprehensive land program. But typical of rural strategies in dependent developing nations, the Land Reform program, unveiled in 1962 as part of the heralded "White Revolution," exacerbated rural tensions, disrupted rural life, and institutionalized capitalist social relations. The main push came in consolidating small rural holdings into larger units, since earlier attempts at reform—the disaggregation of large units and distribution to individual peasant families—had proved inefficient in raising production. Agribusiness enterprises, sponsored and tutored by the Tennessee Valley Authority, seemed promising to the Shah, who encouraged the TVA, claiming that "Iran could be the showcase for all of Asia. America cannot spread its assistance in every country everywhere. Here is the place with the best prospect for a great transformation."[19]

Land reform also implied agricultural mechanization to increase labor productivity. As a result, agricultural production rose 2.2 percent per year, while population increased 3 percent, and consumption of agricultural products jumped 12 percent a year, indicating a sharp demand for agricultural imports. The industrialization of the countryside led to other consequences besides the unintended necessity for greater agricultural imports. The consolidation of land into larger units transformed many peasants into an agricultural proletariat, concerned not for survival but for wages. Those who were unable to find wage work on agricultural enterprises were forced off the land into the cities, a situation analogous to the enclosure movement in England, and there were many caught in it. From 1966-76, over two million villagers left the rural areas to settle in the cities; in 1972-73, the rate of migration had climbed to 8 percent of the population *per year*. These marginal and poor ex-peasants swelled the populations of the already crowded cities, creating a permanent underclass of former rural peasants. Thus in spite of the "urban" nature of the Iranian Revolution, many of the participants were actually rural persons, who happened to live in the city after displacement.[20]

The Shah's modernization program included broad and sweeping social changes as well as the economic transformations of agriculture and industry. Imitating Western societies, the Shah initiated a series of social and educational ventures to bring Iran into the industrial orbit. The age of marriage was raised for women, and the ability of men to obtain easy divorces and to practice polygamy was severely curtailed. The Muslim calendar was replaced. The Minister of Education instructed universities to bar from registration women who insisted on wearing the veil, known as the *chador*.[21] The government seriously cut back its contributions to religious organizations, in 1977 from 80 million dollars to 30 million.[22] This campaign of secularization indicated a shift in Iranian politics towards a Western model of the complete separation of religion and politics, one that would return to haunt the Shah.

The Shah's program achieved few of its desired results. Despite the dramatic rise in per capita income from $176 per annum in 1963-64 to $2,160 in 1977-78, and the rapid acceleration in the rise in gross domestic product—about 9.3 percent per year, which made Iran one of the world's fastest-growing nations—development was marked by persistent inflation that canceled most of the gains. By 1975, when oil revenues suddenly dropped sharply, inflation had become so chaotic that the economy tottered on the brink of collapse. Between March and August 1975, the consumer price index rose 33-38 percent. By far the most significant consequences of the Shah's program of industrialization, however, were social, not economic. The introduction of manufacturing led to the development of an urban working class. From 5 percent in 1953, the labor force had tripled in 1977 to 16 percent.[23] Yet the working class was not incorporated into the political process.

The White Revolution had raised expectations for dramatic improvements in the lives of the people. Although benefits were registered in health, education, and public welfare, 68 percent of the adult population remained illiterate, less than 40 percent of all children completed primary school, and only 60,000 places were open in the universities for over 250,000 applicants. The White Revolution had financed cooperatives and dramatically increased the use of tractors, harvesters, and fertilizers, but 96 percent of all rural villagers did not have electricity, and price controls and lack of access to credit wiped out potential gains. For some, increased access to consumer goods did improve the quality of life. Refrigerators, air conditioners, televisions, cars, and motorcycles proliferated in the cities, but the shanty towns of rural migrants grew even faster. Air pollution, traffic congestion, and hordes of jobless people made Tehran a nightmare according to some American observers.[24]

Among the hardest hit were the *Bazaaris*, the traditional urban lower-middle classes who dealt in the retail trades as small shopkeepers and handicraft workers. The Shah had implemented policies expressly designed to weaken the power of the *Bazaaris*. First, the self-regulating Merchants' Councils were brought under state control, undermining traditional *Bazaari* autonomy. The state also extended its involvement in wholesale and retail trade, setting prices and wages. When inflation triggered by the oil boom threatened to undermine the Shah's development program, he blamed the *Bazaaris* for profiteering from the inflationary spiral and ushered in a price war in the guise of a deliberate "anti-corruption" campaign against the *Bazaaris*.[25] The growth of supermarkets, department stores, and large banks were all seen as threats by the *Bazaaris*, who feared large capital because it threatened their economic autonomy. One shopkeeper told the

New York Times, "If we let him, the Shah will destroy us. The government will flatten our bazaars to make room for the state offices."[26]

Not only was there increasing dissatisfaction among the *Bazaaris*, urban poor, and agricultural workers, but significant opposition also came from religious leaders, who were infuriated by the Shah's resolute secularism. They saw in the Shah's modernization a heretical perversion, a Westernization that bespoke amorality at the heart of his program. Western films and television shows, especially those portraying sexuality, women with uncovered arms, heads, and necks, short skirts and tight pants convinced them that Westerners were utterly morally bankrupt. Rather than relying on popular social support for his policies, the Shah promoted development dependent on foreign capital investment and on political repression through the use of SAVAK, his secret police. Where legitimacy failed his rationalizing authority, terror would maintain it. The gulf between state and society widened into an unbridgeable chasm, maintained by systematic terror.[27]

Such a strategy appeared successful as long as the oil revenues held out. When they faltered, the various displaced and threatened social groups—clerics, *Bazaaris*, urban poor, students and intellectuals, and rural workers—were sufficiently angered to plan a coalition of political opposition against the Shah and his development policies. As with all revolutions, the state had generated its own opposition by moving against many social groups who became increasingly alienated from it. Only one element was missing from the revolutionary coalition, one element that would allow the coalition to gel, for the various elements to hold fast to one another and seize power. That element was a charismatic leader, whose power would allow the final withdrawal of legitimacy from the old regime and the radical break from the past that comprises revolutionary movements.[28]

KHOMEINI AND CHARISMA

Inspired by a seventh-century religious philosophy that claims that religious leaders have the divine right to protect the community from foreigners, to guide the country toward righteousness, exercise power over the elected representatives, and scrutinize the activities of all social groups, Muslim revivalist leaders following the Ayatollah Khomeini led a popular revolution against the Shah in early 1979. The Shah was so weak and cut off from any social support that he had no choice but to flee Iran. Khomeini claimed that the Shah "placed the Iranian people under American bondage. . . . Because America is the land of the dollar and because the Iranian government needs dollars! . . . It is up to the Iranian people to break this chain. It is up to the Iranian Army not to allow such disgraceful happenings in Iran."[29]

Despite Dekmejian's argument that Khomeini's leadership is limited to a small segment of Shi'ite Islam and therefore localistic, "largely a reaction to the repressive politics of a corrupt political order," so that "the movement lacks a leader of charismatic propensity who could provide some focus in terms of spiritual unity and revolutionary activity,"[30] Khomeini embodies many of the characteristics of a charismatic leader, while his authority exemplifies the ideal type of charismatic domination. The source of his authority is more than the religious ethics that underlie his pronouncements. Standing outside the legal-rational order, in opposition to the rationalization of Iranian society under the Shah, Khomeini has come to represent the frustrations and hopes of the dispossessed, those against whom the modernization was accomplished. He is able, one observer writes, to "grasp people's ideas and understand their needs and then move in that direction."[31] What's more, he stands for them, he *is* them. "The Iranian people consider me a symbol," he said. "I talk their language, I listen to their needs, I cry for them."[32]

Khomeini's charismatic authority derives ultimately from his personal characteristics, which are legitimated by recourse to religion. But even here, religion justifies charisma, not the other way around (with charisma only expressing religious ethics). Khomeini understands his role as that of a prophet. He consistently refers to himself as analogous to Moses, and has appropriated the title Imam, suggesting that his role is related to that of the returning Twelfth Imam. His recourse, ultimately, is not to traditional religion, but to God himself. Another Ayatollah said of Khomeini, "By God, his word is the word of God's inspiration and the voice of God,"[33] and Khomeini himself proclaimed, "O God, witness that I give your message."[34] Nonetheless, Khomeini denies his own revolutionary power—"I am not a revolutionary," he claims—but instead hails the revolutionary nature of Islam: "Our international revolutionary spirit comes from the spirit of Islam. The internationalist ideology of Islam has always dominated the nationalist political passions."[35] As charismatic leader, Khomeini lives an ascetic life, denying himself the potential spoils of office. He lives modestly, stoically, himself a disciple of the faith. He is a leader by example, not exhortation. He is uncompromising. He has insisted he would execute his own children if they deserved such punishment.[36]

Once Khomeini's charismatic potential was recognized, it was imperative to indicate the inevitability of his rule. In a sense, this required the rewriting of his biography to indicate that at birth he was destined to rule. Thus, certain events in Khomeini's life were exaggerated and others minimized, to graft historical inevitability onto biography.[37] Fatherless at age two—his father was killed in a dispute with a landlord in 1902, hence the Ayatollah's hatred of landlords—Khomeini was raised by his mother, and in 1919 became a disciple of a well-known conservative ayatollah. In 1920, a divination indicated he would die in Qum, which was taken as a sign by his followers throughout his exile that he would someday return to Iran. From the 1940s, Khomeini was critical of Westernization and modernization under the then Shah, father of Mohammed Reza Pahlevi. When his teacher died in the 1950s, Khomeini became the leading disciple and the chief successor. Khomeini emerged on the political scene in 1963 with an attack on the corruption inherent in the Shah's plans to grant rights to American advisors and military personnel in Iran. His subsequent exile in France backhandedly added charismatic legitimacy to Khomeini's claims. Forced out of his nation by a corrupt Westernizer, he was "forced" to live in Paris, one of the home bases of Mammon. His return to Iran, in turn, was hailed as a religious, not a political, holiday.

Since his return from exile to Iran in February 1979, Khomeini's power has only increased. The source of his charismatic legitimacy is, as for all charismatic leaders, the relationship between leader and followers. They praise his sacredness; he exhorts them to greatness. They exult in his glory; he presses them to search inward for their "Islamic identities."[38] The representatives of the delegation from the First Islamic Parliament praised Khomeini by reference to his divinity: "You [Khomeini] have been able to implement God's divine plan."

> Today, not only the Islamic people of Iran have risen up against the Satans of the Age, but also the enchained peoples from other parts of the world who have heard your Celestial Message, have rushed up against the palaces of oppression inspired with your aspiration to establish the World Islamic Order. . . . Our Imam, Islamic order is a universal order and is a Muslim community that must be formed of all people of the world. We vow to you—you, who have freed all helpless people—that we will spread this victory to the whole world. We promise you that we will spread to the rest of the world *your Holy Teachings*, which are rays of light for all and *whose source is God himself*. The world today must know that Our Islamic order has been reestablished today under *your divine leadership*, whose family linkage reaches back to the Holy Prophet Mohammed. The borders of Iran are too narrow for you, who have, after 14 centuries, brought the fruition of the heroic Shi'ite struggle. *You are too great for Iran. You should rule all living things* because God, who created all living things, entrusted them to his hidden Imam [Mahdi, the twelfth Holy Imam], and you are now his deputy. *You should*, therefore, *rule the world*, a world that is not worthy of you.[39]

Khomeini's response to such adulation is to turn it back to the people. "People who dedicate themselves and everything for Islam are victorious."[40]

Khomeini's charisma, however, is not universally appealing—even in Iran. Vested as it is in the person and not in normative or ethical systems, some are called and some are not. Interestingly, those who hear the call and those who fail to hear it often stratify themselves by class. In Iran, Khomeini's charisma is positively experienced with greatest acuity by the urban poor (the proletariat and new urban migrants) and the traditional petite bourgeoisie, the *Bazaaris*. These groups are, historically, especially susceptible to charismatic movements. They are also precisely the groups most seriously injured by the modernization plans of the Shah, the traditional remnants whose livelihood was undermined by the development of Western social classes.

The goal of Khomeini's charismatic leadership has always been to *restore* traditional authority by returning to a categorically Islamic society. By submerging Iranian society within traditional Islam, Khomeini hopes to reverse the process of Westernization that corrupted Iranian society. Here Khomeini confirms in practice Weber's analysis of Islam. Weber argues that Islam is particularly conducive to charismatic movements because there is no conflict between religion and politics.[41] Weber writes:

> An essentially political character marked all of the chief ordinances of Islam: the elimination of private feuds in the interests of increasing the group's striking power against external foes; the proscription of illegitimate forms of sexual behaviour and the regulation of legitimate sexual relations along strongly patriarchal lines.[42]

Khomeini also understands the essentially political character of his faith. Islam is a "political religion,"[43] he argues, thus "those intellectuals who say that the clergy should leave politics and go back to the mosque speak on behalf of Satan."[44]

Weber argues that there is no conflict between religion and politics in Islam because of the doctrine of salvation by faith, which "directly augments the religious emphasis placed upon vocational activity within the world." Islam promises "redemption from oppression and suffering," he says as a reward for religious consistency. The "assurance that the word of the prophet that God would never permit the congregation of the faithful to fall into error," means that the believer carries promises of world dominion, "in his knapsack, so to speak, as the reward for holy war against all infidels." Moreover, Weber argues salvation by faith presses the believer outward, into the world, to prove faith. Islam

> makes obligatory the violent propagandizing of a true prophecy which consciously eschews universal conversion and enjoins the subjugation of unbelievers under the dominion of a ruling class dedicated to the religious war as one of the basic postulates of its faith, without, however, recognizing the salvation of the subjugated. The practice of coercion poses no problem since God is pleased by the forcible dominion of the faithful over the infidels who are tolerated once they have been subjugated.[45]

Seen in this way, the revolution is a reclamation of territory from Western influence, reclamation of culture from rationalization, reclamation of traditional economic organization from capitalist social relations, reclamation of self-identity from the meaninglessness to which it had been subjected as a result of corrupt and distorted industrialization. Islam is the means and the end of this revolution. The Islamic society is the goal of liberation and surely the sole route to that liberation. "You have everything, rely on your Islamic values and fight the West and Westernization," Khomeini exhorts.[46] "We did not want oil, we did not want independence, we wanted Islam," he remonstrates.[47] The revolution promises a return to the divine origins of Iranian society away from which the Shah had led them. Industrialization, by contrast, had done nothing "except to enrich foreign pockets."[48]

Freedom was what Khomeini promised—freedom to live under Islamic law—and what the Iranian people believe he has delivered, continuing to live as the template of their own freedom. The revolution has changed little materially. Land reform has been virtually non-existent, and rural protests have been frequently subject to serious repression. Industrialization has not progressed much: the initial rejection of all Western consumer goods led to a fall in consumption, but economic development was not what the revolutionary Mullahs promised in the first place. They promised hope, liberation from Western influence, freedom and autonomy, all within a context of recharged traditionalism. The Mullahs have promised a return to an Islamic golden age. The Iranian people are exhorted to believe that they are at its gates. Ultimately the Iranian Revolution is a return to traditionalism, a move from rational-legal authority to traditional authority, accomplished in the only way that theory or politics allows: the personal characteristics of a charismatic leader who promotes the anti-modernist vision.

PART III

The Fate of Charisma in the Modern World

8

Manufactured Charisma and Legitimacy

RONALD M. GLASSMAN

For Max Weber, as Reinhard Bendix has suggested, charisma was more than a sociological category. In his despair over the trends he saw emerging in the modern world, Weber turned to charisma as a potential savior.[1] However, he was always a realist; thus he described two anticharismatic trends in the contemporary world—the "depersonalization" of charisma that occurs after the routinization of charisma, and the "disenchantment" with charisma that emerges from a rational worldview.[2]

The production of "depersonalized" charisma and the inhibition of "pure" charisma in today's rationalized world will be the focus of this analysis. I shall argue that depersonalized charisma, a *manufactured* form of charisma, becomes critical in the legitimation processes of contemporary political systems of all kinds. The influence of the mass media on mass populations becomes a central factor—one that Weber could not have fully foreseen but which fits in neatly as an extension of his theoretical formulations.

ADMINISTRATIVE LEADERSHIP

In terms of human political leadership, we may at the outset differentiate between "task" leadership and "charismatic" leadership. Task leadership is based purely on the skill of an individual at a given task which the group needs to accomplish. There will be many leaders in a group depending on the number of tasks necessitated and the specific differential skills of the individuals in the group. This kind of leadership is never absent from human polities.

Bureaucracy, in its essence, represents the total institutionalization of task leadership. It is an effective, if not always efficient, way to organize and accomplish specific tasks in large-scale, complex societies. Weber has described its structure, Mumford its origins.[3] But since task-accomplishment is never one of the central issues of the political process, humans are always singularly unimpressed by task-officialdom. This attitude is a mixture of blasé acceptance of the necessity of task-officialdom and annoyance when this officialdom impinges upon them and in turn prods them to accomplish some specific task. Bureaucracy gains legitimacy simply because people accept the fact that complex tasks need to be done in large-scale societies.

In fact, bureaucracy is always attached to some other legitimation system. Historically, it has been attached to both traditional kingly authority and to legal-democratic authority. It has also been attached to communist party power in contemporary communist states. Whether bureaucratic leadership can stand alone as a fully legitimated "power elite" in a future technocratic-industrial society, we cannot yet know, though this may be one of the critical questions of our age.[4]

CHARISMATIC LEADERSHIP

Two other more critical processes characterize leadership and politics. The first is power, that is, the need to maintain external protection and territoriality and the need to maintain internal order and distribute life needs (food, shelter, sexuality, childcare). Weber considered power leadership to be a form of *nonlegitimate domination*. But, of course, he recognized that "caesarism," as he termed power leadership, could be long-lived and that the use of excess force could characterize a political system for decades.[5] However, instability would necessarily plague such a political system, since the "acquiescence" engendered by the fear of force could give way to rebellion at any moment within a system where the population does not recognize the right of the leadership to rule. One need only read Machiavelli's *Prince* to gain a clear idea of the instability and resulting need for the use of escalating violence necessitated by a system of nonlegitimate power leadership.

Second, there is leadership based on morale boosting of the individual and of the group, and on group cohesion. This kind of leadership is not related to some specific task, nor is it based on physical force. It is leadership dependent upon the special gift that certain individuals possess of being able to rouse other individuals to greater feats than they thought possible in difficult situations, being able to rouse people from their lethargy when they are depressed or frightened, being able to impart confidence to the group when it is collectively anxious, being able to make the group function as one when conflicts divide it, being able to help the group face crisis situations and the unknown with courage and optimism. This—and more—is what Weber terms "charismatic leadership."[6]

TRANSFERABLE, HERITABLE, "MANUFACTURED," AND INSTITUTIONAL CHARISMA

Whether charisma is transferable may seem like a contradictory question. Technically, of course, charisma should not be transferable. Either an individual has the "gift of grace" or it is absent. In practice, however, close association with the charismatic leader often confers charisma on others. This is so much the case that at the death of a charismatic leader the group will often turn for leadership to one of the individuals closely associated with the charismatic leader. In this sense charisma is transferable, and it is often the case that those close to a charismatic leader can succeed that leader.

In early human societies a close relative or friend of a leader was usually that leader's leadership associate. In most instances, the individual most like the leader and closest to the leader was probably a relative. A brother, near uncle, or son, where leadership was male-monopolized, would often succeed to charismatic leadership. Sometimes a mother or daughter or wife would succeed to such leadership were it not male-monopolized.[7] This process of the transference of charisma becomes important to human societies in terms of the problem of succession to leadership positions. We are faced with the irony that hereditary succession to charismatic leadership—which should be impossible in principle—becomes possible in actuality. Early human societies often came to charismatize a whole family, even a large clan, because of some past association with a great charismatic leader. Weber called this "clan charisma." In this way, succession struggles were eliminated in advance, because anyone born into a charismatic family would possess a certain amount of charisma by the fact of the association.[8]

In late tribal and early agricultural society, when the size and complexity of human societies increased, succession struggles became more extreme. In such societies clan charisma or hereditary charisma was maintained through artificial attempts at stage managing the charismatic process. The key element here was that a leader could be made to appear charismatic, not through his or her personal qualities of leadership, but through artificial, manufactured means. Manufactured charisma had significant ramifications on leadership, succession, and legitimacy.

The critical operation involved in the manufacture of charisma was the successful creation of physical and psychic grandeur through which *any* individual could *appear* charismatic. Special clothing, masks, headdresses, and ornaments which conferred a spectacular appearance upon any individual wearing them were created. If grandeur and beauty were not enough, size and mystery and flair could be added to the charismatizing garb: to grandiose and jewel-bedecked clothing could be added padding and stilts to make the individual look huge, and masks and giant headgear could be used to make the ruler appear frightening, mysterious, even mystical. Magic symbols like animal skins, carved objects, and rare vegetation could be used to evoke awe. In this way, the *office itself*, rather than the specific leader, was charismatized institutionally. That is, the office—with its manufactured charismatic symbols—preexisted any individual who succeeded to it.[9]

As societies grew larger and more differentiated, access to office and the stage management of the charismatic effects became even more limited to fewer and fewer individuals from clearly specified clans, classes, professions, age grades, or sexes. When charisma is extended to only a select segment of society, then the traditionalized charismatization of leadership roles not only produces the charismatic effect of group cohesion and morale boosting, but alienation and resentment also occur, especially among those individuals who aspire to leadership but cannot achieve it because they do not fit the traditionalized succession pattern. Such individuals may become delegitimated from the traditional managed charismatization process and attempt to develop a following of their own against the traditional leadership.

To counteract this latter possibility and to maintain internal order in these larger, more complex societies, the established leadership introduced cooptation, ideological manipulation, force, and terror. Pure charismatic leadership—that is, real or personal charismatic leadership—thus became a revolutionary force in traditional societies.[10]

MANUFACTURED CHARISMA AND POLITICAL LEGITIMACY

Manufactured charisma cannot be understood in its entirety if it is not seen as a component of the legitimacy process. Legitimacy can be roughly defined as "consent to be led."[11] The process of legitimation, or consent giving, in regard to leadership and dominance among group animals, is specific to human groups. Humans have consciousness—that is, the ability to think and reflect together. These capacities lead to what Weber called the "rationality" of humans in their approach to natural and social life, and I shall shortly show that this rationality leads to what I shall call the rational components of legitimacy.[12] But consciousness is a double-edged sword; it also leads to a marked irrationality in human behavior. It is the search for meaning in a seemingly incomprehensible world which produces certain irrational aspects of consciousness. Ironically, the process of attempting to find meanings for life and the world and attempting to alleviate feelings of despair and depression is quite rational indeed. Nonetheless, since rational solutions to this endemic existential problem are probably impossible, irrational solutions are turned to for relief.[13]

This dual nature of humans leads to a conflicting result. Because of the rational component of consciousness, human individuals have the ability to be the least dominated and freest of all animals with group structure, but yet, because of the irrational component of consciousness, humans also can be subjugated more slavishly than all other animals.

The rational components of legitimacy can be separated into several categories: (1) participation in decision making, rule making, rule interpretation, and the selection of leaders and access to leadership offices; (2) limitation of the power and the tenure of leaders (including recall); and (3) law (legal authority) involving debatable, amendable rules for the maintenance of group order, constitution-law guidelines for leaders, and protection for citizens.

There is a direct link between the rational components of legitimacy and democracy. But democracy is not fully coextensive with the rational components of legitimacy. Irrational elements also abound in democracy. Cooptation through gifts and through ideological manipulation and myth-building, and coercion through police, military, and judicial institutions are all parts of democratic political systems. Democracy, however, in its ideal form strives toward purely rational legitimation, whereas kingship or oligarchy or dictatorship does not.

Given the human proneness to irrational as well as rational acts of consciousness, one should not be surprised to find that there are numerous ways of engendering consent through irrational means, and the processes of irrational consent getting are as commonly found in human societies as are the rational factors. The irrational components of legitimacy can be summarized as follows: pure charisma, manufactured charisma, ideological manipulation, cooptation (the buying of consent through direct political, economic, or social gifts), and coercion (the use of psychological terror or physical force or both).

This last category, coercion, is not technically a component of legitimacy. Obviously coercion does not produce voluntary consent, whereas all the other components of legitimacy—rational and irrational—do. There is a debate over whether a system of terror and force can be called a legitimate political structure. E. V. Walter, in *Terror and Resistance*, takes the position that it can be so called simply because of the longevity of such systems and the relative ineffectualness of, and minority participation in, resistance to such leadership.[14] Yet terror and force are not really mechanisms of true legitimacy, regardless of the power they generate. Leaders resort to them only when all else fails. Leaders always desperately attempt to produce other processes of consent getting which will engender the desired voluntary lending of consent by the group. Terror and force are too difficult and costly to maintain over time. Retaliation by the group becomes a nightmare to the leader, disturbing his status desires and inculcating real fears and paranoiac delusions of resistance and rebellion.

No leadership clique maintains itself for long by terror and force alone, but continued use of terror and force may accompany the legitimacy processes, especially where total voluntary consent is never achieved, or where the polity is so large and diverse and complex that some subgroups within the larger society will inevitably be left out of the legitimacy system or will opt out of it. But those societies in which rational and irrational processes of consent giving are operating effectively will use much less coercion than those societies in which legitimacy processes are ineffectual.

In times of massive social change, of course, all legitimacy systems may break down, and the use of terror and force may temporarily emerge as the dominant factor in leadership.[15] But even in such cases, the rise of a great charismatic leader may ease the transition and eliminate the necessity of massive coercion.

CHARISMA AND IRRATIONAL LEGITIMACY

Pure or genuine charisma is the perfect example of an irrational consent relationship between leader and led. Each individual within the charismatizing group feels a special personal relationship with the leader—even if he has never met the leader. This personal relationship creates a bond between the individual and the leader such that the individual fully trusts the leader and consents to the leader in all phases of leadership.

A charismatic leader can usurp enormous amounts of privilege, wealth, and power; yet because of this special, almost superhuman status, the charismatizing group not only will fully consent to these activities but will actually approve of them. Every outward sign that the leader is in truth superhuman raises the group's confidence in the leader and tends to justify the irrational faith which the charismatizing group places in the leader.

Because personal charismatic leadership is the only kind of leadership which combines massive usurpation with total consent giving, and because charisma is transferable, it is no wonder that attempts to manufacture charisma in order to create permanent leadership offices, with carefully designated succession to such offices, were successfully institutionalized. Undoubtedly, the leadership clans, classes, and cliques surrounding the manufactured charismatic leader came to perceive the power relationship in a more rational fashion than the majority of the group. They, after all, often trained the leader and knew him in a close personal way. Furthermore, they participated in the manufacturing process, making sure that robes, scepters, insignia, myths, ideologies, and ceremonies strictly and carefully surrounded the leader at all times. Nevertheless, such elites often believed in the charisma that they manufactured. There is no doubt, too, that the leader himself often fully believed that his charisma was real—especially if the belief was inculcated from childhood. No one could have been more bewildered than a divine king when his divinity was stripped away. Often an entire leadership stratum would be similarly affected.

In agricultural societies the manufacture of charisma essentially took the form of the combination of the aristocratic-clan charisma with the leadership offices of war chief and shaman. The larger populations of agricultural societies and the specialization of labor gave rise to non-food-producing strata for the first time. The war chiefs eventually became a whole stratum of non-food-producing "knights" or full-time warriors. The shamans, too, became a whole stratum of non-food-producing priests. These strata of priests and knights had their succession lines linked directly to, and limited by, the aristocratic clans. Thus true aristocratic classes emerged which dominated all leadership roles in agricultural societies. These aristocratic classes utilized manufactured charisma to the fullest.

The eventual union of the two upper classes, the knightly and the priestly, produced the ultimate in manufactured charisma, a creation never before equaled in the annals of humankind. This was the divine kingship—the divine emperor, the sultanate, and similar leaders. Here the zenith of manufactured charismatic irrationality was reached, for the charismatizing group projected onto the divine king that which it always wanted to project onto a personal charismatic leader anyway, superhuman divinity. The leader became God—not a mediator between humans and gods, but God himself. The led cringed, trembled, crawled, bowed, kissed the feet of, looked away from, the God-leader. Yet the actual human shrouded in a manufactured charismatic veil might be a moron, an incompetent, a child, a senile elder, a woman.

As the aristocratic classes became leisure classes, and as the wealth and complexity of agricultural society increased, a class of noncharismatic task officials was coopted into the leadership structure. Bureaucracy, as a structure of administrative leadership, emerged. A host of bureaucratic officials filled permanently institutionalized offices and performed the functions of task leadership. The charismatic functions of leadership—morale boosting and social cohesion—were still performed by the aristocratic-charismatic classes and the office of divine kingship.

Thus bureaucracy and bureaucratic strata existed under the mantle of traditional authority and manufactured charismatic leadership. In some societies, such as China, the bureaucratic stratum itself developed at least some measure of legitimate authority and even a religious ideology to legitimate it further.[16] Yet even in China, the mandarins, though revered and legitimated beyond any bureaucratic stratum elsewhere, could never gain anything like total consent or full legitimacy but had to hide under the manufactured charismatic veil of the divine kingship. Stripped of this veil, even the centuries-old Mandarin-Confucian legitimation structure proved totally inadequate to justify bureaucratic domination.

In an agricultural society, small leadership cliques surrounding the divine king and dereified from (or not responding to) the manufactured charisma of the deified leader emerged as stage managers of political leadership and partook of—and protected and extended—the usurpations. This leadership clique, or elite, was drawn primarily from the aristocratic classes but also came to include members of the bureaucratic stratum and eventually members of the emerging merchant stratum. The political center or court of the divine king, then, became a separate political arena where elite leadership asserted itself—in a manipulative, usurping way—in which political struggles took on a character of their own, beyond the broader political struggles of the society as a whole.

Thus two levels of politics existed in late agricultural society: the politics of the total society involving all the factors of leadership and legitimacy; and the politics of the elite, courtly, inner circle which operated outside the legitimacy structure but was protected by the manufactured charismatic structure, of which the elite now became caretakers. This process took centuries to develop. However, once the elite court cliques emerged, manipulation of the legitimacy processes and consciously usurping activities became parts of human politics.

MEDIA-MANUFACTURED CHARISMA IN THE MODERN WORLD

Although traditional forms of manufactured charisma have probably disappeared forever, leaderships' elites will continue to exploit new techniques of manufacturing charisma both to achieve societal integration and to legitimize their usurpation of power. We are acutely conscious today of the role of the mass media in manufacturing charisma. Indeed, leadership elites have employed specially trained social science teams to "package" the new media-manufactured charismatic leader in the most successful way.

Newspapers, magazines, and mass-printed posters create an atmosphere in which the political leader seems ever present and larger than life. Since the charismatic relationship functions best when the group feels a personal, trusting, infantilizing bond with the leader, the constant leader presence—in bright images—helps manufacture such leader-led relationships.

Radio is also a medium through which very successful charisma manufacture has occurred. Great and passionate oratory is one of the key ways in which charisma can be generated by a leader. The intersubjective communication or oratorical language can create a spell in which humans become swayed and charismatically linked to a leader. Radio amplifies this oratorical linkage. Hitler and Castro, Roosevelt and Churchill, used radio to raise oratorical charisma to new media-manufactured heights.

All these leaders, however, demonstrated aspects of genuine or "pure" charisma. Since charisma is transferable and heritable, however, their successors and imitators have used and will use media-manufactured techniques to ensure the transfer of charisma to nonnatural heirs. Stalin, for instance, used these techniques to create charisma for himself, where none had existed in the natural sense. Ronald Reagan offers a weekly radio broadcast.

Movies are spectacular in their ability to create manufactured charisma. Just as microphones create an oratory greater than life, so movies create physical beauty and strength far greater than life. Technicolor splendor transforms men and women into gods and goddesses possessing sensuality and strength of charismatic proportions. The movies are larger than life; the voices are smooth and beautiful. Further, the darkness of the theatre puts the individual into a dream state in which fantasy projections and identifications become easy to attain.

Television is still in its infancy as a leadership tool, but it may develop a potential for manufactured charismatic manipulations more far-reaching than any of the other media. Three different processes are already discernible in terms of television's impact on charismatic leadership. First, television through its newscasts, can de-charismatize pure charismatic leaders, as well as enhance their charisma. Second, television helps create manufactured charismatic leaders where pure charisma is lacking. Finally, television (along with movies) creates its own media-manufactured charismatic figures—stars—who then become national celebrities in their own right. Each of these processes merits further consideration.

A test of a political leader's charisma in the modern world is whether his or her charisma can be projected through the media. The kind of charismatic techniques that worked well in the era of public speaking, microphones, and radio do not usually translate well in a television appearance. That is, as McLuhan has pointed out brilliantly, television is a "cool" medium in which "hot" oratory looks out of place—it becomes annoying, grating.[17] The gesticulations seem too flamboyant, facial expressions too twisted and forced, and the voice too small to justify such bodily histrionics. Therefore, the "great orator" does not do well on television. In fact, such oratory is rarely shown directly. Instead, with the speaker in the background and the speaker's voice tuned out, the television newsperson summarizes the main points of the speech with only a few sentences of the actual speaking allowed to go on the air. Not only is the oratorical charisma neutralized, but the newscaster's interpretation of the main points of the speech is all that is conveyed. Only the President, and less often, party chiefs, get uninterrupted speech time on the media in the United States, and even then commentators provided by the networks engage in "instant analysis" and critical summations of the address.

Furthermore, television is unkind to many leaders in that the close-up lens tends to highlight blemishes, pimples, and other physical imperfections. Leaders used to "the stump," but unskilled in the media, often look furrowed, pockmarked, or uncertain on television. Very often they look smaller than life, as contrasted with media stars, who appear larger than life. The lack of media skill, along with a clinging to older oratorical styles, can decharismatize a candidate who cannot adapt to its technical demands. Television in this sense is a de-charismatizing medium.

Some candidates, of course, have just the right combination of good looks, oratorical restraint, wit, and style for the new medium. John Kennedy's looks and style were so well suited to television that he became charismatized through it, while Nixon was so ill-suited to this medium that whatever office charisma the vice-presidency might have carried was largely neutralized by his poor television "presence." The projection of genuine charisma through television is not impossible, then, but demands a different set of techniques than those which enhanced charisma prior to television. Few political leaders have been able to imitate Kennedy's success. There is good reason for this, having more to do with television coverage of political leaders than the leaders' failure to imitate Kennedy.

Certain further decharismatizing processes have become typical in the television medium. It is now evident that even when a political leader learns to master television technique, if television's opinion-forming agents wish to decharismatize such a candidate, they very often can. Television newspeople tend to be cynical and frequently attempt to debunk a candidate. They can be formidable opponents in this regard because *they* manipulate the media situation. They may set out on a careful campaign of slandering the leader's programs, impugning the leader's judgments and choice of aides and friends, or uncovering embarrassing incidents from his or her personal life. They can ask hostile questions during interviews, put the leader on the defensive and never ask the questions which would allow the leader to present a positive, personal point of view. Failure to submit to this ordeal is itself treated as a "news event," while even sponsored programming may subsequently be subjected to critical analysis.

It is because of these problems that modern political leaders have had to learn how to utilize the media to their advantage. They have had to learn how to present themselves on television in both spontaneous and arranged situations, and they have had to hire public relations "image makers" and Madison Avenue "marketing experts" to create television commercials in which their image, their message, and the situation can be manipulated on their behalf. Madison Avenue image making and political commercials are now commonplace phenomena. Media experts can make or break a candidate. "Packaged" versions of candidates are presented to the public regularly. All of these image-making processes represent attempts at media-manufactured charisma. The real candidate is hidden behind the facade as surely as the kings were hidden behind their crowns, robes, and scepters.

This is a "rationalized" world, of course, and therefore the candidates' actions and policies can be analyzed beyond their manufactured images. Thus, sometimes the image-making works, and sometimes it does not. But in either case, the presentation of the leader in today's media dominated world is often a packaged product. Television, then, inhibits the projection of pure charisma and sometimes debunks it when it does emerge, while at the same time structurally encouraging the manufacture of charisma through media techniques.

Finally, if television debunks the pure charisma of political leaders, it also produces charismatic figures of its own. Television, like the movies, produces stars, who are themselves, of course, packaged personalities. We do not know much about the "real" person. The star possesses some modicum of charm, beauty, or other characteristic of importance. Not everyone who is packaged catches on, but the greater part of the personality is manufactured image.

Stars have become potentially powerful as political leaders. C. Wright Mills, so far ahead of his time, wrote of celebrities and how easily they mingled with the politically powerful figures of the United States. He was clearly right when he suggested that the "power elite" would include figures from the world of the celebrities.[18] Figures like Ronald Reagan, Jane Fonda, and Ed Asner have already emerged as political leaders. Even before Ronald Reagan became president, people were talking about Walter Cronkite as a possible candidate. During the Carter-Ford election of 1976, the general opinion in the nation was that Cronkite, in fact, would be more trustworthy and capable than either of them.

Media celebrities, be they movie stars, television stars, sports figures (like Jack Kemp) or astronauts (like John Glenn) are taken seriously as political leaders even though they have no political experience. They are taken seriously because they possess media-manufactured charisma. This manufactured charisma produces an irrational bond between such a figure and a mass audience in typical charismatic fashion. This irrational bond can be utilized to create mass acceptance in the political sphere. The example of Walter Cronkite shows how newscasters can become stars in their own right.

As media celebrities emerged as political leaders, television newscasters also began to stand out as stars—and therefore as potential political leaders. Television news ratings have skyrocketed and news shows have expanded considerably. The newscasters' faces are everywhere, and they command prime time as they "chaperone" and define every critical event. Not only do they debunk the charisma of political leaders, they also can become political leaders themselves, not for their political experience or expertise but as media "personalities." The age of television is truly in its infancy. Size, color, and cable, if newly combined, could produce a "hot" medium of the future in which the manufacture of charisma could reach heady heights indeed.

Instead of leading toward "1984" media-manufactured charismatic political leadership, however, television technology could alternatively lead toward a new kind of rational legitimacy process. Through local and national cable TV hook-ups, a new kind of participation could be generated in which media-monitored town meetings and debates could create a new form of democratic politics. I am not suggesting that the media are neutral entities through which we can do whatever we existentially will—this is not the case. Media definitely affect the process of human interaction. But the use of the media is often variable rather than rigidly singular, and human input and intent are as critical in media adaptation as the structure and effect of the media themselves. The media are only half the message; human participation and will potential are the other half.

SOME IMPEDIMENTS TO THE MANUFACTURE OF CHARISMA IN THE MODERN WORLD

The impediments to the media-manufacture of charisma in the modern world all come under Weber's heading of "rationality." TV commentators in their cynical and probing style, along with newspaper reporters and columnists, tend to produce a kind of debunking rationality in our approach to political life.

Science and social science produce a rational, skeptical, empirical worldview in which humans become an object to themselves. Therefore, attempts at manufactured charisma are analyzed and unveiled by the constant probing and analytical processes of the rational scientific worldview. Of course, at the same time scientists and social scientists are also coopted by elites and utilized to help create manufactured charisma and the new media through which to manufacture charisma. Nonetheless, there will always be other scientists who are not coopted and who will continue to analyze such processes rationally. Thus attempts both to manufacture charisma and to unmask such manufacture will occur in the scientific community. As a worldview, science itself produces a general rationality through which the "average" individual becomes cynical and decharismatized easily, even though media and audience manipulation become ever more sophisticated.

Another factor which makes the media-manufacture of charisma difficult is that modern society is a multigroup, multiclass society. Because of this, any charismatic leader will fail to charismatize certain portions of the population. Such a leader can be, then, decharismatized through active propaganda used against him or her. This process did occur occasionally in traditional societies, but it is intensified today by the rationality of modern groups and by the possibilities of quick travel and media communications. Repression can be used against such activities, but repression does not charismatize the repressed; so the effect of manufactured charisma is never total in multigroup societies of any kind.

Finally, the rise and extension of bureaucratic political organization creates a situation in which charisma is purposefully eliminated from leadership roles and creates instead a structure in which leadership offices are divided and subdivided and organized in a maze of hierarchies. Charismatic leadership is not necessary for cohesion and is instead discouraged. But bureaucratic political leadership creates no legitimacy structure of its own except in terms of performance evaluation, and the alienation and lack of cohesion humans feel when confronted with or absorbed into bureaucratic organizations often drive them toward the desire for charismatic leadership. Thus while bureaucratic political organization actively devalues and destroys charismatic leadership, it produces the concomitant longing for charisma in those individuals alienated by the structure of bureaucracy itself.

Historically, bureaucracy as a political system has never been able to exist apart from some form of charismatic leadership. Thus it may be that the use of bureaucratic organization in all modern societies, capitalist or communist, may drive people toward the easy acceptance of charismatic leadership. However, the rationality of the modern world makes it difficult for individuals to charismatize any leader.

Not only does bureaucracy eliminate and limit charismatic leadership, but bureaucracy also limits the effectiveness of rational political procedures. That is, bureaucracy has a rationality of its own and a hierarchical structure that is anathema to rational forms of political participation, leadership choice, and leadership limitation. Specialization, compartmentalization, and hierarchy—these are the rational structures of bureaucracy, but their rationality is different from that of rational political consent getting.[19]

Thus, bureaucratic organization inhibits both irrational charismatic leadership and rational democratic leadership, leaving the individual in a state of alienation and low morale. Undoubtedly some other forms of political action and consent will have to emerge beyond the modern, purely bureaucratic political and economic organizations.

In communist societies the media-manufacture of charisma is consciously and carefully stage managed by the bureaucratic elite of the Communist Party. Bureaucratic political organization is combined with a cult of the media-manufactured charismatic leader. This has been very effective in the modernizing period, when traditional populations remained the largest grouping in society. With scientific, technocratic, and bureaucratic classes beginning to become majority classes and television spreading, the same kinds of impediments to the manufacture of charisma as emerged in the West are appearing.

In Western societies, the rational processes of consent getting are declining as corporate and governmental bureaucracies increasingly come to dominate political action.[20] Alienation is increasing, and parliamentary democracy is no longer seen as a real vehicle for rational participation by large segments of these societies. A turn toward media-packaged leaders has emerged. But these attempts have been met, so far, with cynicism. Again, whether these media-packaged leaders will gain charismatic currency or whether new forms of rational political leadership procedures will emerge is unclear.

CONCLUSION

Two contradictory trends are emerging powerfully in the modern world: the rational, decharismatizing trend, demanding active participation in the political process and producing alienation where this does not fully occur; and the irrational, infantile trend toward desiring a charismatic leader, genuine or manufactured, who will take care of the individual totally and reintegrate society into a single, loving, cohesive, cooperative group.[21] The tension between the rational and the irrational processes of political action will always exist, and the outcome of this tension can produce very different political structures even in technologically similar societies, depending on the historical, cultural, and structural circumstances of those societies at a given time and upon the existential desires of the individuals within those societies, if they choose to act beyond the limitations which culture, structure, and history impose.

Nonetheless, the cohesion problems of large-scale societies are so complex that pressures toward some kind of irrational unification figure or symbol become almost a necessity, if anomie and social conflict are to be reduced to manageable levels. It is still possible that rational processes of consent getting can be revived and innovated so as to minimize the irrational processes, even if they cannot be discarded, and reciprocal and cooperative rather than usurping and coercive relationships can exist between people and their leaders.

9

The Disenchantment of Charisma: On Revolution in a Rationalized World

WILLIAM H. SWATOS, JR.

Because he never wrote his projected "theory of revolution" chapter for his masterwork *Economy and Society*, most of what has been written about Max Weber and revolution is drawn from his discussion of charisma, which he terms "the specifically creative revolutionary force of history."[1] It is not correct, however, to claim that charismatic revolution is the only source for total change in the sociocultural system. Weber himself speaks of both "traditionalist revolution" and the "revolutionary force" of bureaucratic rationalization.[2] A lack of proper consideraton of these two types of revolution has been, at least in part, the source for much misguided debate on charisma.

In a quest for a positively oriented post-Weberian approach to understanding revolutionary movements and their potentials in modern societies, it is necessary to review Weber's work on both rationalization-disenchantment and charisma. Because there is a clear connection between charisma and enchantment, the basic thrust of this discussion is as much a part of the sociology of religion as it is of politics, domination, or revolution.[3] It is also a question that must be addressed in terms of popular culture as well as theoretical abstractions. The purpose of this essay is not, however, to discuss merely the "fact of change in modern life," or *FutureShock*, as these may be interpreted to mean that everyday things are not the same in modernity as they were before, or that we now recognize this to be true with a greater degree of seriousness than did our forebears. Rather, change that renders the world significantly different from the way it was before, *revolutionary change*, is the focus of this piece.

Whether and how it is possible to bring about major changes in the ways in which people order their lives in bureaucratic society is the major question to be addressed.[4] We will turn first to the rationalization-disenchantment problematic, then to charisma and its transformations, traditionalist and bureaucratic revolutions, and finally to revolutionary potentials in the modern world. In so doing, we will move from a relatively descriptive assessment of Weber's position to a critique and extension of his theoretical framework.

RATIONALIZATION AND DISENCHANTMENT

Weber's sociology is united by the overarching thematic element of the constant refrain of the nature, causes, and effects of *Rationalität* (rationalization). This concept includes not only the development of technical-instrumental processes based upon empirically grounded and efficiency-directed reason (*Zweckrationalität*), but also a rationalization of values, in that ethical-moral thought comes likewise to be grounded in these categories (*Wertrationalität*). Further conceptual elaborations, as Levine has shown, are also possible.[5] The disenchantment of the world (*Entzauberung der Welt*) is the opposite side of the rationalization process, and refers to the progressive demystifying or "desuperempiricalizing" that is a concomitant of rationalization at the systemic level.[6] "The extent and direction of 'rationalization,' " Gerth and Mills say, "is thus measured negatively in terms of the degree to which magical elements of thought are displaced, or positively by the extent to which ideas gain in systematic coherence and naturalistic consistency."[7] Thus, if we explain things in this world's terms (rationalization), we no longer need a supernatural explanation or level of "reality" (hence disenchantment). *Entzauberung* is as much a constitutive definiens of Weber's assessment of the development of the modern world situation as *Rationalität*. Indeed, the one necessarily entails the other.

"Disenchantment" is a rather literal translation of the German *Zauberung* ("enchantment," "magic," or "sorcery") plus the negating prefix *Ent-*. However, whereas the English word "enchantment" has to an extent lost its magical or mystical connotation, the German root still retains this active sense. Thus, to say in German that the world has been *entzaubert* implies that the agencies of magic and spiritual power have lost their grip on human lives and the affairs of nature; the world has been "robbed of gods." The English does not quite convey this sense—"disenchantment" being more a loss of appeal or fascination, a "breaking of the spell" in a figurative but not literal sense. It speaks more of fairy tales, love stories, and career disappointments, than of the center of human existence or of the universe's creative and sustaining power(s). Any other attempt to render the term in useful English does almost as badly, however, in conveying what Weber meant; so there is hardly any reason to break the established translational convention. We may do best to say with S. N. Eisenstadt that *Entzauberung* "denotes the demystification and secularization of the world, the attenuation of charisma and a sort of charismatic neutralism."[8] "Secularization" (*Säkularisation*), a term of lesser importance for Weber but very popular currently, is best understood as the institutional manifestation of disenchantment.[9] It refers not to "worldliness" in the sense of hedonism or crass materialism, but to the processes by which the religious institution and the transcendent system of values it embodies exercise less and less control over the activities of the sociocultural system as a whole.

Weber clearly intends to use disenchantment in a "value neutral" way in his analyses. Disenchantment is not a subjective feeling-state, but a potentially measurable "objective" social reality in the modern world. Yet it is hard to deny that there is also a connotation of loss in his use of the phrase. Though Weber professes himself "unmusical" or even "a cripple" in religious matters, one still gets a strong impression from reading his works that the mystical quality of existence to which religion has addressed itself as a social institution throughout history has value. That value is the price paid for rationalization. Yet—and this is a critically important Weberian paradox—rationalization also has value, for it frees the intellect from the repression of "demonic" forces. Wolfgang Mommsen writes:

> They belonged together: a rational, methodical way of life was in his opinion an essential feature of the personality. . . . The personality needs rational orientation in order to become "itself," to become "free." On the other hand, however, the universal rationalization of all life relationships and the everincreasing demystifying (*Entzauberung*) even of the most intimate aspects of human life, threaten the roots from which the personality derives its power—those values which we can only recognize but cannot motivate.[10]

Thus Weber says that rationalization spreads at the cost of "love, hatred, and all purely personal, irrational, and emotional elements which escape calculation."[11] To this extent, and to this extent only, it is appropriate to refer to the rationalization-disenchantment process as "dehumanizing." Nevertheless, Weber's "rational construction of historical evolution," his assessment of the continually "shifting battle between discipline and the individual charisma," Mommsen says, came to be "overshadowed by a deeply pessimistic fear of a new enslavement to come," in which "the endless struggle between creative charisma and rationalizing bureaucracy" would almost unquestionably be won by the latter.[12]

Weber agonized regularly over the relative worth of the rationalization-disenchantment trade-off, hoping for the best but often overcome by fears of the worst, and the *tension* of the cost-benefit analysis of rationalization-disenchantment was a constant element in his work from the 1890s until his last years.[13] Abramowski indicates that by the time of the 1917-19 Munich lectures this tension was relatively resolved, but in a radically existential way that provided no clear program for action and no comfort for the soul in quest of "ultimate answers."[14] Indeed, it may well be argued that Weber never provided even proximate solutions applicable at a societal level.

Weber was clearly personally involved in the rationalization-disenchantment problematic, though he generally held his passions in check by embracing the *wertfrei* ("value free") canon. There is perhaps no more succinct illustration of the difficulty as he saw it than in a reference that he makes almost offhandedly in his discussion of heterophony in Russian folk songs in *The Rational and Social Foundations of Music*: "As in all ancient folk music, the heterophonic development of the theme is improvised. The several voices do not disturb each other either rhythmically or melodically only because of an established communal tradition. People of different villages cannot sing together in a many-voiced fashion."[15] So questions may be posed: Does each have a voice in a little community, achieving "unity in diversity," but remaining isolated from others? Or, do people come from many villages but sing without differentiation, in only one dimension? Or, is a technical solution imposed, in this case harmony? If so, then to what extent does music become "reified" to serve exterior technical purposes, rather than purposes "of the soul"? To what extent is music now valued for its technical complexity or musicians for their "technical virtuosity" rather than for the inner "spiritual" value of what is expressed? Here, in a disarmingly simple passage, Weber has captured the whole problem of modernity and set it out for public view. In this context, it is important that his readers not become so taken with the wide range of Weber's own technical competency—from agricultural law, to capitalist modes of production, to Chinese religion, to Russian music—that the sense of the burning issue that fired his imagination is lost.

Weber's fears can thus hardly be said to be extrinsic to his "real" work. While rationalization-disenchantment is a global concept for civilizational analysis, it never loses specific application to the lived experience of human beings. Yet Weber is neither anti-rationalistic nor pro-religious. This, so to speak, is Weber's curse: he dreaded the old gods of the pre-Judeo-Christian era, but feared that the ultimate consequence of Judeo-Christianity as it was developing in Western history was an equally barbaric, mechanized bureaucracy in which the old gods would reappear "disenchanted" as impersonal "forces" trying to gain power in our lives, and destroying freedom and creativity in the process. The Weberian is cursed because he must live on a tightrope drawn between an intellectual sacrifice to religion or a similar one to uncontrolled bureaucracy. In his many pessimistic moments, Weber seems sure that people will cling to one option or the other, with little difference in the results, rather than risk falling into the apparent abyss.

Yet Weber is not *absolutely* pessimistic. Because he never embraces determinism or inexorable evolutionism or a naive faith in "progress," positive options always exist in Weber's sociology. Of course, these options are not ahistorical. The future is not one of limitless possibilities but one of real probabilities for responsible decision making. The choice that Weber gives is one of living in full consciousness of ambiguity—which is part of what is bound up in the political and scientific vocation essays—or falling before some "absolute" (which is always historically proved to be a pseudoabsolute on the level of concrete experience). A commitment to uncertainty is Weber's hope for the world, for only by rejecting "final solutions" on an empirical plane are we freed to criticize, inquire, remake, and create. This is why Weber refused to allow the lecture hall to become a site for pulpiteering or politics, and why the ability to say "In spite of all!" is essential to the political vocation: "Man would not have attained the possible unless time and again he had reached out for the impossible."[16] This is how Weber was able to combine science and politics in his own person. His goal was always articulated in terms of proximate answers and a strong sense of the frequently shifting sands upon which all sociocultural houses were built.[17] His own awareness of the irony of human life—of the unforeseen consequences of human thought and activity throughout human history—gave him a perspective that taught the value of cherishing the present without ignoring the future. Part of Weber's faith here, at least, lay in the social potential of *charisma*.

CHARISMA AND ITS TRANSFORMATIONS

"The attempt to write a sociology of culture and a social psychology in a single set of sentences," Clifford Geertz remarks, "is what gives Weber's work its orchestral complexity and harmonic depth. But," he continues, "it is also what gives it, especially to ears less attuned to polyphony, its chronic elusiveness."[18] Certainly, use of the concept "charisma" today is so sloppy that it is easy to despair of ever recalling its roots in Weber.[19] A generation of social and political scientists, journalists and media experts has somewhere along its educational career found out about charisma. Whatever else it may be, they have learned, charisma is what makes leaders leaders. Popes and presidents are elected because of their "charisma." A football player or musician who doesn't have charisma won't make it to "stardom." Favorite ministers and professors are said to have charisma, and in some of the most bureaucratic churches, there is an active "Charismatic Movement." Indeed, one can read all about it in the magazine *Charisma*. Some sociologists have even suggested that corporations and their products—their "names"—have charisma. As a result of this admixture of accretions there must be an effort, among sociologists at least, to unearth within the rough ground of Weber's own work the meaning of this concept and its place in his typology of authority/domination. This is not to urge a conceptual rigidity—something which

Weber clearly eschewed—but rather because "typologies continue to be used with clarity only when they are used in their original frame of reference."[20]

It is both ironic and disappointing that when Weber specifically indicates, at the outset of his discussion of the types of domination, both the nature and function of ideal types as methodological devices,[21] and later indicates —again in detail—that in practical application authority systems actually contain a mixture of the various typological elements,[22] writers claiming to present analyses in the Weberian mode act as if he had proposed a taxonomic scheme. The only proper Weberian response to the question, "Is 'X' a charismatic leader?," for example, is "Compared to whom?"

As with rationalization-disenchantment, so here too Weber's interest lay in types of social authority or domination and not in the psychological profiles of leaders. Weber's charismatic authority type is *not* to be identified with the psychohistorical "great man" tradition, as Gerth and Mills rightly note. *Charisma is fundamentally social.* First, though formally always a leader's claim to obedience by followers as a duty, as an objective legitimate system of domination charisma is *always* subject to validation by the followers, based upon some "proof" to the followers that the leader is what he or she claims to be. Charisma is always contingent upon a *shared belief* on the part of *both leader and followers* in the genuineness of the leader's charismatic possession. Furthermore, the "activation" of charisma, according to Weber, is predicated on "extraordinary" social circumstances. The typical case is not one of a person arising in everyday activity to proclaim himself, or even be proclaimed, a new leader—much less the so-called charisma of theatrical, musical, or sports personalities.[23] Rather, the extraordinary nature of the *times* calls forth a charismatic *authority structure.*

The leader is but a part—albeit a critically important part—of a *structure* of domination. Indeed, Eisenstadt rightly observes that "throughout his discussion of charisma Weber emphasizes not so much the charismatic leader, but the charismatic group or band."[24] Authority structures that correspond closely to this pure type in the context of an empirical analysis Weber refers to as based upon "genuine charisma." Here charisma is "the specifically creative revolutionary force of history," but it exists only briefly, "*in statu nascendi,*" before being transformed or routinized into some more stable form.[25]

Transformed Charisma

It is at this point that confusion arises in many attempts at Weberian analysis, as others have also noted: the failure to understand that Weber makes a consistent distinction between "genuine charisma" and routinized or transformed "stable" forms. Genuine charisma is revolutionary in nature and short-lived. Routinized charisma—whether hereditary, democratic, or the "charisma of office"—is a stable form of domination that enters into a mix with either traditional or rational-legal structures of both.[26] Since all authority is in a sense fallout from charismatic explosions, various transformations and routinizations will appear in both traditional and rational-legal types of societies, or as Shils puts it, "charismatic sensitivity can slumber within the rational-legal and traditional legitimations of authority."[27] The hereditary "charismatic" leader, for example, is to be understood as succeeding from and existing in reference to some "genuine" charismatic leader who preceded him or her, but the two are not identical.

It is thus possible and correct to speak of persons as "charismatic" figures within traditional or rational-legal systems *in varying degrees*, because pure type systems are methodological constructs rather than empirical realities. Dow, following Peter Berger and W. G. Runciman, gives several examples of this phenomenon, and Constas speaks of "charismatic bureaucracy."[28] Alan Berger's discussion earlier compares manifestations of charisma among Hasidic Jews and in the Unification Church as, respectively, traditional and bureaucratic routinizations of charisma. Weber himself writes that "traditional domination possesses a charismatic duality of rule that is tradition bound as well as free from tradition."[29] "Charismatic" figures in such routinized settings, however, must be carefully distinguished from the "genuine" charismatic leader and his or her revolutionary impact. A critical analytical difference pertains between charismatic figures or elements in noncharismatic authority structures and the charismatic type of domination per se. Concern here is with the latter. Admittedly, many personages or events in both traditionalistic—especially patrimonial—and rational-legal systems have charismatic qualities, but this is transformed charisma routinized into an authority structure corresponding to a different type of domination.

One of the most comprehensive attempts to extend our understanding of charisma beyond Weber's foci has been a series of essays by Edward Shils. Published for the most part in the early 1960s and now conveniently collected into a single volume, Shils' writings represent a conscious effort to give "charisma" a new footing and wider application. In so doing, Shils elaborates the conjoint notion of "center and periphery" as a vehicle for understanding individual-societal structural relations as conducive to and maintaining consensus-based order. Charisma becomes in this interpretation the attractive "power" of the center that enables it to keep the societal periphery in order. Thus Shils maintains that "charisma not only disrupts social order; it also maintains or conserves it," and again that "the charismatic propensity is a function of the need for order."[30] Charisma is in this sense, as Eisenstadt notes, an institution *building* process:

> Institution building is based not only on the direct or indirect exchange of . . . resources . . . for the implementation of . . . discrete, instrumental goals but in addition also necessarily includes interaction between, on the one hand, those individuals or groups who are able to articulate varied collective goals and crystallize acceptable norms [i.e., the charismatic types] and, on the other, those individuals, groups, or strata that are willing to accept such regulations and norms.[31]

Historically the church—or common religious convictions in the absence of a formally organized body—served as the agency for the continuous integration of the periphery from the center. In modern society, on the other hand, Shils contends, charisma has become dispersed as participation in the center has extended to more and more of the population. Yet, "a center still exists and must always exist," in part because "the propensity to seek contact with transcendent powers and to impute charisma is rooted in the *neural constitution* of the human organism."[32] According to this logic, Weber's emphasis on disenchantment is fundamentally erroneous, an unfortunate by-product of the temporal limits of anyone's vision of the future.

It is precisely here, however, that Shils' proposals seem to founder, for they rest upon assumptions difficult to verify. Charisma becomes so dispersed that it apepars practically everywhere as a *definitional* necessity, rather than as an independent attribute. Dow argues perceptively that "Shils' attempt to attribute charismatic elements to a wide range of ordinary secular roles, institutions, and strata of persons" creates a setting in which "charisma ceases to have any independent descriptive or analytic value."[33] Shils vitiates the critical defining component of a *special* "gift of grace," a gift that is by its very nature inexplicable in empirical terms. The dilemma is better phrased, then, by saying that modernity presents not dispersion, but an *absent* center from which genuine charisma is excluded.[34] Shils accurately observes that "a society entirely without tradition is inconceivable,"[35] but it is the traditionalist routinization of charisma, rather than the "dispersion" of charisma, that should be the focus of attention here. By attempting a reformulation of "charisma," Shils deflects our attention from *the true condition of modernity* which *is not disintegration* (as he correctly notes), *but disenchantment.*

The charismatic figure—or the charismatic band—is enchanted, and without enchantment genuine charisma is impossible. This, of course, does not mean that charisma will appear within channels of institutionalized religion. Rather, it is more likely that charisma will often appear irreligious in the eyes of the "legitimate" religious structures—though not so completely foreign to the religious constitution of the society as to "make no sense." It is for this very reason preferable to speak in terms of enchantment-disenchantment than, for example, religion-secularization. So it follows that in a rationalized world charismatic revolution is impossible, as is the appearance of genuine charisma—at least with respect to the ideal-typical context. In Weber's use "charisma" is irrational. Thus Vinson is mistaken when, following Shils, he says that IBM has "charisma."[36] What IBM has is technical competence, not only in what it produces, but also in management, service, and advertising. At most, this is the "charisma of office," but even this is stretching a genuinely bureaucratic element—the virtue of efficiency—too far. Genuine charisma depends upon the mysterious above-and-beyond, and this is neither the mere ability to confuse or deceive nor speculative "scientific" insight into the potentially knowable empirical future.[37]

Manufactured Pseudocharisma

Weber indicated—perhaps more prophetically than he realized—the possibility that bureaucratic structures in a democratic society might have to use "mass effects" and the "charisma of rhetoric" to create "charismatic hero worship" in order to build the emotional support necessary for the maintenance of power (illegitimate domination).[38] In short, charisma might, as Glassman has put it, have to be *manufactured*: rationality might have to "create" irrationality. From the viewpoint of its creators in modernity (as contrasted with traditionalistic manufacturers of charisma, where enchantment still prevailed), then, this would be a completely *rational* activity intended to remain within clearly nonrevolutionary bounds. It would maintain the status quo rather than overthrow it; hence it could hardly be identified with either genuine charisma or its traditional transformations. Here we should adopt Bensman and Givant's term "pseudocharisma," and recognize that this is a step beyond the "normal" transformations of charisma to which Weber refers.

Pseudocharisma is not an incorporation of charismatic elements into a more structured everyday form, but the calculated rational construction of superficial charismatic "signals" to maintain everyday forms. Paradoxically, pseudocharisma uses revolutionary signals, rhetoric, and effects to prevent genuine revolution. It is a rationalization of social science prophecy —i.e., man's dependence on charisma, emotional and irrational signals of supermundane power, for survival. Pseudocharisma is an unforeseen, and probably unfortunate, by-product of Weber's own research. His demonstration of the place of charisma in the history of human societies and his delineation of its empirical features have not been without their practical applications by skillful political "advisers." The production of "charisma" (i.e., pseudocharisma) is now an established part of applied political science. This has been noted most eloquently and with application to mass culture by writers like Lowenthal, Adorno, Marcuse, and even Boorstin.[39]

What is involved in pseudocharisma, then, is the construction of a pseudoreligious experience. In his analysis of pilgrimage centers, for example, Victor Turner delineates the characteristics of liminality, anti-structure, and communitas.[40] All three of these aspects of the religious experience are cultivated and managed in pseudocharisma. The pseudocharismatic leader gives a sense of crossing the threshold from everyday life to something beyond-though-unclear. There is the rhetoric of new interpretations of social relations and new interaction patterns, and there is the pseudo-*Gemeinschaft* of thinking that one belongs to a distinct community of followers. All of this, of course, is manufactured and unreal, lacking even the possibilities of transcendence that are part of enchanted religion. The quest for transcendence is channeled, controlled, and subjected to processes of reason in a structured game-like setting that vents affect while changing nothing. The "charismatic" politician manufactured in this way makes as little contribution to positive and far-reaching social change as an electrified rock star, NFL football hero, or celluloid space cadet. All are managed efforts to keep things as they are; "of the last stage of this cultural development, it might well truly be said: 'Specialists without spirit, sensualists without heart'."[41]

Weber was not aware of the telecommunications revolution as he wrote, nor of its impact upon Western culture. He died before radio had reached its heyday, and television, computerization, satellite transmission, and the like were merely glimmers in the eyes of a handful of scientists. The possibilities for the manufacture of charisma through these means seem limitless. Yet Glassman suggests that ironically this increasingly sophisticated technology in its very rationality is potentially "decharismatizing." The control of the media is critical here. In societies where control is completely in the hands of the power structure, the manufacture of charisma by those in power, while at the same time those without power are systematically excluded, can extend almost beyond imagination. Small wonder that the first target for revolutionaries in these societies is often the national broadcasting facilities. In societies where some measure of democratic control is exercised through the public or private sectors, on the other hand, the media can have a tremendously decharismatizing effect by providing "instant analysis"—i.e., criticism—of any figure or event. The extraordinary and the everyday are so merged here as to become indistinguishable, and of course, one may at any time turn the dial elsewhere or turn the tube off.[42]

Karl Loewenstein thus observes correctly that although

> democratization has strengthened beyond all expectations the plebiscitary components in the power process . . . at the same time it has decidedly diminished the chances for the development and operation of true charisma. . . . The leader who shows himself daily . . . is less magical and magnetic than the leader who is not seen at all, or only rarely on occasions especially favorable to him. Far from reinforcing charisma and spreading its magic in a wider context, the mass media in an

open society act as disenchantments. . . . It would appear that charisma . . . has become a victim of modern technology. In the last analysis, as a basis of rule, it possesses a historical reality. Or, to put it differently: charismatic authority in politics is a phenomenon of the pre-Cartesian world.[43]

As Weber remarks that the "charismatic glorification of 'Reason,' which found a characteristic expression in its apotheosis by Robespierre, is the last form that charisma has adopted on its fateful historical course," so prophetically charismatic Reason, once transformed and routinized, reasons away charisma.[44] The hero, magician, or other fearless leader competes with dozens of "charismatic" media personalities for attention "every day." For contemporary Western society, it is this de-charismatizing effect of the media—not a nonrevolutionary effect, but rather one that is bureaucratic in type—that is of greatest significance.

TRADITIONALIST REVOLUTION

Weber does not say a great deal about traditionalist revolution. It is perhaps sufficient that he indicates that "it is directed against the master or his servant personally, the accusation being that he failed to observe the traditional limits of his power," rather than being directed against "the system as such."[45] This also implies, however, the possibility of a restorationist revolution, bringing about systemic change toward a previous system state. The Glorious Revolution against James II in England is a classic example. The ousting of Richard Nixon, though less dramatic, is a possible contemporary illustration of some of the same dynamics, as is the Islamic Revolution in Iran and elsewhere. Many of the governments systematically replaced by "revolutions" (in pre-Marxist Latin America, for example) are also subject to this same analysis. Since Weber introduces this concept under the section "Traditional Authority" in the chapter "Types of Legitimate Domination," he apparently does not think that charismatic leadership is a necessary condition here, and elsewhere he explicitly distinguished the charismatic claim from traditional bases of authority.[46]

It is especially important, however, to recognize that like charismatic authority, traditional authority itself is largely *personal* in character. A traditionalist revolutionary who commands loyalty over against the incumbent is *not* the type of figure to whom Weber refers when he uses the term "charismatic." Such a person is more accurately conceptualized as a "virtuoso" in a patrimonial system of domination. The loyalty commanded here is based on personal embodiment of the social tradition. "Charismatics proclaim a message," Michael Hill observes, "virtuosi proclaim a method."[47] The patrimonial figure and the charismatic leader, though they may appear very much alike in their mass effect, stand at opposite theoretical poles.[48] The potential patrimonial revolutionary calls the current officeholders to account by claiming "It is written!" The charismatic cries "Nothing is written!" Weber illustrates the difference between the great Biblical prophets, scribes, and holy warriors on the one hand: "Moses says, so do." And the charismatic Christ on the other hand: "Moses says this, *but I say*. . . ." In more contemporary terms, although the analogy is not perfect, this is the contrast between Billy Graham and the Reverend Moon.

The movie *Star Wars* is an excellent example of traditionalist revolution in a futuristic setting, not at all different in general form from the American Western.[49] Its popularity comes from the fact that despite its setting it is nostalgic, and nostalgia is currently running strong in our culture. Nostalgia and charisma, however, are not the same thing. Luke Skywalker, though a hero, does not become a leader. He is a soldier dedicated to and successful in restoring an earlier form of domination. Although the film has often been described by viewers as "religious," the clearly *im*personal nature of "the Force" must not escape our attention: the old gods risen from their graves in a disenchanted world as impersonal forces. The success of *Star Wars* derives not from the hope of charismatic revolution but, rather, from its nature as an icon of popular culture. It projects our current nostalgic feelings into the future and says, in effect, that our own way of life isn't so bad after all. This theme is extended and confirmed by the specific search for "earth" by the "rag tag band" of the same author's *Battlestar Gallactica.*

It is thus a mistake to think of "traditionalist revolution" as something that has passed away with the development of modern technology. Unlike charisma, traditionalism as a political force is not necessarily dependent upon enchantment. Personal loyalty to a leader—patrimony, or sultanism in its extreme form—may arise from purely secular origins. Tradition-bureaucracy cannot be reduced to a sacred-secular dichotomy. *Both* tradition and bureaucracy are essentially secular routinizations of the extraordinary "sacred" demonstration of authority that is the cornerstone of charisma. "The disenchantment of the world," then, does not mean a decline of the authority structures that Weber discusses as traditional. Just as it is possible to speak of the Roman Empire as a bureaucratic authority structure,[50] while not denying the extreme rationalizations of our own era, so one may not use the term "pre-modern" to imply that traditionalism or traditionalist revolution cannot occur in contemporary post-industrial society. Traditional authority structures can and do make use of modern technology apart from ideal-typical bureaucratic rationalizations. From a Weberian standpoint, it is very possible to speak of traditionalist revolution in modern society without engaging in either typological or semantic confusion.

The relationship between nostalgia, tradition, and fascist revolution must be discussed in this context. Consideration of this question is forced on us not merely academically but because of the tremendous similarities that pertain between the contemporary world and pre-Nazi Europe.[51] Here we must first struggle to separate fascism as an authority structure from Hitler's personal insanity. If we do so, fascism appears as a basically traditionalist form of domination, essentially patrimonial, with some elements of manufactured charisma. Admittedly the tradition bears no relationship to "objective" history. But that is just the point, as Wallerstein astutely observes:

> The "traditional" . . . always is an aspect of and creation of the present, never of the past. It may in fact be taken as a general sociological principle that, at any given point of time, what is thought to be traditional is of more recent origin than people generally imagine it to be, and represents primarily the conservative instincts of some group threatened with declining social status. Indeed, there seems to be nothing which emerges and evolves as quickly as a "tradition" when the need presents itself.[52]

Kimball and McClellan have accurately distinguished the fascist from the Marxist when they describe the former by saying, "if, when the lines are drawn, he still marches with his nation rather than with his class, he no longer does so out of motives that he can defend to his own intellect [i.e., rational calculation], but rather out of deep, irrational urges."[53] Nostalgia for the "good old days," though it may begin in what appears to be innocent fantasy, is a prime breeding ground for thoughts of former glories, "fatherland," and ancient god-kings. Fascist leaders promise a return to *the way things were.* Though they ostensibly criticize the current system (qua system) more than the ideal type of traditionalism would suggest, their criticism is ultimately of the people who embody the system. Their remedy is a return to the "traditional" system as it was before the current power-people came into domination. To this end they generate personal loyalty from their followers, while often identifying the hated power-people as a class. Displacement of that class of usurpers of the "tradition" becomes the primary goal of the revolution. Eugene Genovese comments from the perspective of a historian of slavery:

> The brutal fact remains that when conservatives are not extreme *laissez-faire* liberals, or apolitical literary men [Weber's "Ink bottle Romantics"] . . . , they have difficulty in not ending as fascists. To have a world without marketplace values you must have a world without a market place at its center. . . . The reconstruction and consolidation of an archaic world order being an impossibility, all attempts at a prebourgeois restoration can only end as the counter-revolution of the bourgeoisie itself.[54]

Viewed from this perspective, fascism represents a live possibility for traditionalist revolution in our time—in spite of superficial bureaucratic appearances (i.e., gray-flannel fascism). Such a revolution would *not* be charismatic in its essential nature. The only "charisma" its patrimonial leadership would have is what it manufactured as a result of the technical resources generated by modern industrial society. It is, however, possible that such a traditionalist revolution, if sufficiently comprehensive and prolonged, might bring a certain level of reenchantment in its wake—the personality of the leader being ascribed god-like qualities, for example. This may be what is happening in Iran; it is implicit in the growing trend toward fundamentalism on a global scale. Then, with an irony Weber would have appreciated, the possibility for authentic charismatic leadership would resurface, and a charismatic revolution might follow. Clearly, this would involve a tremendous change in the ordering of the modern world-system, but one which certainly is not impossible. Jimmy Carter's defeat marked, both at home and abroad, a major traditonalist resurgence against the rationalist internationalism of the Trilateral Commission, for example. Indeed, although Shils himself does not address this whole topic as aggressively as he might, the very exposition of "center and periphery" that he offers gives some theoretical basis for these developments.

BUREAUCRATIC REVOLUTION

The bureaucratic form of revolution is explicitly compared and contrasted with charismatic revolution as an anti-traditional force. Bureaucracy, Weber says, revolutionizes "from without," while charisma revolutionizes "from within." It is tempting here to think by way of example of the industrial revolution. But it is much more important and instructive to realize that virtually all "modern socialist"—i.e., Marxist and neo-Marxist—revolutions are of this type. Although there is a large theoretical literature within Marxism that has absorbed Weber's overarching concern with bureaucratic routinization and has thus become self-critical, nevertheless the primary intent of such revolutions in practice is to impose a new system of action that will alter the mode of production and the nature of social organization. It is rational calculation that is at the core of liberal ideology, of which Marxism is but one strain.[55] Likewise, central to the Marxist analysis of world problems is the belief that they reside first—if not totally—in the material order. For those who hold such principles, the place to initiate change is in the "external" system of production. Revolutionary alterations here, it is believed, will bring about the necessary changes in the hearts and minds of the men and women involved. Romantic socialists often overlook the fundamentally bureaucratic nature of actual socialist societies, whereas Weber himself spoke prophetically of a "dictatorship of the bureaucrats" that would in practice replace the theoretical "dictatorship of the proletariat."[56] This is epitomized clearly, for example, in the term that the Soviets have used for their ruling cadre—the polit*bureau*.

Marx and Weber shared a fundamental concern for the welfare of human beings and a commitment to empirical investigation. Both were also politically active, though Weber was highly critical of the use of the teaching platform as a political rostrum (which principle Marx, working almost entirely outside the academy, never violated). Marx's goal was clearly to reduce the alienation of the worker from his or her essential self that had occurred as a result of the rise of capitalism and the industrial revolution. Weber recognized that the "iron cage" effect of bureaucratic rationalization was a part of this same process. Karl Jaspers paints a picture of Weber as a passionate humanist who "gave the most urgent thought to the question of how . . . when the masses on the plains of Mississippi and Siberia would be rigorously confined to rigid estates and corporations, . . . the individual might preserve his rationality and personality."[57] One can thus no more lay Gulag on Marx than Nazism on Weber. Indeed, Weber at least, once he had overcome his anger, would probably find a pathetic amusement in how his own work on history's ironies could apply to these cases as well. Nevertheless, the fact remains that there is a wide gulf between academic or "religious" Marxism—the Marxism of Marx, as it were—on the one hand, and societies that have undergone "Marxist" revolutions on the other.[58] In Marxist societies which attain political-economic stability, bureaucracy is a central operating principle.

In spite of constant complaints, contemporary American society is less bureaucratized than it seems. Personal considerations often enter into decision making. Weber himself points out that the elected officials of our government—and to an extent their administrative staffs as well—represent routinized charisma. "They are not 'bureaucratic' types. . . . Such an administrative structure [as that of the U.S.] is greatly inferior as a precision instrument compared to the bureaucratic type with its appointed officials."[59] Although local representatives of federal agencies and their immediate superiors appear as "bureaucrats," their ultimate responsibility is to elected officials and to rules made with considerations other than those of technical efficiency in mind. The American system is a mixed type in which rational administration is sought for purposes that *include* personal considerations. Irritation with "bureaucracy" may well reflect the structural constraints of such a system, as well as the larger question of whether human beings can ever approximate a social order based upon a mechanical model.

THE FUTURE PRESENT

The December 1979 issue of *Saturday Review* gave major attention to the inaccuracies and foibles of futurologists of the sixties and seventies. Weber also made much of the strange contortions that took place as ideas worked themselves out over time in social settings. Perhaps it is for this reason that he did not move beyond his excellent analyses of bureaucratic domination and instrumental rationality to critical reflection about how they can be controlled or at least how their destructive effects could be softened. Weber simply did not solve the problems unfolding from his own commitment to modern rationalism, in spite of his assertion in *Economy and Society* that the extreme instrumental rationality of modernity is linked to great substantive irrationality. The commitment of the scientist to unremitting uncertainty that Weber applauds in "Science as a Vocation," is a clue but cannot resolve this contradiction—particularly as he limits science to the sphere of instrumental rationality. His reference to "ethical paradoxes" in "Politics as a Vocation," likewise recognizes yet does not solve the problem.

Weber acknowledges the sociological sense—made explicit, for example, by Berger and Luckmann in *The Social Construction of Reality*—that human nature is a historically relative concept. Yet he also asserts, as noted earlier, that bureaucratic rationalization spreads at the cost of "love, hatred, and all purely personal, irrational and emotional elements which escape calculation." Instrumental rationality advances, to some degree, as other action orientations shrink in importance; in so doing it limits the range of human experience—feelings of loss and alienation result. The disenchanted world is thus often portrayed as a sad one in which unrelenting bureaucratization reduces creativity, spontaneity, and freedom to meaninglessness. We constantly seek "experiences" but are left unfulfilled.

In some of Weber's writings this pessimistic *Weltanschauung* has no corrective; yet such a position is clearly un-Weberian in its determinism. If history is totally controlled by rationalization, then there is nothing to commend Weber's work over that of Marx or any other "force" theorist.[60] Voluntarism gives humanity more credit for its destiny, without being historically naive. Our future is certainly conditioned by our past, but to speak of driving forces is to lose touch with our ability to recreate the nature and purpose of human existence. The quest for meaningful experience, then, and its lack of fulfillment become in part definitive for human being in our time and space—the preconditions for the permanent suspension of the natural attitude that Ernest Gellner refers to as the "second secularisation."[61] The two options for resolution that appear most obvious—traditionalist or bureaucratic revolution—both constitute *mauvais foi*: Nostalgia for a world that can never be because it never was, or capitulation before a mechanized system of action that denies the irrational and transcendent potential of human existence.[62]

Although Weber is vague in setting it out, one cannot help but think that he looked toward another option, a more profound idea of the movement of modern reason that provides a basis for hope. This option—far more revolutionary in its consequences should it be effected—is living in and with a rational and thoroughly disenchanted awareness of the inevitability of unfulfillment that is at the same time fully cognizant of and unwilling to exploit the irrational elements of our personalities. Such an attitude has neither the eerie nor exciting, mysterious nor miserable, possibilities of quests for "final solutions": "Politics is a strong and slow boring of hard boards. It takes both passion and perspective. And even those who are neither leaders nor heroes must arm themselves with that steadfastness of heart which can brave even the crumbling of all hopes.''[63] This attitude also radically distinguishes our time and potential futures from all of human existence heretofore. At all times past a society could look with confidence toward an above-and-beyond that would provide meaningful answers to present problems as well as ''ultimate concerns.'' Neither the United States nor, even less, the world-system can do so today.

It is an oversimplification to say that there are no answers. The truth is that we make our own answers. A full and deep consciousness of this elementary fact of life in a rationalized-disenchanted world opens a wide horizon for creativity, even as it forces us back upon our own tragically wounded and terribly mortal existence.[64] As social scientists we cannot give the metaphysical guarantees Weber rightly criticized the ''rostrum prophets'' of his own day for attempting to create. But we can make explicit the meaning systems of the different institutions of our complex society and champion the importance to human civilization of what Berger and Neuhaus term ''mediating structures''—family, religion, voluntary associations, and the like.[65] This approach—rather than trying to find a ''wholeness'' that is not there—places individual experience and consciousness into an empirical sociocultural framework that makes responsible decision making possible even in the face of operational agnosticism. It denies neither irrationality nor transcendence but places them in a perspective that makes rationality work for, rather than against, a humane social order. In short, we need a dereification of rationality that celebrates its human roots and thus grasps limitation as a principle *for* action, rather than as nonsense that ''will not compute.''[66]

Accomplishing this task falls as a moral obligation upon those who see both its reality and the destructive potential of other alternatives. Here the stage will be set for a purposive and participatory construction of a worldview that gives meaning to the simple fact that life does go on, in spite of disenchantment. Instead of searching for ''new mysteries,'' or ''reenchantment,'' we recognize that the mystery is in the search itself. The here-and-now *is* lived experience and takes on meaning from that fact. This requires commitment to an ethic of limitation—to a frank and fresh awareness that we will never have or never know all that there is—and to an ethic of human worth. Given *scarcity* as a basic principle, the personal, social, and cultural development of the person as an interacting being takes on renewed importance. We must teach and urge people to live for the future present—never to deny today because of the glories of tomorrow, but never to waste today so that there is no tomorrow. If the natural gas industry's commercial message, "The future belongs to the efficient,'' has any meaning beyond self-glorification, it is to distinguish between efficiency and expediency as goals of production and ultimately as forms of domination. Genuine efficiency recognizes the value of resources and their limits. It maximizes these for both short- and long-run ends, acknowledging that the global system is now the only legitimate basis for reliable calculations.

Weber's lack of faith in the doctrine of "progress" stands ultimately vindicated. The era of mindless expansion appears increasingly as an anomaly across the broad sweep of history. The technological advances that have come with it have obvious destructive power as well as productive potentials. The task is to develop a new system of authority that is historically sensitive to the abysses that lie on either side of us—including those models for society which guarantee a terminus in rationality and freedom but can at the same time be used as rationalizations for brutalizing people in the short run, which is when they live their lives. The social and cultural sciences as genuine humanities offer to those who will hear the potential for a new construction of reality. The danger is that in the absence of either transcendent or instrumental meaningful futures, ennui and apathy may set in. It was specifically this that Weber insisted be conquered through a commitment to meet "the demands of the day."[67]

10

Hitler's Dictatorial Charisma

ARTHUR SCHWEITZER

The central concern of this case study of Hitler's charisma is Weber's "basically authoritarian principle of charismatic legitimation."[1] Our interpretation of Hitler's record will proceed in terms of Weber's theory. We shall seek to identify the dictatorial components in the charismatic qualities, and analyze the specific subtypes of alternative and cumulative charismata personified by Hitler. The last section will compare the unconditional authority of dictatorial charisma with the arbitrary authority and illegitimacy of despotic power.

PERSONAL MAGNETISM

Hitler's exceptionally great impact upon his listeners is attributable to the compulsive self-inflation of his personality that differed in two respects from ordinary self-image. First, Hitler displayed extraordinary self-confidence; he *alone* could be the leader of the movement. He incorporated desirable objects, such as the fatherland or the deeds of others, into his own personality. In many of his speeches he claimed to be the founder as well as *the* promoter of the party, who had built up this organization by his own hands. His self-esteem grew to such an extent that he lost his sense of reality and proclaimed: "Nothing is impossible; one can do everything if one has the necessary will."[2]

Self-inflation was often followed by Hitler's second psychological ability, his self-intoxication in front of audiences. To be sure, Hitler prepared himself carefully for his speeches; he studied his own gestures in front of a full-length mirror; he acted the culminating points of his speeches during dictation; he reread and endlessly corrected the typescript in order to remember each argument and find the most expressive word for each thought.[3] As a result, Hitler did not merely act in front of an audience but intoxicated himself by his own emotions until he reached the point of near hysteria. The quality of his voice changed as his passion succeeded in reaching the inner springs of his listeners. They not only lost their own distinctiveness in the mass, but also came into the ban of the speaker's will. He pulled them toward himself as if he possessed an irresistible magnetic power. The magnet was his ability to turn the feelings of masses into an ecstasy.

In the moment of overexcitement, Hitler was able to lead his listeners into two, logically speaking, opposite directions. He singled out *the* enemy, defamed and insulted him in the extreme and aroused his audience into unlimited hatred. As he said himself: "If a people is to become free, it needs pride and will power, defiance, and hate, hate, and once again, hate."[4] Hatred of the enemy was followed by exaltation of the party and movement, by expressions of fraternal love or at least concern for his followers. The other line was self-glorification, when Hitler presented himself as the savior of the nation and the movement who would free both by his own personal will power. The result was usually a tremendous enthusiasm for the leader who promised to lead the masses into a glorious future.

The final act of his emotional intoxication and the ecstasy of the masses came when Hitler found the appropriate words to express the emotional bond that united leaders and followers. At a meeting of 30,000 SA-men (Storm Troopers) in January 1936, he said: "I have founded this SA. . . . I have led you for the last fourteen years. I have learned to know you. Everything that you are, you have become through me; everything that I am, I have been able to do only because of you."[5] This emotional union which Weber regarded as the culmination of natural charisma, was here achieved through the psychological process of mutual identification of the leader and the led.

The readiness to be attracted by Hitler's magnetism was so great in the German middle class that millions of them participated in what Weber would have called this "epileptical ecstasy." Even intellectuals, such as Albert Speer, became the victims of Hitler's gripping appeal.[6] There existed only two general conditions that created a limit to Hitler's magnetism. One resided in the ideological or religious beliefs of voting groups that were committed to the Catholic, Social Democratic, or Communist parties. This immunity of ideological groups points to the fact that it was primarily a clash between ideologies, not foremost emotional resistance, that reduced the impact of Hitler's appeal. The other could be found in the status consciousness of many members of the upper class. Their critical attitude was expressed early by General von Lossow, commanding officer of the *Reichswehr* in Munich during the time of Hitler's coup in November 1923. He subsequently testified in court:

> The well-known eloquence of Hitler at first made a strong impression upon me. But the more I heard him, the fainter this impression became. I realized that his long speeches were almost always about the same thing, that his views were partly a matter of course for any German nationalist, and partly showed that Hitler lacked a sense of reality and the ability to see what was practicable.[7]

Believers in oppositional ideologies and bearers of a status honor were thus immune to Hitler's charismatic appeal.

These two external limits were more than compensated for by favorable conditions that greatly enhanced Hitler's magnetism. Related to his ecstatic ability was the technological invention of the microphone that permitted Hitler to communicate his emotions to many listeners and dominate huge mass meetings. Eventual exclusive control over the radio brought millions of others under his spell. Charismatic dispositions as mass phenomena came into being only in periods of extreme stress, such as the hyperinflation and the Great Depression, in which misery and frustration created the socio-psychological readiness for accepting unconditionally one man as savior of the nation. If any of these favorable conditions had been missing, the impact of Hitler's magnetism would have been substantially reduced.

SUPERNATURAL CHARISMA

Whenever Hitler tried to explain the psychological excitement he created at his meetings, he leaned towards his well known theory of the masses as an object of manipulation. In a speech to the businessmen of Hamburg in February 1926, Hitler summarized in one sentence his attitude toward the masses: "What the great mass has to feel is the triumph of one's own power, the contempt of the enemy, and especially the conviction of their own right" as a group.[8] But this manipulative interpretation failed him when he tried to explain his own capacity to excite the masses in his meetings. He then turned to transcendental terms of supernatural calling, to his infallibility, and to the right of the leader to command obedience from others.

For Hitler, his calling as a political leader had a supernatural origin. His decision to become a politician, he said was made during his sickness shortly after World War I. "As I lay in the veterans' hospital, I said to the Almighty—if I do regain my eyesight, I shall take that as a sign that I should become a politician. When I could later see again I was so deeply stirred that I regarded my recovery as a heavenly act of calling me to a higher task."[9] The Almighty thus not only made Hitler healthy again but also indicated what kind of vocation he should choose.

The semi-divine calling came at the right time after the defeat of Germany. A military victory in World War I would have been, Hitler asserted, a misfortune for Germany. A state based exclusively upon military power would not have found the way to a rejuvenation of the German blood. "By having to go through a catastrophe but being saved from the abyss, Germany escaped the danger of internal disintegration. . . . A wise proverb applies fully to us: The love of providence for his people expresses itself in the form of punishment."[10] Hitler thus said in 1937 that the postwar misery was a sign of God's wrath which had the effect of generating the socio-psychological conditions for the origin of national socialism.

This punishment was beneficial because the Germans were held by Hitler to be God's chosen people. In 1937, he proclaimed:

> Not men but God who watches over all of us has created the German people. He has formed this folk; we have grown according to His will, and because of our will Germany shall live eternally. . . . One folk has been resurrected, our *Reich* has been created new. The German has found himself and, in doing so, he has lived up to the will of his maker. . . . One strong state, one proud people, so great and noble that every German can happily confess: I am a German and I am proud to be and remain a German.[11]

The belief in a chosen people thus was turned by Hitler into an extreme form of national self-glorification.

Linking religious with nationalistic beliefs prepared the ground for the claim of charismatic leadership. National unity and internal renewal could come only through faith in the leader. "Great tasks have been accomplished only by strong leaders but even the strongest leader will labor in vain if behind him there is not a truly united and faithful people."[12]

In Hitler's view, his leadership was the apogee of faith charisma. Faith was here the synthesis of his will, his belief in himself, his belief in a supernatural assignment by a God as well as the people's faith in a God, and the personal endowment granted to one leader by the Almighty. It was because of this synthesized faith that Hitler felt a calling to be the savior of the German nation. He saw in himself the incarnation of God's will in the political sphere. His calling as a kind of political apostle by a superhuman being generated a feeling of commitment to his task and aroused in him a sense of responsibility to devote all his energies to his fight. Goebbels said Hitler

> acts intuitively in his great decisions. He begins to hibernate for days whenever he has to arrive at a great decision. It is as if he tried to listen to an inner voice. He suffers even physical pain during this period of gestation. He has often confessed to me his physical pain—and how wonderful he feels when a decision has been reached and action can begin. He places his ear to the ground to listen to his fate.[13]

When, in 1931, Hitler looked out of the window of his Brown House to the residence of the Pope's representative in Munich, he said: "I do not question the infallibility of the Holy Father in Rome in all religious matters. But nobody can dispute that I do understand more about politics than anyone else in the World. I thus proclaim for myself and my successor the right to political infallibility."[14] It was because of this belief in having unerring judgment that he claimed the right to make all the major decisions in party and state. Repeatedly he rejected the notion that he could or did ever make a mistake. In deadly seriousness he tried to establish a causal nexus between faith in his person and his ultimate infallibility. A mistaken decision would be corrected by the unswerving loyalty of the whole nation to him personally.

In all there was a relationship of reciprocal reenforcement between Hitler's magnetism, the absolute faith in his personality, and the faith of the leader and led in a supernatural selection. Confidence in him received much of its credibility through the emotional experience of his magnetic power. The feeling of interacting ecstasy of the leader and the led was lifted from the psychological to the moral level through the absolute faith each had in the other and in the Almighty. The recurrently reenforced psychological and moral forces, blessed from above, achieved one great result: both created Hitler's faith charisma and generated the legitimacy for his charismatic authority up to the beginning of 1938.

RELIGIOUS LIMITS TO CHARISMA

It was Hitler's practice to justify his belief in his personality by claiming the moral support of the Almighty. Most of the key terms in his charisma—calling, chosen people, faith, blessing, salvation—came from or were strikingly similar to the expressions of the Christian prophets.[15] It seemed to many of his followers that Hitler regarded belief in the Christian God as indispensable for authenticating his charisma. Such an expectation had assisted the Nazis in gaining the confidence of many church people during the years of hunger in the depression.

In a confidential speech of November 1937, Hitler described the new division of functions between party and churches. "We will give you [the churches] unconditional freedom in your teachings and in your conception of God. . . . The churches may dispose of the German men in the other world, but the nation shall decide through its leaders over the worldly views of the Germans." This separation of functions involved a constraint for the party. "The organization of national socialism is the movement of the people, but under no circumstances will we engage in any kind of religious cult of rituals."[16]

From 1937 to the middle of 1939, great ingenuity was employed to sever all connections between party and churches. Churches were no longer allowed to use public buildings or to have priests and sisters teach in public schools. Religious instruction was curtailed by allowing pupils to excuse themselves from such classes. Teachers could no longer act as organists or choirmasters in their churches. School classes could not be obligated to participate in church affairs outside of school.[17] Governmental employees were specifically authorized to give up their church membership.

Most detailed were the instructions of Himmler to the police whose members were to refrain from assisting churches while on duty. At the same time all help was to be granted to those *Schutzstaffel* (SS) men who resigned their church membership provided they confessed a belief in a church-free deity. Atheists were instructed to give up their nonbelief, or else their personnel dossiers had to be sent in immediately. Hitler's assured freedom of religion thus turned into pressure to become a believer in a non-Christian deity. The internal statistics of religious affiliations record the results of such pressures.[18]

Consistently Hitler expressed his disbelief in Catholic teachings or practice. In January 1940, for instance, he said in a private conversation to Rosenberg,

> I have never allowed any church representative to address a party meeting or to bury a party comrade. The Christian-Jewish pestilence is coming close to the end of its influence. It is a degrading situation that there once was an influential religion which demanded of its believers to eat their God in the act of Holy Communion. Good deeds of Christians were believed to be religiously significant only if one enjoyed the grace of God. And it was the privilege of the church leaders to decide who deserved his grace.[19]

In place of the Christian God and doctrines, Hitler expounded the notion of a creative God who had the power to create life, to give some individuals extraordinary abilities, and who endowed each nation with certain racial qualities. The greatest values are those that give us the knowledge to recognize our racial endowment and to educate the young in the art of maintaining and purifying the racial strains. This belief in a creative God was accompanied by a racial concept of a religious prophet. Hitler informed his followers that "Jesus was an Aryan. But Paul distorted his teachings so as to mobilize the underworld and to prepare the ground for the rise of a pre-Bolshevism."[20] Hitler thus felt himself to be an especially endowed individual selected by this creative God. Because of his endowment, Hitler felt a mission to be a political prophet who had a right to claim charismatic authority in party, state, and nation.

Unlike the religious prophets, however, Hitler did not expound any religious doctrine or lead an exemplary life to be imitated by others. Explicitly he emphasized his disinterest in specifying new religious beliefs or accepting the concept of another world for the faithful. He saw before him only the rise of an Olympus "in which I will enter, and in which I will find the most enlightened minds of all times."[21]

Over time there developed a twofold religious limit to Hitler's supernatural charisma. One resulted from the charge of blasphemy by the church leaders. Hitler's racial ideology prevented him from sincerely believing in Christ and most Christian teachings; thus he was prone to derive his calling directly from God and to present himself as the incarnation of God's will, thereby preempting the traditional place of Christ. Since he could not assume the role of the *anti*-Christ, however, prior to the war he had no choice but to accept the blasphemy limit to his charisma.

The victorious *Blitzkriegs* inflated his self-esteem to such an extent that he saw himself as a charismatic hero. Any restrictions upon his power became increasingly unbearable for him, while his success emboldened him to formulate his "last great task." In allowing the first steps toward a religious counterrevolution by Bormann and others, Hitler saw the elimination of the churches as an ideological crusade, similar to the fight against liberalism and Marxism. While the preparatory attack upon the churches affected only their power, not their existence, many Christians regarded these actions as an assault upon religion. The danger of a religious war, constituting the second limit, thus forced Hitler to refrain from openly linking his belief in a pagan deity with his charisma.

PROVIDENTIAL CHARISMA

What kinds of changes did the two religious limits and the internal disputes engender in Hitler's charisma? Was he forced to give up his claim to a supernatural origin of his charisma?

There is no evidence that Hitler ever considered giving up his claim to the supernatural origin of his calling. In public proclamations, Hitler continued to express a neutral position on the churches. In the Nazi setting, however, there developed a coexistence of personal charisma and a semi-religious cult. There was an extensive worship of party, ideology, and top leader. While not directly connected with his charisma, his skillfully repeated propaganda produced the effect that Hitler became much more popular than his party.[22] Not churches or sects but the Nazi party and its affiliates transformed themselves into cultic organizations.

Hitler's natural charisma was especially effective with the young people who possessed the greatest capacity for enthusiasm. Awakening was accompanied by a renewal of ecstatic feelings. One listener describes the repeated impact of Hitler's voice:

> Always when I hear his voice I go home deeply stirred. I feel that I was permitted to see how he could be, how he should be and how he really is. His voice awakens my

conscience and lets me appreciate the good. He shows everyone the general goal but reveals to everyone . . . his particular goal. The most gratifying feeling is, however, that his voice creates the courage to realize this goal; the voice strengthens one's will and confidence in one's own energies. . . . The voice is a helper, acts like a shield, is a true magnet, an illuminating star in the dark.[23]

Unfortunately, this was not a single or exceptional experience, since whole groups could be stirred to tears simultaneously. At a demonstration in Breslau in 1938, the following happened:

When the folk comrades of the Sudetenland passed Hitler, a wall suddenly built itself in front of Hitler. . . . The people who had come . . . to look into the beloved face of this man could not be prodded to march on. Weeping women came up to the *Führer* to touch his hand. One could hardly understand what they said to him, for their voices were choked by their tears.[24]

Inconceivable though it seemed to enemies of the Nazi regime, Hitler not only generated temporary ecstasy in his followers, but was also able to incite their lasting love of, and veneration for, their leader.

Cultic actions were transformed into rituals. In special prayers children had to thank God for giving the country a leader, the savior of Germany. All subleaders of the party had to swear loyalty to the leader each February in a ceremony broadcast to every corner of the nation. Each affiliated organization formulated its own oath to the leader. Most extensive was the worship of the various Nazi flags. The sixteen victims of the Nazi revolt of 1923 were declared martyrs of the movement. The flag carried at that occasion was called the "blood flag." Each year Hitler touched the blood flag as he dedicated the flags of regional party or affiliated organizations. The consecrated flags were to be kept as relics at the respective headquarters. Hitler and his consorts marched every year through the streets of Munich, reenacting the abortive revolt of 1923. A whole host of Nazi songs praised the political struggle and worshipped the movement. Indeed, it was in these songs that Nazi beliefs and worship found their most vivid expression.[25] At the center of the Nazi cult stood Hitler, who was the main performer as well as the subject of the performance.

HEROIC CHARISMA

The simultaneous belief in providential and heroic charisma, coupled with cult and infallibility, produced the effect that Hitler became for his most ardent followers the only person to be worshipped.

Heroic charisma manifested itself early in 1938 when Hitler dismissed the top leaders of the army, demoted or pensioned off many of the leading generals, promoted younger careerists, assumed the role (but not the title) of the minister of war, and claimed the right to determine military strategy for the *Reich*.[26] At the same time, Hitler reorganized the top agencies of the state in such a way that his four secretaries for administrative, military, party, and presidential affairs, as well as his delegate in economic matters, reported exclusively to him. They all had to be ready to formulate and execute his commands.[27]

This purge and reorganization of 1938 cannot be adequately explained by either providential charisma or personality cult. The former existed previously; the latter was greatly magnified by the purge and its consequences. After Hitler had overcome his self-doubt about providential charisma, there occurred a significant rise in his own self-esteem. He linked his notions of indispensability and infallibility with the problem of military expansion. The new living space "had to be gained during his life. Coming generations could not provide a solution. He alone could settle the question."[28]

How could the corporal of World War I believe that he would possess the military competence to direct a series of wars effectively? There are two answers to this question. Politically, he convinced himself that his success in Germany could be readily repeated in Europe.[29] Charismatically, he increasingly believed that his exceptional ability extended also to the art of leading large-scale wars. A shift set in to the charismatic hero. It began shortly after the incorporation of Austria when Hitler wallowed in a huge wave of enthusiasm. The leading newspaper of the party greeted him at his arrival in Munich with the words: "Return of the Victorious War Lord."[30] His many victories in the first years of the war, especially the defeat of France, induced an increasing number of his followers to share his belief and worship his heroic charisma. Personality cult thus culminated in hero worship.

PLEBISCITARY CHARISMA

Parallel to faith and providential charismata, to personality cult and infallibility, runs the development of plebiscitary charisma. This additional kind of charisma resulted from two contradictory motives. Plebiscites were used as a deliberate tactic of disguising the dictatorial nature of Hitler's charisma and policies; but they also sprang from the desire to provide the people with a form of affectual participation in Hitler's great deeds.

The failure of the *Putsch* in 1923 had convinced Hitler that he could come to power only if he would pretend to seek power by a vote of confidence by the majority of voters. The purpose of this strategem was to gain sympathizers, steal the voters of other parties, and undermine them prior to taking over power. There also was the tactical aim of preventing the democratic government from suppressing the Nazis because of their obvious intent to tear apart the constitution.

There was only one occasion when Hitler exploited for his purpose the plebiscite provided for in the Weimar Constitution. In the presidential election of 1932, Hitler was able to run against the incumbent President von Hindenburg. It was not a contest between parties but between personalities. In comparison with 1930, the Nazis doubled their votes. Von Hindenburg received 53 and Hitler 47 percent of the votes. In a democratic process, the loser should have accepted his defeat gracefully, but Hitler took this charismatic contest as a vital step in his push for power. It was not by majority vote, however, but by an alliance with reactionary forces that Hitler was appointed presidential chancellor of Germany in 1933.

After his ascent to power Hitler granted himself the right to call at will for a "plebiscite of the people." Deviously he said: "In every year I shall give the German people the opportunity to determine the extent of my power."[31] Actually, what happened was a shift from a democratic plebiscite with two or more candidates to a dictatorial plebiscite offering the voters only the right to vote for or against the single leader.

Each of the major surprise attacks against foreign states prior to the war was followed by Hitler calling a plebiscite. After the march into the Rhineland he said: "I cannot conclude this historical period of restoring our honor and freedom without asking the German people to give me and all my coworkers the subsequent approval for all the seemingly arbitrary decisions and all the great sacrifices I had to ask of you during these years."[32] Often popular affirmation was accompanied by a reelection of the German parliament. But there was only one list of candidates, so voting amounted to a mere affirmation of the leader's actions.

Actually there was a clear distinction between a democratic and a dictatorial caesarism. The former could be criticized and terminated by the voters; the latter could not. Each plebiscite was at the center of a deliberately contrived and manipulated personality campaign that made it a national obligation for everyone to acclaim the leader by his vote. The space for "no" on the ballot was extremely small, whereas the one for "yes" was greatly magnified so that voters could have no doubts about what was expected of them. Anyone who did not vote or who rejected the claim of the "superman" was identified and punished. Secrecy was eliminated from the ballot box and voting became coercive. These contrived excitements and threats became so clearly identified with the plebiscites that this kind of caesarism fell into the dictatorial category.

GIGANTIC CHARISMA IN DICTATORSHIP

What does this case study reveal for the theory of dictatorial charisma? Hitler was undoubtedly an outstanding example of a charismatic giant. Magnification sprang from the belief that he derived his extraordinary qualities from natural as well as supernatural sources, from developing different subtypes of unconditional authority, and from combining various forms of exceptional actions into an unusual kind of cumulative charisma. On top of these were grafted his personality cult and belief in his infallibility.

Magnification expressed itself most visibly in the larger number of charismatic features of the dictatorial giant. Most obvious was the addition of the personality cult and of the idolatry that are usually missing in democratic charismatic giants. This raises the question of how these semicharismatic features were combined with the genuine charismatic qualities.

Another case of magnification was the diverted alternative charisma. In regard to the supernatural sources. Hitler was compelled to give up a religiously oriented faith charisma and to adopt in its place providential charisma. But the shift had either very little significance for the attached followers or could be compensated for by greater emphasis upon loyalty and discipline. Hitler's doubt and uncertainty in the year 1936-37 were removed by his belief in a creative God. His extreme self-confidence was not diminished in the slightest, and his course of action became decidedly more aggressive. The alternative to a pagan calling was thus considered and accepted secretly by Hitler but did not hinder or change his plans or policies.

Closely associated with magnification was cumulative charisma. A distinction emerged between the roles and the personality of charisma. Various roles were performed by the same leader. From 1933 to 1938, Hitler desired to demonstrate his popularity and called for dictatorial plebiscites. Charisma of the plebiscite was coupled with providential charisma. Heroic charisma began with the march into Austria and continued until the severe defeat at Stalingrad. Providential and heroic charisma coexisted during his political and military victories and reenforced each other without becoming identical. In cumulative charisma the leader's power was not only derived form his original qualities, but his prestige and political position were greatly enhanced by his exceptional deeds. No other mortal could legitimately challenge his authority and get away with it. Cumulative charisma thus lent itself readily to dictatorial rule by a supreme commander.

Most original was the symbiotic relationship between natural charisma and personality cult on the one hand, and between supernatural charisma and idolatry on the other. The two sets of components remained inherently dissimilar, but they became so intimately associated in specific situations that the leader could readily shift from one to the other, and most of the believers did not or could not readily identify the line of distinction.

A similar link was established between natural charisma and personality cult. Love and hatred became equally important components in Hitler's interpretation of natural charisma. The hatred was directed towards one specific enemy: international Jewry. This enemy had to be destroyed at any price. The leader was the only man who could lead in this fight to reveal and terminate the conspiracy of the enemy. Hatred of the enemy and his destruction provided one source for the indispensability of the leader. The other source was the emotional attraction of the followers that turned into love of the leader. It was quite natural for many followers to turn in their fraternal or erotic love to glorifying and worshipping the leader in the form of various cults and rituals. Love turned into glorification and natural charisma was linked with personality cult, in spite of the obvious contrivances used in the latter. Paladins, engaged in building up the contrivances, such as Goebbels or Albert Speer, did not fall for the cult, but they retained their fraternal love almost to the final defeat.

The twofold symbiotic relationship goes far in explaining the paradoxical fact that the followers loved their dictator. For the true believers as well as worshippers, the leader was not a dictator but a genuine savior of the nation. Hatred of the enemy and the desire for his destruction were for them only the other side of the coin of loving the leader, of accepting voluntarily his rule, and of regarding the punishment of disbelievers and deserters as morally justified and politically indispensable. Personality cult and glorification of a superman extended the spell and power of the leader even to those who did not feel deep love or were not consumed by hatred of the enemy.

These three sociopsychic processes effectively explain the success of gigantic charisma in a dictatorship. Magnification by means of the two charismatic sources presents the reason for the continued inner consistency and the absence of fickleness of the charismatic quality. Cumulation of several kinds of charismata in the same leader constitutes the cause for the rising strength of the leader and the charismatic movement. The two kinds of symbiosis explain the persistence of the affectual participation of the masses in most of the leader's appeals and policies. Each of the processes contained an element of reciprocity of the followers to the actions of the leader and vice versa. It is the fatal defect of the alternative theories of either a demoniac or mob leadership that they do not identify these processes and miss their respective reciprocity.[33]

What were the major "dictatorial" components in Hitler's charismatic leadership?[34] There was, first and foremost, an emotional exploitation of the followers by the leader. In natural charisma, emotional union contained a mutual taking and giving that brought satisfaction and permitted affectual participation of the masses in the leader's appeal and action. In the personality cult, however, the emotional union was transformed by the leader into an unquestioned and one-sided glorification or worship of his person per se. Admiration in natural charisma was contingent upon exceptional deeds, performed or expected. The intensified feeling in worship served only the leader, who derived from the concentrated emotions an enlargement of his power and privileges. These advantages were obtained without the intention and explicit consent of the worshippers. When the expected and demanded worship was not forthcoming, then the attempted emotional exploitation was followed by compulsion. Refusal of worship was punished whether the withholding sprang from distaste, disinterest, disbelief, disloyalty, or emotional desertion. The leader had to be glorified or the nongiving follower punished.[35]

The second dictatorial element was contained in the new meaning given to legitimacy as a justifier of charismatic authority. In democracy, legitimacy contains the voluntary approval of the leader's right to lead as well as the followers' readiness to comply with his decisions. In the single party dictatorship, however, charismatic authority was no longer dependent upon the approval of the followers. The right to lead was said to be automatically justified by the two interacting sources of his exceptional qualities. Approval was replaced by the sanctification of the already enjoyed and justified power. The inner willingness of the followers to comply with the leader's wishes was superseded by unlimited obedience. The voluntary elements in legitimacy were replaced by compulsion. Instead of authority resulting from legitimacy, sanctified authority was the cause of obedience.

The third dictatorial element consisted in the widening of the unconditional authority of the leader. In the first phase of the Nazi regime, not all contingent authority had been removed. There coexisted a normative and prerogative state.[36] But the rights of the courts to review the laws and administrative rulings diminished rapidly from 1938 onwards, and the orders of the leader were increasingly held to be above the law. The prerogative state was enlarged when parliament was deprived of its legislative function, when the presidency was combined with the office of the chancellor, when the cabinet was reduced to a mere administrative agency, when the leader became the *de facto* head and actual commander of the armed forces. Combining offices and centralizing power for the charismatic leader became the indicators for eliminating the previously existing authorities of coresponsiibility and the rise of his authority. The leader became all-powerful in the political sphere.

The fourth dictatorial element resided in the increased claims of the leader for justifying obedience to his unconditional authority and applying it to particular situations and groups. Similar to the religious prophet who "preaches, creates, or demands new obligations by virtue . . . of his own inspiration or of his own will,"[37] Hitler insisted that it was the moral duty of paladins and followers to accept and implement his orders. This dutiful authority was demanded in general appeals.

For specific groups or actions, however, Hitler created three other kinds of authority. Instead of being satisfied with admiration and enthusiasm, he institutionalized oath-taking authority. All officials in the Nazi movement had to swear unlimited loyalty to the leader annually. The oath translated emotional attachment into a norm that morally committed all members of the movement to be eternally loyal to him personally. A plebiscitary authority was fashioned for the voters. Phenomenal deeds of the leader were to be affirmed by all eligible voters. Whoever refused to partake in the plebiscite was punished by the secret police. Finally, there was the invention of disciplinary authority. Each state official and soldier had to swear unlimited fealty to the leader personally. "A charismatic hero may make use of discipline . . . if he wishes to expand his sphere of domination."[38] What was said of Napoleon fitted Hitler perfectly. Of these four kinds of charismatic authority—dutiful, oath-taking, plebiscitary, and disciplinary—the last one increased in relative significance and became predominant during the years of defensive wars.

As a desired side-effect of the dictatorial elements, the personality cult linked charisma with idolatry. Under conditions of a monopoly of all means of mass manipulation, the personality cult transformed the leader into a superman. His supremacy became so great that even disbelievers acquiesced to his rule and opponents felt the futility of resistance. Acquiescence of the nonfollowers became an effective substitute for charismatic authority. The leader himself became a victim of self-aggrandizement when he mistook his claimed infallibility as an extension of his superhuman qualities. The personality cult linked genuine beliefs with idolatry when superman and infallibility became adjuncts to dictatorial charisma.

This leads to the question of arbitrary authority and illegitimacy. What was the place of violence in dictatorial charisma? How far did the compulsory elements in dictatorial charisma justify violence? Or, was there a normative political limit to violence even for the charismatic dictator?

Weber tried to establish a twofold relationship between revolutionary charisma and violence. One is the thesis of a distortion of charisma. Minimal violence is compatible with charisma if it is limited to the mere act of overthrowing the old regime and of protecting the leader against assassination. Any violence going beyond these limits leads to a distortion of the values implicit in revolutionary charisma. The other thesis culminated in the prediction of an unintended self-destruction of revolutionary charisma. Adopting wholesale violence, whether by the masses or by a revolutionary dictator, breeds a military dictatorship that suppresses revolution by force. Did these two theses also apply to Hitler's dictatorial charisma?

Hitler's earlier violence was neither minimal nor distortive of his charismatic qualities and appeals. His concealed civil war shortly after his appointment as chancellor was minimal in the sense of neutralizing the regular police and armed forces, but maximal in destroying all democratic and leftist groups and wantonly killing many of their leaders. The same was true of the murder of SA leaders, although they merely disagreed with him politically, and did not threaten him or his leadership. Instead of being limited to the period of violent upheaval, secret police and concentration camps became permanent instruments of violence, serving the goals and policies of the leader. Rather than diluting his charismatic quality, the two occasions of concerted violence in 1933 and 1934 and the new agents of violence greatly increased Hitler's appeal as well as popular fear. There was a shift from compliance to obedience for the believers, and an increasing acquiescence of the nonbelievers, undercutting any effective opposition within the movement and rendering hopeless any nonviolent resistance of his opponents to him and his regime. In fact, the two occasions and the use of instruments of violence were sanctified by the loyal and disciplinary authority of dictatorial charisma and supported by affirmative and submissive obedience.

Other wholesale kinds of violence were either justified as acts of self-defense or as retaliations for insults to the leader or the German people. Deception took the place of charismatic legitimacy. Claiming the right to call German soldiers to war and death was justified as an act of self-defense against foreign aggression. Killing hostages in occupied lands, killing allied paratroopers landing in Germany, closing universities and decimating intellectuals in dominated countries, were all falsely defended as retaliations for criminal acts against the German people or armed forces.

The three greatest atrocities, however—the systematic mercy killings of hapless victims, the deliberate starvation of the Russian prisoners of war, and the expropriation, deportation, and extermination of the Jewish people—were kept secret from the majority of the German people. The reaction of those who heard of it did not indicate a limit of authority: "The *Führer* does not know these things, otherwise he would put a stop to it." Hitler himself drew a private line against violence incompatible with his charismatic authority. He refused to invite Himmler to his social parties by saying: "I need such policemen . . . but I don't like them."[39] But his personal dislike was not enough. When the mercy killings threatened to become a public scandal, Hitler was forced to stop this particular violence. Reluctantly, he had to admit that even dictatorial charisma did not legitimize deliberate killings of hapless victims for reasons of populational-racist policies.

Racist genocide continued as charismatically illegitmate campaigns. To be sure, the agents of extermination excused themselves with blind obedience and disciplinary authority. Commander Hoess of the Auschwitz extermination camp confessed subsequently: "It did not occur to me at all that I would be kept responsible. You see, in Germany it was understood that if something went wrong, then the man who gave the order was responsible."[40] While the political and military leaders were given detailed reports by Himmler on extermination, he declared emphatically "that the *Führer*'s name must never be linked with these deeds." Himmler assumed personal responsibility for the massacre by the SS. But at the same time he boasted that the extermination policy was "carried out . . . without our men and our leaders suffering the slightest damage to spirit and soul."[41] His reference was not to charismatic legitimacy but to Nazi ideology.

Instead of self-destruction of charisma, racial and imperialist violence coexisted with dictatorial charisma. There were three reasons for this coexistence. One was the veil of secrecy covering the despicable atrocities. The second was Hitler's belief in his creative God that called upon him to purify the German blood from any form of racial pollution. The third and most important reason was Hitler's particular ideology that replaced his charismatic message and that demanded of him the extermination of the racial enemy. In living up to this ideological obligation, going far beyond dictatorial charisma, Hitler established a form of racist and eventually also of political despotism that is truly unique in modern history.

11

The Historic Fate of the Charisma of Reason

PETER KIVISTO

While Albert Salomon may have overstated the case when he wrote that Weber's sociohistorical problematic was profoundly shaped by "a long and intense dialogue with the ghost of Marx,"[1] there are good reasons to suggest that many twentieth-century Western Marxists, particularly those who see Marxism as a mode of critique rather than a science in positivistic terms, sought to explicate the form and content of the human predicament in the modern world with the ghost of Weber hovering over their shoulders. Indeed, it might well be contended that despite both their Marxist credentials and the attacks that they frequently leveled at Weber, their lack of concern for such traditional Marxian themes as the emiseration of the proletariat, surplus value, and the falling rate of profit, for example, was related to their concentration on *Weber's* major thematic focus, the causes and consequences of the thoroughgoing rationalization of all spheres of human endeavor. Weber and his critics shared a similar fear that rationality was itself yielding to irrationality, and that a rationalized civilization, the liberator of the individual from barbarism, was itself becoming a prison house for the creative and sentient person. Yet, despite these assessments, we confront what might appear to be a paradox: far from becoming romantic critics of a rationalized world, they viewed themselves as confronting its disenchantment as partisans of reason.

Without seeking to detail the Enlightenment concept of reason, I will argue that the criticism directed at Weber by his critics on the left is due largely to his inability to accept what Ernst Cassirer saw as the cornerstone of the Enlightenment's concept, "a belief in the unity and immutability of reason."[2] Giving up the quest for certitude, Weber treated reason and a rational life as goals only. For this he was perceived to be engaged in a depreciation of reason. In contrast, from a Weberian standpoint, his critics were engaged in a rehabilitation of reason that was primarily motivated by the mythopoeic appeal of a new harmony transcending the terribly discordant modern world.

What follows will proceed by tracing the major threads of Weber's work regarding the historical fate of reason, and comparing and contrasting his assessment to those of Georg Lukács, Herbert Marcuse, and Theodor Adorno and Max Horkheimer—major figures in the movement, in Lichtheim's felicitous phrase, "from Marx to Hegel."[3] In seeking clues that can serve to explicate the general thrust of Weber's *oeuvre*, attention will focus on his discussion of the "charisma of reason." The differences between his neo-Kantian conclusions and those proffered by these critical Marxists will be illustrated by reviewing, in the case of Lukács, the issue of the revolutionary subject and the concept of totality; Marcuse's understanding of reason and revolt, eros and liberation; and Horkheimer and Adorno's analysis of the "dialectic of enlightenment." Given the sometimes opaque, sometimes shifting definitions utilized by these authors, especially in defining reason and rationality, one could quickly get mired in exegetical issues. To avoid this, I will merely note at the outset that this is intended to be a symptomatic reading predicated on the belief that Weber and his critics defined these terms, in fundamental respects, in a congruent manner.[4]

THE CHARISMA OF REASON

Max Weber's understanding of the fate of charisma in the modern world is not an entirely unambiguous matter, and charisma's relationship to reason is even more complex. In the first place, his work is not as systematic as it might be,[5] but more important, his analyses of charisma are not always explicitly integrated into his views on sociohistorical development. In addition, exegetical efforts are inevitably shaped by the interpretive filters of scholars who have chosen to emphasize various aspects, nuances, and modalities of the Weberian corpus at the expense of others, and have been willing to fill in perceived lacunae in his treatment of the topic while claiming to remain faithful to his intentions.

In the section in *Economy and Society* on "Sect, Church, and Democracy," Weber makes a fascinating statement concerning the historical role of charisma in the modern world that has, until recently, escaped critical scrutiny. While discussing the role of Protestant sects in promoting fundamental individual rights against all forms of domination (political, hierocratic, or patriarchal), beginning with freedom of conscience—and here he agrees with George Jellinek—Weber comments on the expansion of individual civil rights in the writings of Enlightenment thinkers. The justification for such rights is made possible, he argues, by the Enlightenment's faith in the efficacy of unimpeded reason in creating "the at least relatively best of all worlds." He then adds a sentence pregnant with meaning: "This charismatic glorification of 'Reason' which found a characteristic expression in its apotheosis by Robespierre, is the last form that charisma has adopted in its fateful historical course."[6]

Weber does not explain his reason for singling out Robespierre. He may have seen in Robespierre's biography the psychological tension between reason and the emotions and in his political career an inherent tension between the pursuit of private interests and the promotion of the general will—both brought into sharp relief by the French Revolution. Robespierre was, during the early phase of his public life, able to locate these tensions within the parameters of the *ancien régime*, and in a Manichean fashion suggested that they could be overcome with the advent of the new social order. He defined his actions in terms of moral principles and could agree with the twentieth-century historian of the French Revolution, George Lefebvre, that "Revolutionary action takes place in the realm of the Spirit."[7] However, as Therimidor approached, he became increasingly intent on basing the legitimacy of the new order, not on ends predicated on absolute values, but on rules. His introduction of religious *fêtes* to the Supreme Being was a consequence of his twin fears: that powers had been unleashed that the leaders could no longer contain and that the people were incapable of being enlightened. Thus near the end, in what Norman Hampson has depicted as a "rambling speech" delivered to the Convention on July 26, 1794, he despairingly declared that, "My reason, but not my heart, is on the point of doubting that virtuous republic whose plan I had traced out for myself."[8] This tragic split between head and heart, between is and ought, was obviously not lost on Weber.

This reference to the charisma of reason is all the more remarkable because in the sections of *Economy and Society* that explicitly treat the nature of charisma in its pristine and attenuated forms, no mention is made of a type of charisma located in ideas rather than vested in people. Recently, both Guenther Roth and Wolfgang Schluchter have explored this neglected and underdeveloped aspect of charisma. My analysis builds upon their work, as well as the inquiries of other Weberian exegetes.

Schluchter's study of Weber's specification of the major factors contributing to the rise of Western rationalism provides an important historical contextualization of the transformations of charisma, flushing out certain latent implications while seeking fidelity to the general thrust of the work. As he observes, Weber equates charisma with the extraordinary, denoting it as the "specifically 'creative' revolutionary force in history."[9] In emphasizing the creative quality of charisma, Schluchter argues that charisma is itself transformed over time "by the developmental logic of rationalization."[10] He suggests that Weber depicts, without providing an adequate analytical articulation of the differences, three types of charisma that in a general way suggest historical stages: magical charisma, religious charisma, and the charisma of reason. Schluchter treats the charisma of reason, then, as a new stage, a "last form," that further extends the impersonalization of charisma arising in the transition from magical to religious charisma, wherein "the idea of god has arisen," thus permitting the religious mission to be "stabilized against" a particular carrier-magician.[11] Though Schluchter does not think that charismatics will necessarily disappear, the uncoupling of charismatic ideas from individuals presumed to be endowed with gifts of grace is a significant formal difference with historical consequences.

Roth is in complete agreement with Schluchter: "There is an historical movement from revolutionary challenges inherent in the personal charisma of men with magical powers, such as Jesus . . . or Thomas Munzer . . . , to the charisma of self-evident rights that no longer need a charismatic personification."[12] Like Schluchter, Roth does not explicitly describe the key factors contributing to the transition to the final form of charisma, but it is clear that the intimate link between rationalization and secularization is crucial, since rationalization serves to effect the disenchantment of the world by calling into doubt the authoritativeness of sacro-magical definitions of reality.[13] Without exploring further the issue of the extent to which Occidental religion "carried the seeds of secularization within itself," it is important to note the "shrinkage in the scope of sacred reality" that resulted because of the Protestant Reformation.[14] A decline in the efficacy of religious solutions to the problem of meaning raises new questions and poses new dilemmas for secularized groups and individuals who are in need of an existential grounding that will help them to comprehend their condition, thereby providing the motives for meaningful action. Weber, using the term in a broader sense than that of Christian theology, refers to this as the continuing need for theodicies; it is not a question of being driven by material need, "but by an inner compulsion to understand the world as a meaningful cosmos and to take up a position toward it."[15]

While Weber stresses the multiplicity of possible solutions to the problem of meaning,[16] he contends that for certain strata (including the modern proletariat) and for various segments of the intelligentsia, a solution predicated upon reason is chosen. Reason is seen as a medium of emancipation from existing modes of domination. As such, faith in reason provides the basis for an eschatological belief in the total transformation of the social world, a soteriology that, despite their differences, was shared by radical bourgeois liberals and socialists. The historicizing of reason leads to notions of progress, predicated on reason's ability to overcome the illusions of the past, while gaining for the first time control over human destiny. As such, reason can be seen, in the ebullient terms of the young Marx, as "the solution of the riddle of history and knows itself to be this solution."[17]

Such utopian thinking was anathema to Weber. His inability to conceive of such a resolution is reflected in his understanding of the political implications of the charisma of reason. While he does not provide a sustained discussion, his views can be interpolated by observing something of the treatment of the types of legitimate order in *Economy and Society* in light of his earlier presentation of types of social action. Martin Barker has recently called attention to the fact that while Weber distinguishes four types of social action, noting in the process that they may not exhaust the possibilities—instrumentally rational, value-rational, affectual, and traditional—he cites only three types of legitimate authority, predicated on traditional, rational, and charismatic grounds.[18] In this scenario, charismatic authority located in individuals is seen as rooted in affectual action. However, the charisma of reason would seem to differ, being best identified with value-rationality, which, if a goal be pursued without regard for consequences, is as irrational as affectual action. Value-rational action differs from affectual action, however, insofar as the former entails a conscious articulation of values.

Articulating values, nevertheless, is not the same as arriving at a general societal consensus concerning their respective truth claims. Weber's demand for a value-neutral methodology is not merely an epistemological ploy. Rather, his neo-Kantian divorce of facts from values, of is from ought, precludes consideration of an ultimate, transcendental rational grounding of values. As such, a metacritique of various modes of instrumental rationality is not possible. Instead, there is great variability in the relationship between value-rational action and instrumentally rational action.[19]

What was desirable for Weber was a situation where reason informed value commitments. The choice, nonetheless, entailed a leap of faith. In this sense, of course, his thinking is part of the tradition going through Kierkegaard to Luther, and pushing further back, to Augustine and Paul. Roth describes this as a "decisionist" philosophy of history, and suggests that this saves Weber from abject pessimism.[20] The implications of this decisionism are nowhere more evident than in the vocational essays written during the latter years of Weber's life.

In this connection, Thomas Dow's analysis of Weber's understanding of charisma is particularly insightful. Dow stresses the ecstatic character of charisma in Weber's formulations, seeing charismatic authority as representing "a pattern of psychological, social, and economic release" from the past and present demands of everyday life.[21] As Weber's hostility toward the irrationalism of mystics and mystifiers attests, emotional release contained a fundamental irresponsibility, refusing to "meet the demands of the day." In direct response to this refusal, the vocational essays urge not simply an ethic of responsibility, but a passonate commitment to conduct guided by "a feeling of responsibility [*Verantwortungsgefuhl*], and a sense of proportion [*Augenmass*]."[22] To be called to one's vocation, to be capable of saying *Ich kann nicht anders, hier stehe ich*, entails an ability to overcome the morally deadening routinization of the age of bureaucracy without being able to obtain the keys to unlock the mysteries of the universe. The charisma of reason fails in its mission by proving itself incapable of providing us with certitude. Weber accepted this and argued that, rather than capitulating to unreason, we must understand not only the limits of reason, but its virtue as well: namely, its ability to provide us with clarity.

Reason is to be pressed into service by the ethic of responsibility. Only then, as Dow writes, is it possible to "rescue man from the immaturity and inhumanity of both unexamined routine and irresponsible release."[23] Reason will not save us; however, it is possible that we may save ourselves. Learning to live with this burden as well as learning to live with uncertainty and ambiguity does not mean that our lives are devoid of hope. Weber's sociology is thus infused with an acceptance of the world that entails both taking a stand on the critical issues of the day and resigning oneself to the world's intractibility in the face of our wishes that things might be otherwise.

SECULAR REJECTIONS OF THE WORLD AND THEIR DIRECTIONS

The Revolutionary Subject and the Cunning of Reason

It is precisely Weber's resigned acceptance of the disenchantment of the world and the limits of reason in overcoming the reified character of modern culture that caused key figures associated with Hegelianized Marxism to challenge his work so vigorously. They did so, it should be noted, not from the vantage of winners, but losers. Perry Anderson is correct when he writes that the "hidden hallmark of Western Marxism as a whole is thus that it is a product of defeat."[24]

This is nowhere more evident than in the case of Georg Lukács, that "orthodox heretic" and "romantic Stalinist,"[25] whose ambiguous legacy has informed and continues to inform the main currents of philosophical Marxism. This Hungarian philosopher was the first critical Marxist in this century who went behind Marx to rediscover the Hegelian origins of Marx's thought, and in so doing sought to overcome what he perceived to be the historically specific antinomies of bourgeois thought. His collection of essays published in 1922 under the title *History and Class Consciousness* has been rightly hailed as a "truly extraordinary work."[26] Its overarching quest was to discover a grounding for the forging of a unity of theory and praxis, an impossibility if one's philosophical starting point was the neo-Kantian dissociation of facts and values. Of particular importance is his response to his former teacher, Georg Simmel, and his former associate, Max Weber, for as he wrote in the 1967 preface to the volume, he had earlier approached Marx "through spectacles tinged" by both scholars.[27] His understanding of reification was clearly shaped by Simmel, while his treatments of rationalization and bureaucratization were similarly influended by Weber.

Moveover, his diagnosis of the problem of the age is markedly similar to both, though he seeks to locate his analysis within the materialist ontology of Marx and within the historically specific parameters of the capitalist mode of production. Reification, the perception of the results of human activity as alien objects existing independently of the subject is, thus, linked to the commodity character of capitalist production. His essay on "Reification and the Consciousness of the Proletariat" is thus, in essence, a fusion of insights derived from Simmel's *Philosophy of Money* and the first chapter of *Capital.*

According to Lukács, in the age of capitalism the commodity becomes the universal mediator of human relationships, as it simultaneously becomes the crucial element in the subjugation of human consciousness. The market becomes tantamount to a second nature as the transformation of production from use-value to exchange-value comes to be seen as an eternal, taken-for-granted given. Linking this to bourgeois rationalism, he concurs with Weber's characterization of the increasingly ossified quality of social life which is increasingly incapable of providing a setting for the realization of human liberation.

In his aesthetic writing on the novel as a distinctively bourgeois mode of expression, Lukács describes the implications of this situation: the modern novel, with its emphasis on moral education, treats freedom as becoming an entirely subjective phenomenon.[28] The external world moves further away from the emotional inner world of the human subject. Relating this to specifically Weberian themes, he writes: "Only in this context can the problem of modern bureaucracy be properly understood. Bureaucracy implies the adjustment of one's way of life, mode of work, and hence consciousness, to the socio-economic premises of the capitalist economy, similar to that which we have observed in the case of the worker in particular business concerns."[29]

The diagnostic similarities of Weber and Lukács only serve to accentuate the radically different remedies proffered.[30] For Lukács the ethic of responsibility postulated by Weber must be condemned, not merely because it is a bourgeois ethic of one who has learned to accept the given world as is, but because it postulates an "ought" divorced from "is," in particular, divorced from objective possibility. While he sees this as a manifestation of rank subjectivism, he is no less severe in assessing ethical socialism.[31] To overcome the heterogeneity of purposes and the multiplicity of meanings that are accepted as immutable givens by Weber, Lukács employs Marxism as a method, convinced that contained within historical materialism is the self-knowledge of capitalism.[32] The key concept for Lukács is "totality," for the concrete, historically specific totality is "the category that governs reality."[33] In apprehending the totality, the limits to our understanding are overcome, thereby freeing us from the tragic view of life that he sees offered by Weberian thought. However, this apprehension does not entail a flight into mysticism, for the totality can only be grasped through praxis—or more specifically, through achieving the unity of theory and praxis.

But, Lukács is at pains to argue, this cannot be achieved at a merely subjective or psychological level. Confronting the sheer facticity of the objective world as well as its pre-constituted meanings, the individual can "never become the measure of all things."[34] Individuals as knowledgeable agents creating their destiny are therefore replaced by classes as the true subjects of history, for only classes "can relate to the whole of reality in a practical revolutionary way."[35] More specifically, in the capitalist epoch, it is the modern proletariat that becomes the historical subject capable of societal transformation. Only it can find a way out of the impasse created by capitalism. It alone is the class capable of uniting theory and praxis, for it is the one class that has no interest in maintaining itself as a class. The truly self-interested praxis of this class pursues an ultimate course, not of strengthening its position, but one of eliminating itself as a class by destroying the socially antagonistic relations inherent in capitalism. "When the proletariat furthers its own class-aims, it simultaneously achieves the conscious realization of the—objective—aims of society."[36]

However, for the proletariat to grasp its historical mission, which it "cannot abdicate,"[37] it must achieve class consciousness: the "fate of mankind will depend . . . on its class consciousness."[38] Armed with truth as a weapon, the proletariat becomes the embodiment of reason, the vehicle through which the cunning of reason overcomes alienation and reconciles humans to their fellow humans, to their social world, and to themselves. For Lukács, the proletariat constitutes at once the repersonalization of charisma and a refurbished charismatic glorification of reason.

As he seemed acutely aware, however, this burden did not rest lightly on the shoulders of proletarians, and their psychological states seemed less than promising in terms of letting the scales fall from their eyes—the necessary precondition for realizing their historical mission via revolutionary praxis. Unlike Rosa Luxemburg, he was unwilling to accept the conviction that the proletariat was capable of spontaneously developing class consciousness. The divide between the theoretical proletariat and flesh-and-blood proletarians was enormous. The capacity of the latter to adopt various modes of "false consciousness" appeared unlimited. Thus, Lukács adhered to the Leninist view of the role of the party, depicting it as "the bearer of the class consciousness of the proletariat and the conscience of its historical vocation."[39] Equipped with this view, he was prepared to defend the party in all circumstances and was equally prepared to attack as enemies anyone challenging the party's dictates and actions. What others might see as a sacrifice of the intellect was perceived by Lukács as the route to total reason, a reason capable of comprehending a deeper level of reality beneath the flux of empirical existence.

It is not surprising, therefore, that his writing exhibited a "peculiar esotericism,"[40] for his belief in the myth of total reason propelled him into the role of theologian, his primary duty being to ferret out the heresies of the age which perverted the Church of Reason with doctrines of relativism and subjectivism. In *The Destruction of Reason* Lukács engaged in a wide-ranging attack on nineteenth- and twentieth-century modernist thought. The polemical bludgeoning meted out to Heidegger, Jaspers, Sartre, Adorno, and many others has been described by George Lichtheim as an exercise in "the art of sinking."[41] What Lukács could not abide was their apparent willingness to accept the powerlessness of thinking, the limits to reason—in short, the routinization of the charisma of reason.

Eros and Techné

Marcuse was one of the heretics attacked by Lukácsian orthodoxy, and from the Hungarian's vantage, there would, indeed, appear to be good reasons for challenging him. First, Marcuse does not view the working class as the subject of history, and often appears to be engaged in a quest for substitutes—particularly in his later work on the counterculture. Capitalism, furthermore, is treated as only one manifestation of a larger problematic, for when Marcuse speaks about one-dimensional society, he is speaking about advanced industrial societies, whether they be in the capitalist West or the state socialist Soviet bloc. In this regard, of course, his thought is distinctly similar to that of Weber. Finally, in his attempt to incorporate Freud into Marxian discourse, Marcuse focuses on the sensuous individual in a manner quite foreign to the thought of Lukács.

Both share a fundamental Hegelian undergirding, however, that suggests that reason is reality, though reality is not something perceptible at the level of immediate sense experience. Indeed, as Marcuse writes, "the world in which we find ourselves living . . . must be comprehended, transformed, even subverted in order to become that which it really is."[42] In *Reason and Revolution*, he refers to this process of comprehension as the "power of negative thinking."[43] Marcuse does not see "the rational is real" as an endorsement of the established order since he treats the rational as, in Paul Robinson's words, a "projection of human and historical potentialities."[44]

But human potentiality is not well-articulated in Marxian thought. Marx's philosophical anthropology is at best vague, and especially in *The Paris Manuscripts*, he tends to imply an infinite psychological malleability. Its rather inarticulate utopianism conspired against it, leading a number of twentieth-century Marxists, including Fromm, Reich, Roheim, and Marcuse, to look to contemporary developments in psychology, especially the work of Freud. *Eros and Civilization* constitutes Marcuse's principal contribution to this discussion.

There is a paradoxical quality to Marcuse's intentions. His formulation is posed as defense of Freud against various neo-Freudian interpreters—including Marcuse's former associate at Frankfurt, Erich Fromm—who are criticized for downplaying depth psychology's centrality of the unconscious, the import of sexuality, and the existence of a death instinct. In contrast to ego-psychology's more sanguine view concerning the ability of the rational core of personality to achieve a greater degree of autonomy from the unconscious than Freud was willing to grant, Marcuse seems to want to emphasize a bedrock irrationality lurking beneath the surface of conscious life. However, while claiming a greater fidelity to Freud than the revisionists by preserving what he refers to as the depth of Freud's formulations, Marcuse simultaneously revamps the ahistorical, immutable character of the instincts so as to treat them as subject to historical modification.[45] Whereas for Freud civilization was predicated upon the transformation of the pleasure principle into the reality principle—the immutable tension between the individual and society being not only the bedrock of civilization but also the source of individual discontents—Marcuse augments Freud's universal categories with sociohistorically specific terms: surplus-repression and performance principle.[46]

If Freud saw work as necessary unpleasantness, as possible only through sexual renunciation, he did so because he considered material scarcity to be the eternal human condition. Marcuse agrees that this has, in fact, been the case in all prior periods of history. However, the very success of the performance principle, the fruits of the achievement-oriented capitalist entrepreneur as the prevailing historical form of the reality principle, has established the preconditions for its obsolescence and the possiblity of its demise. Industrial civilization affords the possibility that, with the elimination of surplus-repression, the work situation itself will be transformed into a humane form of interaction and production. Marcuse at this point is in accord with Marx: labor is not eliminated, but transformed from a situation of alienation to that characterized by the flowering of the individual.

To the extent that the individual is liberated from an instrumental role in the labor process, the body is capable of being resexualized, resulting, in contrast to Reich, in "a resurgence of pregenital polymorphous sexuality and in a decline of genital supremacy."[47] Thus Eros triumphs in Marcuse's utopia not, as with Norman O. Brown, at the expense of civilization, but in the interest of a nonrepressive civilization, since Marcuse believes that necessary sublimation can automatically emerge out of the polymorphous state. This, however, constitutes a significant misreading of Freud, who not only argues that genital sexuality is *biologically* determined rather than being subject to historical modification, but who also treats sublimation, or the substitution of object-catheses, as being made possible precisely by the achievement of genital sexuality. Furthermore, whereas for Freud sexual development in the manner he describes poses the means by which the aggressive and destructive instincts are controlled, Marcuse's advocacy of sexual regression (a term he admittedly would not accept) appears oblivious to the potentially nihilistic consequences of unleashing the aggressive instincts. Statements in the text notwithstanding, Marcuse seems actually to harbor a view predicated on the natural harmony of humans and their world.

Marcuse's linking of Marx and Freud hinges on his equation of desexualization and alienation. But if, as Morton Schoolman has argued, the organization of the instincts at the genital stage is a purely biological phenomenon, and therefore not social, one cannot term this process of maturation either repression or alienation.[48] Repression acquires a sociological dimension only when the individual's subliminal strivings for gratification are impeded by such factors as political constraints and the negative consequences of the division of labor.[49] Such are the concerns, as Marx would remind us, not of a natural being, but of a natural human being, which is to say, a being endowed with the capacity to think critically and act due to a sometimes weak but nonetheless crafty ego, rather than a being guided by unconstrained or unmodified instinctual drives. In this sense, the neo-Freudians, whom Marcuse so scathingly attacks, are the faithful adherents to Freud's dictum: where there was id, let ego be. Conicidentally, ego-psychology appears to be more congruent with Marx's *homo faber* than with Marcuse's polymorphously sexual individual.

But Marcuse has no truck with the solipsism of inner-directed therapies, for the potential for individual psychic liberation can be actualized only if one-dimensional society is radically transformed. Marcuse's diagnosis is remarkably similar to that of Weber, for it is the domination of "technical reason" that serves as the basis of contemporary servitude. Stylistically, his writing during his American exile bears striking similarities to various critics of mass society, ranging from Riesman to Daniel Bell to Mills, with a touch of Burroughsesque "airconditioned nightmare" panache, evident in the opening sentence of *One-Dimensional Man:* "A comfortable, smooth, reasonable, democratic unfreedom prevails in industrial civilization, a token of technical progress."[50]

Appropriating the Hegelian notion of the negation of the negation, he then argues that this very technical progress provides the basis for its transcendence by creating, for the first time in history, post-scarcity societies. It provides the basis for the reconstitution of science and technology themselves, "the turn of quantity into quality."[51] Thus, as Anthony Giddens has perceptively observed, Marcuse does not share the pessimism of either his former Frankfurt School colleagues or Weber. Marcuse's theory is a utopian thesis that does not deem such thinking as a flight from reality or from history. Rather, his writing's central theme is that "utopian possibilities are contained in the very technical organization of the advanced industrial order."[52] In this hope, Marcuse is much more a direct descendant of the original Enlightenment thinkers than Lukács, for he reintroduces the link between reason, nature, and history—seeing in reason triumphant the elimination of the domination of not only people, but nature as well. While he concurs with Weber that in this iron cage it "is difficult to see reason at all,"[53] he nonetheless affirms a possible future that Weber largely disavows.

The Melancholy Left and the Dialectic of Enlightenment

Diametrically opposed to the optimism contained in the writings of Marcuse, the two central figures of the Frankfurt School, Theodor Adorno and Max Horkheimer,[54] evince an unremitting pessimism that led Walter Benjamin to characterize them as representatives of the "Melancholy Left," figures who, like the depiction of the angel in the Klee painting, looked at history and saw "one single catastrophe which kept piling wreckage upon wreckage."[55] Thus, in terms of temperament, Adorno and Horkheimer are seen by some as sharing an affinity with Weber, prompting H. C. Griesman, for example, to contend that they manifest a "cosmic pessimism."[56]

Beyond temperament, these two are much more Weberian than Marxist in a number of substantive areas. Unlike the model of Marxian orthodoxy, Lukács, they do not share a materialist ontology inherited from Marx. Neither do they adhere to the Lukácsian identity theory derived from Hegel.[57] They are also not prepared to adopt the concept of totality, as Adorno's oft-quoted aphorism attests: "The whole is the untrue." Their inability to follow Lukács is related to their unwillingness to see the proletariat as the subject of history, forcing the Critical Theory that they construct to engage in an immanent critique of social life without recourse to, as Martin Jay writes, a "real historical 'subject,' " and thus they write from a "position of 'transcendence.' "[58] As paradigmatic homeless intellectuals, this lack of historical grounding severed any attempted linkage between theory and praxis, their work being essentially devoid of immediate, realizable political implications. They, in a very real sense, have no politics.

The problematic Adorno and Horkheimer seek to explicate is more expansive than that of Marxism, having its roots in an earlier time than the rise of capitalism. As they contend at the outset of the *Dialectic of Enlightenment*, "In the most general sense of progressive thought, the Enlightenment has always aimed at liberating men from fear and establishing their sovereignty. Yet the fully enlightened earth radiates disaster triumphant."[59] The very success of reason marked its failure; the moment of its zenith is simultaneously the moment of its eclipse. At issue is the conflict between humanity and nature, the consequence of the former's domination over the latter. The combination of external and internal nature, achieved by pressing reason into service and effecting the disenchantment of the world, constitutes the very essence of the Enlightenment project.

> If one were to speak of a disease affecting reason, this disease would be understood not as having stricken reason at some historical moment, but as being inseparable from the nature of reason in civilization as we have known it so far. The disease of reason is that reason was born from man's urge to dominate nature, and the "recovery" depends on insight into the nature of the original disease, not on a cure of its latest symptoms.[60]

Implied here is a belief that "true" reason has been perverted in the process of being used as a mode of domination. When knowledge is equated with power, Enlightenment, the destroyer of tradition and myth, itself reverts to myth and paves the way for a new barbarism. Horkheimer and Adorno are particularly hostile to modern science dating from Bacon, for critical thought is presumed to be lost in the obsessive quest for methodological techniques aimed at the utilitarian desire to control. As Zoltán Tar writes, they contend that "Concepts such as substance and quality, activity and suffering [*Leiden*], being and existence had been declared metaphysical and banned from science."[61] Devoid of a critical dimension, reason serves to ratify the status quo by becoming incapable of conceptualizing alternatives to what is. As Adorno writes, "The power of reason today is the blind reason of those who currently hold power."[62] Conceived in these terms, Enlightenment becomes a mode of "mass deception,"[63] and thus, turning to the realm of culture, the arena wherein societal values are articulated, Horkheimer and Adorno present many of their most penetrating and insightful analyses.

As "heirs of the Enlightenment," however, they also believed that there was no turning back. Thus, Adorno's criticism of Stravinsky is premised on his belief that the composer sought to achieve through his music an ersatz harmonization of humankind and nature. Similarly, his scathing indictment of modern jazz proclaims the falsity of its "programmed spontaneity" and its attempt to capture a pristine primitivism. In contrast, he hears in Schönberg's music, with its painful dissonances, a critical truthfulness that unveils the alienated condition of the present age without reveling in it.

If there is no turning back, or if turning back entails a return to barbarism, then a secular soteriology must be future-oriented. Thus, what Marshall Berman has written of Marx applies equally well to Horkheimer and Adorno: they hoped to "heal the wounds of modernity through a fuller and deeper modernity."[64] In *Eclipse of Reason*, Horkheimer provides what is perhaps their most cogent assessment of the current status of reason and the remedy needed. Distinguishing between "objective reason" and "subjective reason," he contends that it is the former that is in a state of eclipse, with the latter constituting the dominant type of reason in advanced industrial societies. Since these terms are essentially equivalent to Weber's distinction between formal and substantive rationality, his assessment of the ossified quality of contemporary social life is distinctly Weberian. In terms of assessing the prospects for transcending this situation and achieving social and personal emancipation, the Critical Theorists are decidedly ambiguous. They seem to concur with Weber's conclusion that there are fatal flaws in any attempt to reachieve the charismatic glorification of reason. Unlike Weber, who seemed content to explore the various modes of human relatedness to society, Horkheimer and Adorno also sought to comprehend humanity's relationship to the natural world. Habermas is quite right when he observes that they "entertained doubts that the emancipation of humanity is possible without the resurrection of nature."[65]

Programmatically and praxiologically, however, their work offers precious little. While much of their writing—and this is especially true of the work that Adorno authored alone—is opaque and purposively elusive, Horkheimer stresses the need to appreciate the necessary interrelatedness of subjective and objective reason and the need to strike a balance between the two.[66] Despite their stress on the ethical implications of Critical Theory, they nevertheless do not proceed to develop an argument concerning how to make concrete the reconstituted harmony between the two types of reason.

In a very real way, the work of Horkheimer and Adorno moves full circle back to Weber. The limits to reason of which Weber appeared to be so acutely aware also seemed to be appreciated by the Critical Theorists, witnessed in Horkheimer's existentialist thoughts on religion: "In a really free mind the concept of infinity is preserved in the awareness of the finality of human life and of the inalterable aloneness of men, and it keeps society from indulging in a thoughtless optimism, an inflation of its own knowledge into a new religion."[67] But the stoic resignation of Weber which led not to despair, but to the vocational essays, is not paralleled in Horkheimer and Adorno. In Adorno's case, his thought veered toward a nihilistic retreat, in Lukács's depiction taking "up residence in the 'Grand Hotel Abyss.' "[68] In the case of Horkheimer, his thinking ultimately manifested a religious "yearning for another world."[69]

CONCLUSION

If the intellectual trajectories of these critics of Weber suggest anything, it is that Weber is vindicated in his claim that the charisma of reason reached its zenith in the eighteenth century. Thereafter, the ascendance of instrumental or technical reason marked the process of its routinization. The attempt to rekindle the charismatic spark, to seek a future circumscribed by triumphant reason, led Lukács and Marcuse to abandon genuinely critical thought. It also led them into blind alleys, the result of their shared conviction that intellectual solutions to the problems of modernity were isomorphic with praxiological solutions. In the case of Lukács, this led him to endorse the revolutionary violence of Bolshevism, promoting, in the words of Ernst Bloch, "the categorical imperative with a revolver in the hand."[70] This landed him in the intellectual mausoleum erected by Stalin, where his thought would remain hermetically sealed from the fresh air of free inquiry. For Marcuse, an optimistic philosophical anthropology which claimed that the alienated condition of the modern world could be attributed solely to historical factors culminated in his romantic endorsement of the 1960s counterculture, replete with its anti-intellectual and antinomian strains.[71]

Only Horkheimer and Adorno paralleled Weber in rationally stripping away as many illusions as possible, including illusions about reason itself. Only they share with him a demand to preserve the integrity of critical inquiry. Ultimately, all three reached the painful point where critical thought reaches its limits in terms of its ability to understand not only what is, but also what is objectively possible. At that point, as thought and desire are interwoven, the trio found themselves wrestling with the ambiguous and uneasy relationship between critical thinking and wishful thinking.

Epilogue: Charisma and Social Structure—The Success or Failure of Charismatic Leadership

RONALD M. GLASSMAN

In his essay "Reflections on Charismatic Leadership," Reinhard Bendix writes: "In referring now to Weber's specifications of the term 'charisma' I confine myself to the concept of 'charismatic leadership,' *leaving out the 'routinization of charisma' . . . as well as the positive or negative relations between charisma and social structure*" (emphasis added). Where Bendix leaves off, this essay begins. Whereas Bendix focused centrally on charismatic leadership as such, I shall emphasize the social structure within which charismatic leadership is enmeshed and attempts at the routinization of charisma. "The positive or negative relations between charisma and social structure" will be the major focus, leading to a discussion of the way in which this relationship affects the success or failure of the charismatic leader in determining the *direction of the routinization* of charismatic authority.

CHARISMA AND POLITICAL THEORY

Weber's conception of charisma is one of the great contributions to political theory. It links the "great man" theory of history to an analysis of *form of government* and *social structure.* Weber, of course, never embraced a simplistic "great man" approach to history; rather as C. Wright Mills observed in *The Sociological Imagination*, Weber combined the study of "history, biography, and social structure."[1]

Historians of Weber's day were wont to write as if history were a story of great men's lives, or a chronicle of battles, kings, and dates.[2] Political scientists, on the other hand, tended to concentrate on governmental form, while the sociologists put their main effort into the analysis of social structure. Weber synthesized these in one great sweep with his category "charismatic authority," for the charismatic leader is always analyzed within a specific, comparative sociohistorical context, and the form of government emergent from the eventual routinization of charisma is always also specified by Weber.

Weber's conception of the charismatic leader is tied to periods of social crises. These may arise from conditions that are primarily external to the society—invasion, flood, famine—or they may be the result of massive social change in which the old authority structure breaks down, but a new one has not yet emerged. In the former case, if the crisis is successfully withstood, the society will not change; whereas in the periods of massive social change, the crisis is endemic to the structure itself. Here charismatic authority takes on a special function: it creates order and stability during the period of transition, and it may help to direct the society toward the institutionalization of a new authority structure.

The "new" authority structure may represent a progressive or regressive form of authority—no unilinear teleological schema of history is endorsed by Weber. He makes it clear that once charismatic authority is established, its routinization may go in either a democratic or a despotic direction. It may reinstitute a form of traditional domination, or it may become absorbed into a rational-bureaucratic legitimacy system.

Weber divides the processes of charismatic leadership into: (1) the period of the establishment of charismatic authority, centering on the leader, the loyal followers and paladins; and (2) the period of the routinization of charisma, in which a more permanent authority structure is constructed, and through which the dependence upon charismatic authority can be reduced. Weber discusses both the establishment of charismatic authority and the routinization of charisma in its varying directions.[3]

Certain questions, however, arise from Weber's discussion of charisma. Some are answered elsewhere in Weber's work. They are nevertheless valuably raised, for they help illuminate the relationship between "history, biography, and social structure" implicit in Weber's theorizing:

1. What determines the success or failure of charismatic leadership in a situation in which a society is undergoing change?
2. What determines the direction of the routinization of charisma—that is, what determines the new form of authority that will emerge?
3. Can a charismatic leader move a society in *any* political direction he or she wishes?
4. Can *force* be used by a charismatic leader (or a "caesarist" power leader) to move a society in *any* direction desired?
5. Can force be used to move a society in a democratic direction?
6. What role does the personality of the charismatic leader play in (a) the direction of the routinization and (b) the style or character of domination?

The answers to these questions may be found through an analysis of the causal relationships between *form of domination* (legitimate or illegitimate) and *social structure.* Weber is absolutely explicit in his analysis of forms of domination (legitimate domination and power regimes). He is somewhat less explicit in his analysis of social structure. From his critical writings on the Marxian conception of social structure and social change, however, we can piece together a consistent Weberian conception of social structure and social change. Once we establish this, we can turn to the central problem of the success, failure, and direction of the routinization of charismatic authority.

WEBER'S THEORY OF SOCIAL STRUCTURE AND SOCIOHISTORICAL CHANGE

Weber writes that it is *not* his "aim to substitute for a one-sided materialistic an equally one-sided spiritualistic causal interpretation of culture and history. Each is equally possible," he adds, "but each, if it does not serve as the preparation, but as the conclusion of an investigation, accomplishes equally little in the interest of historical truth."[4] Weber's conception of social structure and social change thus provides us with a multi-dimensional description of the various causal processes of social action which create the social organization of society.

His analysis includes: (1) the material, or economic, organization of society, the type of administration, and the types of military and religious institutions which characterize a given society;[5] and (2) an analysis of the strata engendered by these institutions (and the material and ideal interests carried by these strata);[6] these strata include: (a) classes linked to the economy, (b) status groups, whose base may be political, military, religious, or even administrative, and (c) ethnic groups, as groups in their own right, in independent causal interaction with the social structure. Taken together, economic classes, status groups, and ethnic groups form a *complex stratification system*, which is the hallmark of Weberian social-structural analysis.[7]

In terms of the causality of social change, again partially in reaction to Marxism, Weber attempted to present a more *balanced* view in which political, military, ideological, and cultural-historical elements are given an equal causal role with economic elements in the social organization, social stratification, and social alteration which emerge in history.[8] Weber made it clear that he did not wish to replace the Marxian material view of history with a spiritual one, but to present a view of social structure and social change in which economic, political, and ideological factors were all included as potentially independent causal spheres of social action.

Form of Government and Social Structure

Political analysis in its inception combined the study of form of government with the study of social structure. Plato and Aristotle both linked the social structure of a society directly to the form of government that emerges from it. For both, too, the form of government—through the mobilization of power—could act back upon the social structure to alter it as well; thus the direction of causality might emanate from either institutional sphere. The relationship between the form of government and the social structure became the central focus of political analysis for Plato and Aristotle.[9]

After the writings of Machiavelli and Hobbes, however, political science as a discipline tended to concentrate upon the study of the power of political leaders, political parties, and the precise structure of the form of government, with little emphasis placed upon the analysis of social structure.[10] In a corollary way, sociology after Marx and Durkheim tended to place its emphasis upon the analysis of social structure, as if the power and political institutions were mere reflections of the social structure.[11]

Weber's political sociology resynthesizes the study of power and the form of the state with the study of social structure and the legitimation processes linking the two spheres. Aristotle had made the link between form of government and social structure explicit. He utilized the theoretical tool of classes—rich, middle, poor, and slave—as the basis of his theory of politics.[12] Marx had developed the theory of classes beyond Aristotle, linking the conception of social structure more closely to the mode of production and to sociohistorical change. For Weber, however, Marx had over-emphasized the causal action of economic classes on the form of government. Weber then revived a formulation—closer to the Aristotelian one—which, though it incorporated the Marxian principle that the form of government emerges from the specific social structure, presents a more complex analysis of the social structure, and asserts (with Aristotle) that the form of government, once institutionalized, develops power sources and legitimation processes which enable it to act upon, and alter, the social structure.[13]

Weber's theory of social structure, then, includes a complex class and stratum analysis, while his theory of social change emphasizes the independent causal action of ideas, military conquests, and the power of state and administrative apparatuses, along with economic causalities (and even including civilizational peculiarities).[14] Finally, Weber's theory of the link between form of government and social structure includes the potentiality for the state to act back upon the social structure in an attempt to determine its form.

The Peculiar Nature of Social Structure During Periods of Massive Social Change

In the analysis of cases of charismatic authority, the social structure will necessarily be in a peculiar state. It will be in a state of major transition, in which parts of the old collapsing social structure will remain, while parts of the new social structure will have already emerged.

The facts that must be determined in each specific historical case are:

(1) How ingrained are old economic and political institutions and the ideologies linked with them? (2) How powerful are the old classes and status groups? and (3) How powerful have new classes and status groups, linked to new economic and political institutions carrying new ideologies, become? In addition, we must determine whether outside forces are involved in supporting one portion of the social structure as opposed to another, for the power of any section can be shored up or undermined by outside forces. This, of course, can completely alter the social structure as a whole. These outside forces can manifest their influence through political, military, economic, or ideological "interferences."

With this outline of Weber's conception of social structure and sociohistorical change as a backdrop, I now wish to analyze some historical cases in which charismatic leaders have attempted to bring their societies through a period of social change and to routinize their charisma in one direction or another. From these historical cases of acknowledged charismatic authority, we can attempt to establish some regularities for hypothesis construction.

THE SUCCESS AND FAILURE OF THE ROUTINIZATION OF CHARISMATIC AUTHORITY

In most cases in this section we will be dealing with charismatic leaders who were able to come to power but either (1) could or could not maintain themselves in power, or (2) could or could not routinize their charisma in the desired direction (i.e., the direction the leader and most of the followers believed in).

Just as Bendix earlier presented capsule descriptions of the lives and times of the charismatic leaders he was analyzing, I will present capsule descriptions of the social structures in which the charismatic leaders I am analyzing functioned. Bendix establishes that the structural and cultural nexus in which a charismatic leader functions may influence the political results emerging from the charismatic authority. Though the charismatic leader arises during a period of massive social change, the structure and culture of the past—the classes, the ideology, the institutions—have not evaporated, though they have declined. The problem, then, is to analyze the structural and cultural context in which various charismatic leaders have functioned and to evaluate the causal influences these structural and cultural factors have had upon the direction of the routinization—or the failure of routinization—that occurred. A charismatic leader can also act on the social and cultural structure and in some cases alter it in the desired direction.

Bolivar and Washington

As both Bendix and Richard Bell have mentioned George Washington in their essays, I propose to begin my series of capsule analyses by comparing him and his social setting to Simon Bolivar, "the George Washington of Latin America," and the structural-cultural nexus in which his charisma functioned. Both of these leaders and certainly some of their followers were influenced by the democratic-capitalist ideas emanating from seventeenth- and eighteenth-century England, Holland, and France. Both leaders led their troops to victory over colonial overlords and thus came to power. But Washington and his coterie succeeded in routinizing his leadership in the desired direction, whereas Bolivar and his followers failed—and Bolivar died brokenhearted.

Bolivar

In Latin America the economy was a cash-crop "latifundia" and mining economy. The production of raw materials for export predominated. The cash-crop and mining organization was semi-feudal, controlled by Spanish landlords using local overseers and serf-like laborers.[15] Though money was involved, it was used by the lords to buy luxury goods and expand their aristocratic lifestyle, rather than for constant reinvestment and capital expansion for its own sake—the hallmark of capitalism according to Weber.[16] The feudal aristocracy owned the land and dominated the serfs, who were often of Indian and African heritage. They utilized the money gained for luxury and power display but had little or no interest in industrialism or commerce.

The aristocratic feudal class was very powerful, while the peasant or serf class was the majority of the population by an enormous margin. The middle class was relatively weak in numbers, but actually quite wealthy because they handled the overseas trade which the aristocracy desired. Therefore, this commercial upper-middle class, though it was in political and ideological struggle with the feudal aristocracy was itself almost an upper class in lifestyle.

The cultural influence of the Spanish feudal aristocracy was all pervasive: "Every man an *hidalgo* [lord]"; the "macho" complex (Don Juanism); a disdain for the masses, who were made to serve. For a short time the ideas of the North American and French revolutions were introduced by the commercial upper-middle class. These ideas, centering on freedom and democracy and commercial development, excited the intellectuals of the Latin American commercial class and were absorbed by the leaders of the downtrodden peasants, who sought freedom, dignity, and control of their own land. But such ideas never really became internalized in Latin America, for the feudal aristocracy rejected them outright, the majority of the commercial class clung to their own version of the *hidalgo* complex, and the peasants, mostly Indians and Mestizos, though desiring freedom from Spanish domination, knew nothing of law, capital, or private property. Furthermore, the Roman Catholic Church, linked to the Spanish lords, was very powerful, and reinforced the feudal political, social, and ideological structures.

The form of government was Spanish-feudal. The central authority was weak and corrupt. Pay-offs (*mordidas*) for all services were demanded by officials. Vassalage ties were weak—each lord was a king unto himself. The feudal aristocracy preferred to live in the cities and leave overseers on their estates. Thus they did not allow the commercial upper-middle class the freedom of the cities (as their English and Dutch counterparts had), but vied for control of the cities with them, producing the kind of patrician feuding that characterized the northern Italian cities of the Renaissance.

The social structure and cultural nexus of Latin America were hardly compatible with the establishment of the legal-democratic form of government or capitalist-industrialization which Bolivar would champion. If this were not enough, outside interference from externally powerful nation-states would make the situation worse.

The United States and England "interfered" in an unpredictable way. While promulgating democratic and capitalist ideology, they actually inhibited the growth of the indigenous commercial class, because American and English merchants wanted the profits to be gained from control of the raw material and cash-crop trade, and did not want industrial competition from Latin American businessmen. Thus the Americans and English, after the defeat of Spain by the merchant-peasant armies of Bolivar, formed an alliance with the Latin American feudal aristocracy. They shored up the feudal class militarily and monetarily, helped repress the peasants (seeking freedom and small plots of land for subsistence, rather than cash-crop production), and inhibited the growth of the democratic-capitalist upper-middle class.

As a result, the political institutions and ideologies carried by Bolivar—parliamentary government and constitutional law—collapsed. Bolivar had been a genuinely charismatic leader, holding his rag-tag troops together against the Spanish feudal forces in a long bloody campaign similar to the United States' Revolutionary War. When his independence war against Spain was won, Bolivar came to power. He set up electoral and legal-governmental institutions, but they were undermined, attacked by the still powerful indigenous feudal class, opposed by the Church, misunderstood by the Indian and African serfs, barely supported by the feudal-enthralled commercial class itself, and subverted by British and American foreign power. Parliamentary democracy collapsed like a house of cards. Bolivar died in misery, realizing that his dream had not been achieved.

Washington

In North America, we find a social structure almost fully consonant with the routinization of charismatic authority desired by Washington. The English revolution—and the Dutch, I might add—had been over for nearly a century and a half when the American revolt against England occurred.[17] Therefore, unlike Latin America, no fully feudal aristocracy existed, and except for Afro-American slavery in the South, all the peasants were free farmers. The transition in the United States, then, was not really a transition to a completely new social structure. However, as Lord Acton makes clear, the elimination of the property qualification for voting and office-holding was radical step toward democratization first established in the United States and long resisted in England.[18] Furthermore, becoming a new nation was a traumatic process, and the war with England had been long and inconclusive. Washington's presence as first civilian leader helped to produce order and stability.

The United States was characterized by pre-industrial capitalist merchant-trade on a large scale. The upper class, though retaining gentry-aristocratic airs, also was fully involved in "money-making for the sake of money-making"[19]—Weber's aforementioned distinction between feudal lords who want only what money can buy, and capitalist businessmen who want to deal with money for its own sake being resolved toward the latter (whereas the Latin feudal "lords" disdained it). Farm production also moved rapidly to capitalist market-oriented production, for North American farmers were not bound by feudal lords, but were free peasants who became small businessmen early on.

Class divisions were weaker in the United States, because the gentry were weakened by the expulsion of the Tories, and the middle class strengthened by the prosperity of the small farmers, artisans, and shopkeepers. The upper class was rapidly becoming fully commercialized in its world orientation, and no Roman Catholic hegemony existed to reinforce feudal values.[20] Instead, Calvinist sectarians—representing the dominant religious worldview—produced a profound ideological influence, reinforcing individualism, hard work, egalitarianism, anti-aristocratic asceticism, and legitimating money—*wealth in itself* (rather than its symbolic accouterments or lineage-perpetuating functions) as the sign of heavenly grace.

Instead of establishing giant estates with serfs and servants, the North American frontier saw business-oriented, Calvinist-inspired, small property owners. Therefore the feudal-aristocratic, or even oligarchic-patrician, tendencies of the upper class became inhibited—though they never entirely disappeared. In Aristotelian terms, the lower-middle and middle classes formed the large majority, while the poor were few indeed, especially in comparative perspective.

The ideas of democracy and capitalism were carried by all the classes in North America. No feudal ideology existed to compete with this, and Calvinism was consonant with it. With the farmers and artisans prosperous, resources plentiful, and no large, impoverished working class yet in existence, the ideologies of democracy and capitalism were totally dominant. The political structure of parliamentary democracy and constitutional law was fully accepted, actually deeply revered—more so even than in England. With the majority in the United States holding property, democratic processes became the passion of the new nation, its claim to world fame.

Since kingship was completely eliminated in the United States (a significant difference from both England and Holland, where constitutional monarchy still produced a traditional authority aura), the presidency took on a much more symbolic and actual power potential than the office of prime minister. Therefore Washington's military heroism was transferred into an official "charism" that produced a spellbinding effect on the population—witness the numbers of places and things named after the "Father of his Country"—in relative disregard for the far greater systematic contributions of other revolutionary figures (e.g., Jefferson).

The British and French continued to attempt to interfere in the affairs of the First New Nation. The French reinforced the democratic traditions, while the English attempted to shore up the gentry-patriciate or to retard the growth of the rapidly expanding commercial upper-middle class, having their greatest success in the cash-crop, slave-holding, quasiaristocratic upper class in the South. In fact, this one nonconsonant area produced the need for further transition, and the trauma of this transition—the trial by combat—produced the need for further charismatic authority.

The quasifeudal squirearchic slave society of the South could not be integrated with the democratic-capitalist society of the North and Midwest. Barrington Moore has rightly observed that the American Civil War was actually the last phase of the transition from feudal to capitalist-democratic society that had begun in Western Europe and England in the 16th century.[21] Whereas this was a major social change, a charismatic leader could ease the transition. Lincoln became that leader, though like Washington, his charisma was far more forced upon him than the classical type might suggest.[22] Lincoln's sudden death left America without the charismatic authority to ease the transition (even though it may actually have enhanced Lincoln's stature as a hero).

This latter point is theoretically important: If the social structure is strongly nonconsonant, or large segments of the social structure cling to the old structure and culture, the charismatic leader may not only be rendered ineffective, but even killed either by those he seeks to move toward change or someone acting out violence in the period of anomie in which normative inhibitions to violence greatly weaken.[23] We can also add Gandhi's death in India at the hands of a Hindu fanatic, and Martin Luther King's assassination under not so mysterious circumstances in Memphis. This is a topic to which we will return in the conclusion of this essay.

Sun Yatzen and Mao Zedong

Both these leaders were acknowledged in China at different points in its transition to modernity as charismatic leaders. Both came to power and remained rulers until their deaths. Sun, however, could not move China in the direction he wished. Mao could and did.

The economy of China was typical of a kingly-bureaucratic empire—peasant agricultural production, plus large-scale corvée labor projects, all directed and coordinated by a well-developed Mandarin bureaucracy connected to the divine-kingly state. China's economy had been structured in this manner since around the fourth century B.C.! By Sun Yatzen's time, European and Japanese industrial capitalists had established foreign-owned industries in Shanghai and elsewhere. The organization of peasant production, however, remained locally communal, with some lands alienable and others held in common. The bureaucratic regulation and distribution of food, though it included aristocratic and bureaucratic usurpation (leading to enormous luxury for the emperor, the aristocrats, and the bureaucratic elite), was communal in its orientation to the peasants, who made up the bulk of the population and were linked to the high status, powerful class of bureaucratic officials.[24]

The aristocracy was relatively weak in China, because of their conquest origins and the centuries of Chinese isolation from attack. The kingship was often controlled by the Mandarin bureaucrats. Merchants in China were numerous and often wealthy, but their status was dramatically lower than their wealth, and they had to buy into the Mandarin bureaucracy to attain higher status and political power.[25] A small working class emerged, connected to the foreign capitalists. A class of Western-educated intellectuals also emerged, but connected to no clear European colonial tradition.

The ideologies of democracy and capitalist industrialization were spread by the intellectuals, but the peasants, mandarins, aristocrats, and even the merchants did not respect any ideas from the Western "barbarians." Even among the intellectuals themselves, there were factions who championed Chinese superiority in ideas and social relations. Confucianism was a powerful, and relatively rational, ideology carried by the educated Chinese, and this counteracted Western influences to a great extent.[26] The prior spread of mystic Buddhism, too, as more consistent with the rational-ethical Confucianism, inhibited the spread of Christianity in any form, as well as of individualistic, free-choice, free-will ideology in general. In particular, democracy and laissez-faire capitalist economy were remarkably nonconsonant forms of polity and economy in a China in which the sultanate-bureaucratic state with its hierarchical authority structure and communal economy still existed, and had existed for thousands of years.

Outside interference was crucial in China, for the "colonial" period was not long and stable or dominated by one power whose institutions and ideologies could be emulated. This period, rather, was short, horribly violent, and disruptive. The "opium war" produced degeneracy in social relations, while thousands died in just a few days in the Boxer Rebellion. China was torn apart by the competition between the rising industrial powers.

As the old social structure of China began to collapse, Sun Yatzen arose as a genuine charismatic leader, surrounded by a charismatized following embodied in the Kuomintang. Yet when Sun and the Kuomintang attempted to routinize charismatic authority in the direction of parliamentary democracy and capitalist industrial production, along with capitalist farm production, this routinization did not succeed. The peasantry would not modernize production in a capitalist direction, resisting the well-intentioned efforts of the Kuomintang mightily—nor did they understand or approve of the nondeferential political actions of parliamentary democracy and the concomitant Western ideas. The great hopes of Sun Yatzen began to crumble, and Sun, who idolized the American system, began instead to look toward the Russian system in his later years. The Kuomintang split into factions, with Mao Zedong advocating the Russian model and Chiang Kai-shek, the American.

After Sun Yatzen's death, Chiang was not able to routinize Sun's charismatic legacy in a democratic direction. He was pushed to resort to force in order to maintain the parliamentary system and institute the capitalist industrial economic system. Chiang resorted to greater and greater amounts of force, so that he was himself undermining the routinization of charisma in a legitimate, democratic direction. "The last of the War Lords," as he came to be called (hardly an evocation of democratic leadership), had drifted toward "neo-fascist" military dictatorship, and China split in civil war.

From Aristotle to Machiavelli to Hobbes, political theorists have taught that naked power can triumph in politics—even Weber recognizes this in the political vocation essay.[27] One should not be surprised, then, that Chiang initially defeated Mao. Chiang's military forces were superior. He had Western support. And Mao was not yet a well-known figure, while Chiang, as heir to Sun Yatzen, retained some of the charisma still attached to the Kuomintang.

Mao's charisma might never have become a factor in China had not World War II intervened to dissolve China further. After the war a revitalized Maoist group, which had proved its effectiveness in peasant-agricultural reorganization and its efficiency and fairness in political administration, fought a weakened Chiang faction and won. What is most significant is that once Mao took power, he did not encounter the same difficulties that Sun Yatzen had encountered. Mao utilized more power than Sun, but less than Chiang. The key was that Mao's program simply was more consonant with the social structure and culture of China. When the charismatic leader Sun attempted to routinize his charisma in a direction nonconsonant with the social structure (even though the social structure was disintegrating), he failed. When Mao routinized his charisma in a more consonant direction, he succeeded.

There is no absolute, unilinear principle in this. Sun could have used massive force to alter the social structure in the desired direction, for example. Sun, enthralled with Western ideas, did not realize that it would be difficult to institutionalize such ideas on the very different structural-cultural base of China, whereas Mao could see this. Furthermore, Mao's modernization program was so consistent with Chinese culture and structure that it later had to be modified away from the mandarin-communal model established for the rural provinces in which he spent his exile during World War II.

We shall return to the question of force, too, but before that I want to take up the cases of two other leaders and assess the success or failure of their routinizations of charisma.

Nasser and Castro

Nasser

Egypt's economy at the start of the twentieth century was still based on river-flood agriculture as it had been practiced since 10,000 B.C. The carefully coordinated centralized bureaucratic empires' corvée and slave projects had disappeared centuries earlier during the later Roman epoch. The "Nomarchs," or Mandarins of Egypt, had disappeared with the hieroglyphics. Peasant production was haphazard and subsistence-oriented. Since the days of the Hellenic era, furthermore, small business, trade, and shopkeeping, emanating from Alexandria, had become a major career line in Egypt. This orientation was stimulated by foreigners—e.g., Greeks, Armenians, Jews, Lebanese—who had trade links throughout the Middle East. The aristocracy was weakened by centuries of foreign domination, and the peasants and shopkeepers clearly formed a majority. Wealthy merchants formed an upper stratum, but were often of foreign background with foreign ties—and purely mercantile, rather than industrial-capitalist, in orientation.

Islam, with its powerful "Moslem Brotherhood" organization, its venerated *Ulema* (rabbinate or scholar-priests), and its powerful hold on the minds of the people, openly opposed both communist ideology and institutions and democratic-capitalist structures and ideas—all "Western" ways were decried by Islam. The family structure, backed by Islamic ideology, resisted women's liberation mightily and also opposed the idealization of "work" (i.e., the "protestant" work ethic) for men. As Weber has shown, Islam is a religion which rewards warriorhood for men, traditional casuistic Koranic learning for priests (*Ulema*), and chaste household service for women, possibly in polygamous marriage.[28]

In the countryside, the peasant family (and religious structure) resisted attempts at both modernization and commercialization, and continued to overpopulate and underproduce. These processes sent millions to Egypt's cities, and to these unemployed, displaced peasants, Nasser had a charismatic appeal.

Nasser rose as a charismatic leader at the point at which Egypt's condition was economically disastrous. French and English colonialism finally ended with World War II and with the last of its kings (Faruk I) and the last of the colonialists gone, Egypt had to find its own way into the modern world. Nasser was not able, however, to generate enough jobs on his own to absorb the mass of *lumpen*-peasants accumulating in the cities. He turned to Russia to help develop an economic infrastructure, but even the Aswan dam was not enough to improve the dire economic situation. He then embarked on a confrontation policy with Israel, attempting to lead the Arab world to victory against the new state.

The Egyptians had by far the largest population of all the Arab countries. The problem was that the Egyptians were not Arabs. They did not have a tradition of warrior heroism, in spite of Islamic ideology. The wars with Israel went badly. The troops fought poorly. Thousands died, while additional thousands were captured. *Egypt* had nothing substantial to gain from the wars, and everything to lose. *Nasser* gambled on a high-stakes game for his own purposes and also lost.

What is significant about Egypt is that after centuries of Greek, then Roman, then Arabic, then European rule, no indigenous, respected, legitimated political structure remained. Rather, the indigenous Egyptian population became skeptical of, and resistant to, all political regimes.

Nasser did rouse the population in charismatic adulation and unity for a short moment—even the foreign small business-people (some Jewish) admired him, though they knew he might "nationalize" their holdings and expel them. However, he attempted to lead the population in a direction in which they refused to go—toward a strong, militarized government, with repression of small business and small peasant activities. The communist emphasis on "work," atheism, and the equality of women was hardly consonant with Islam, which proved a powerful impediment to communism —which it accurately perceives as a "Western" ideology—as it has all over the Moslem world, from Syria to Indonesia. Furthermore, in Egypt Islam lacked the warrior-charisma which is associated with it in Arabia. This made Nasser's power tenuous indeed, and it is a testament to his genuine, if short-lived, charisma that he was able to excite the Egyptians into a number of skirmishes with Israel before Egyptian rebellion. The ethnic merchants did not welcome communism either. They had prospered under trade-capitalism. Nasser expelled many of the ethnics, especially the Jews, but also the Greeks. Instead of creating prosperity for the Egyptian merchants who remained, however, this produced ruin, since the Jews and Greeks had had most of the international trade connections and stimulated the trade-capitalist sector.

In addition, the Russian technicians were viewed by the Egyptians as arrogant and domineering. At Nasser's death, his entire dream collapsed overnight. Sadat, with overwhelming support from all factions, brought

Egypt back into the capitalist orbit and made peace with Israel and the Islamic brotherhood. Nasser failed to create anything like a Marxist-Leninist style polity and economy, and the majority of shopkeepers and free peasants, with their deep attachment to Islam, welcomed Sadat and approved of the break with Russia.[29]

Castro

The case of Castro in Cuba is particularly fascinating, for it exhibits the Weberian theory of change quite convincingly. The same nexus of structural and cultural forces which had created an anarchic stalemate in the rest of Latin America,[30] and which had operated to prevent the routinization of charisma in every direction attempted,[31] also originally existed in Cuba. *Unique historical events*, however, occurred which would alter this situation.

Since the days of the Spanish-American War United States business influence was so strong in Cuba's sugar, tobacco, and other export industries that it actually undermined the Cuban aristocracy. In most Latin American countries, American business interests shored up the aristocracy, but because of the near-colonial relationship the United States had with Cuba, the results were quite different. Additionally, the proximity to the North American mainland created a tourist and gambling industry unprecedented elsewhere. The tourist industry became so vice-ridden under the influence of the American crime syndicates who ran the gambling operations that it began to shock the Cuban middle and upper classes.[32] The corruption of the Batista regime and its direct links to United States business and crime produced such a revulsion in the Cubans, that Castro—whose army on a purely military basis was too weak to succeed—was allowed to come to power. Not only the lower classes backed Castro enthusiastically, but the commercial upper-middle and middle classes, who were relatively strong for Latin America, also welcomed Castro into Havana—"duty bound," as it were, to charismatize him in the genuine sense.

Castro had not led the upper or middle classes to believe that he had communist leanings. He had not been supported by the Cuban communist party (which had direct links to the Soviet Union), but had, rather, been espousing the mild reformist doctrines which typified "*Caudillo*" leaders throughout Latin America.[33] Once he came to power, however, Castro realized that with United States business, United States criminal syndicates, and the Cuban commercial upper-middle class holding the balance of power in Cuba, his days in office, like those of so many other *Caudillo*-reformist leaders, were numbered. In a bold stroke, which the United States has never gotten over, he allied himself with the Cuban communist party, sought, and quickly received, Russian military support, expelled the American businessmen and mobsters, and then, boldest of all, he exiled the majority of an entire Cuban class—the wealthy commercial upper-middle class (along with what was left of the aristocracy) to Miami.

With the Americans and wealthy Cubans gone, and with Russian military and economic support, Castro was able to routinize his charisma in a direction that probably would have otherwise been impossible, given the sociocultural structure as it existed. Furthermore, to those Cubans who remained—the poor, the black, and the peasant—Castro was a genuinely charismatic hero whom they would follow to the death. We shall discuss in the conclusion whether charismatic leaders can always alter the social structure in the direction they wish, but for now, we may accept the fact that this is precisely what Castro was able to achieve.

The political structure of most Latin American countries, typified by a bastardized, nonlegitimated parliamentary façade corrupted by Spanish-style payoffs (*mordida*), graft and institutionalized corruption, and dominated behind the scenes by an American-armed military, has been a monumental impediment to charismatic leaders attempting to establish true legal-democracy.[34] Castro dismantled most of this, however, and created a Russian-style dictatorship of communist party officials, along with a modern bureaucracy. Backed by Russian money, technicians, and military power, and supported by the poor, it has taken root. The presence of a black majority in the lower classes particularly aided Castro's legitimation. Castro played to the blacks and received strong support from them, as they assumed American intervention would reinforce anti-black racism.

In terms of outside interference, the Americans, embarrassed by Batista's corruption, allowed Castro to come to power. They, too, thought he was a liberal reformer. No communist leader had ever seized power in Latin America,[35] and the communist parties there had been rather ineffective. Russian influence up to that point had been weak. Once Castro allied himself with Russia and established a Marxist-Leninist state, the United States decided he had to go. By this time, however, the powerful, American-linked, upper and middle classes had been exiled; thus the CIA plot which was formulated—similar to that in Guatemala when Arbenz was ousted—lacked indigenous support. In the meantime, Kennedy had been elected president, and though anxious to oust Castro, he refused to allow a full-scale American air and ground invasion, believing that the Guatemalan-style coup would suffice.[36] Given the heavy Russian military support and the charismatic link of Castro with the majority-poor, however, the invasion by the upper-middle classes was doomed to failure. After the invasion attempt, Castro "encouraged" even more of the middle class to leave. Thus, the social structure that remained was consonant with the routinization which Castro established. Even then, the Russians had to shore up the economic system with billions of rubles per year, to make up for the loss of cash-crop capital from the United States.

Hitler and Perón

Arthur Schweitzer's essay in this collection describes Hitler's genuine and manufactured charisma. He makes the point strongly, which Weber made somewhat weakly, that a charismatic leader may not wish to move his or her society in an "advanced" direction. In fact, however, a charismatic leader may attempt to routinize charisma in a despotic direction or return to a form of society like that which has disintegrated—or both. If old classes, institutions, ideologies, and historical circumstances are strong enough, a new form of authority embodying elements of the old is possible. The Ayatollah Khomeini is proving this in Iran, as Kimmel and Tavakol have shown in their essay in this volume.

However, the charismatically engendered conservative, or nativist, social structure will never be the old social structure as it existed,[37] as Swatos points out, but rather something new, retaining elements of the old social and cultural structure shored up by the charismatic (or pseudocharismatic) authority of the new leader. Such conservative charisma may or may not become permanently routinized, but charismatic leaders, such as Hitler and Mussolini, certainly attempted such routinization.

Hitler

In Germany, the economic structure was a peculiar mixture of industrial capitalism in the West, and feudalism in the East. Capitalist farming had been institutionalized in Western Germany for many years, while in Prussia feudal production was still typical[38] and the feudal aristocracy was still powerful. They held land as a gentry class in Prussia and other provinces, and, unlike their English counterparts, exhibited a feudal, rather than a bourgeois ideology.[39] They maintained dueling fraternities, took pride in dueling scars, and generally held onto a knightly mentality. This aristocracy also held key government posts in the military and civilian bureaucracy.

The capitalist rich were a growing class in Germany, but they needed the help of the feudal aristocracy in government, because Britain was ahead in industrial technology and production and held most of the overseas raw materials markets. Therefore, protectionist and imperialist support from government was sought. The feudal aristocracy in the government formed a partnership with the upper bourgeoisie in the industrialization process. The working class in Germany, furthermore, was socialist in orientation and revolutionary in character. After the "Spartacist" revolt, the upper bourgeoisie depended even more upon the feudal aristocracy for support —both in repressing the socialist workers and in promoting competition with Britain. The peasants in many provinces were still markedly feudal in orientation. Thus the Weimar Republic was not really supported by large sectors of the populace, and most critically, not even by the capitalist class (upper and middle) who had generated this form of government in the first place. Germany still had a feudal majority.

The classes who wanted a return to "military" government believed that such a dictatorship would be like that of Napoleon III—a semi-monarchical regime with a functional, efficient bureaucracy, as in Bismarck's Germany.

Fantasies of the German barbarian invasions of Rome, the German-dominated Holy Roman Empire, and the Order of the Teutonic Knights, however, also danced in the German mind. Such heroic military visions were kept alive by composers such as Wagner and Liszt, and vivified by feudal-oriented intellectuals such as Hegel, Von Treitzke, Fichte, and Nietzsche. Even Weber describes with awe the Nordic "berserk" warriors—the blond beasts—who were kept in cages by their Arab captors.[40] Some even consider Weber's whole notion of charisma as a heroic-romantic German conception derived from Nietzsche.[41] Weber, however, hated the dueling fraternities, was a champion of the Weimar Republic, and exhibited no protofascist sympathies—as his friend, Michels, for example, did. Weber's liberalism was hardly typical of German thought, however, as feudal-heroic images of the Fatherland excited the imagination of the Germans.

In terms of political structure, the existence of a functioning bureaucratic state dominated by feudal-military strata plays a crucial role in Germany: These bureaucratic and feudal strata would as soon follow a dictatorial leader as deal with the "inefficiencies" of a parliamentary government. Hitler's militarism—his paramilitary party, his paramilitary police, and his revival of the heroic-military history of the German past—when linked to his genuine charisma, was consonant with the structure, culture, and the state of mind of the Germany of the 1930s, and provided exactly the authority structure the Germans were searching for. Blaming the Jews for the loss of World War I, finally, turned the workers and the small shopkeepers toward his charisma and away from socialism, capitalism, and democracy, all of which seemed to have failed them.

There were outside interferences which also turned Germany in on its own vision of its past. The Germans felt trapped between England and Russia, and they also felt unduly punished by the terms of the Versailles Treaty.[42] They felt betrayed by America's entrance into the war, and the resulting tip of the balance toward Britain. All these factors, plus the Great Depression, contributed toward the charismatization of Hitler by most segments of German society.

Perón

I have already described the Latin American social structure in the capsule descriptions of Bolivar and Castro. What is interesting for us here is that Perón, a genuine charismatic leader to all Argentinians but the aristocratic class, attempted to establish a fascist style regme in Argentina but failed.

The economic system of Argentina was controlled by American and European industrialists, who opposed fascism. The feudal aristocracy wanted dictatorship, but under their control, and in no case with ties to the lower classes. The working class (the "shirtless ones") loved Perón, but wanted him to be a socialist charismatic leader. They also loved Evita for her charity toward them, and saw them as a charismatic couple. The lower classes viewed Perón as a *Caudillo*, a hero of the downtrodden, but they did not really desire a rigid, orderly, military state.[43] Many of the peasants, far away from Buenos Aires, knew little of Perón and remained attached to their feudal lords or rancheros.

The Latin ideology was *machismo*, Don Juanish, *hidalgo*, but it harbored no dreams of world conquest, military heroism, or industrial-productive leadership. No racist ideology of superiority was contained in Latin culture. The Latins considered themselves superior because they were racially *mixed*—the "cosmic race," embodying all races, and sired by the "Spanish Stallions," the Conquistadores.[44]

Argentina was characterized by a loose, decentralized, corrupt government, and patrician-family-dominated political parties. Strong government of any kind was suspect, as was parliamentary democratic government, which was perceived to give the masses too much liberty.[45] There were Germans and Italians in Argentina who had brought the fascist ideology with them, but they also carried socialist and anarchist ideologies. There were Jews in Argentina, and they did become scapegoats. However, the whole culture of Latin America deemphasizes ethnicity and race, and since Argentina was multi-ethnic, the Jews could not be easily singled out, as they were in Germany.

Fascism was an imported idea. The bulk of Argentinians did not take it seriously, as they did not take democracy and capitalism seriously. In addition, the influence of the United States, although muted during World War II, was powerful thereafter. Contemporary leftist critiques notwithstanding, the United States moderated fascist tendencies all over Latin America, and actively opposed such tendencies after World War II. The United States did not oppose military dictatorship—we supported the military wherever we could out of fear of communism—but dictatorships built on fascist ideology and principles were opposed.

Perón tried numerous times to establish a neo-fascist style of government, but failed each time.

SOME TENTATIVE HYPOTHESES CONCERNING THE SUCCESS OR FAILURE OF CHARISMATIC LEADERSHIP AND THE DIRECTION OF THE ROUTINIZATION OF CHARISMATIC AUTHORITY

I. The success or failure of a charismatic leader in coming to power and remaining in power is causally related to the relative *consonance* or *nonconsonance* of the leader's charismatic authority with the social structure. If a leader's support and program are extremely nonconsonant with the social structure, he may not come to power at all; if he comes to power, he will be unable to remain in power. Such leaders as

Zapata, Bolivar, and Nkrumah come to mind as charismatics who could not maintain their power. The Gracchi brothers of Rome similarly attempted to gain power, but failed to achieve control of the polity. Julius Caesar, too, can be viewed in this way.

II. The success or failure of charismatic authority *as a bridge* between an old and a new form of authority is determined by the *intended direction of the routinization* and its consonance or nonconsonance with the social structure as it stands.

A. If the social structure is near consonance with the desired direction of routinization, then the presence of a charismatic leader helps ease the transition to the new form of authority, because the charismatic leader is able to move in his direction certain segments of the population (classes, strata, religious or ethnic groups) who, without charismatic authority, might resist. Cromwell comes to mind here, for through his charismatic authority the radicalism of the Levellers was negated and the oligarchic demands of the gentry were at least partially and temporarily reduced.[46] Washington played a similar role in the United States,[47] though Cromwell's task was far more monumental in England.

B. If, however, the desired direction of routinization is markedly nonconsonant with the structure, powerful segments of the population will resist change, and *no longer recognize the leader as charismatic.* The charismatic relationship is a fragile sociopsychological relationship, and charismatic awe can disappear like a burst balloon in the face of the nonconsonant structural superiority of segments of the population. Sun Yatzen—with all of his acknowledged, genuine charisma—could not establish the routinization of charisma in the direction he desired. So, too, Bolivar. Sukarno, in Indonesia, could not routinize his fully acknowledged charisma in a Marxist-Leninist direction, and fell from power during a violent rebellion against him when he attempted to do so. Yet Ho Chi Minh, with no Moslem brotherhood against him (as it was against Sukarno), and even in the face of French and American outside power, was able to establish Marxist-Leninism in Viet Nam. Sukarno and Ho were similar charismatic figures fighting similar colonial powers, but the social structures in which they were enmeshed were different indeed.

Yet, according to both Aristotle and Weber, the power of government can be used to act back on the social structure; therefore:

III. Physical or ideological force can be used by a charismatic leader (or by a noncharismatic power-leader—a caesarist leader in Weber's terms, or a dictator or military junta in modern parlance) to maintain a political system that is nonconsonant with the social structure.

A. Force can be used by a charismatic leader to attempt to alter the social structure so that it is brought into consonance with the desired direction of routinization. In this regard, charismatic leaders may have to exert less force than dictatorial leaders in order to create social structural change, simply because of their charismatic hold on certain segments of the population. Again, Cromwell comes to mind, because, while he used force against the agrarian-socialists, he quashed their rebellion with very little exercise of it because of his great charisma. Castro used force against the upper and upper-middle classes, but again, did not need massive force in order to reduce their opposition. If one contrasts the force used by Stalin, for example, with that of Lenin, one can see that the non-charismatic power-leader, Stalin, relied solely on force and terror to achieve his alteration of social structure in the agrarian sector of the population, whereas Lenin had exerted charismatic authority—genuine and manufactured—in order to move the peasants in his direction. Though Lenin did not succeed in moving the peasants toward communal production while he was alive, the communist system he was establishing was not in danger of collapse.

   Stalin's utilization of force to alter the social structure is proof enough that a power-leader can move the social structure in the direction he desires, but that lacking charisma, the amount of force needed becomes massive, and the human sacrifices barbaric. The irony of the case of Hitler is that he, with his awesome charisma—genuine, and then reinforced through manufactured means—did *not* need to resort to much force, since the social structure of Germany was consonant with his desired routinization. Mad with murderous racism and teutonic military fantasies, he committed massive atrocities quite independently of his need to maintain authority. This shows that the personality of the charismatic leader can influence the determination of the direction of the routinization of charismatic authority quite apart from system needs.

B. If the social structure is markedly nonconsonant with the desired routinization of the charismatic leader, *even force may fail* to bring about the stability of the charismatic regime or the desired changes in the social structure. Instead, the charismatic regime may fail.

   Robespierre and his "Reign of Terror" come to mind here. Force failed to democratize radically France's government, and Robespierre himself ended up on the guillotine. Chiang Kai-shek used increasing amounts of force in China, but ended up losing whatever charisma he had gained through association with Sun Yatzen and failing to alter the structure.

C. Force, for the maintenance or suppression of a charismatic regime, or for the alteration of the social structure in a desired direction, can come from *internal* or *external* sources.

1. In terms of *internal* sources, the charismatic regime itself may attempt to alter the social structure by: (a) repressing or expelling certain elements of it, and by shoring up others, (b) by creating a political structure which can maintain itself through power, while it attempts to alter the social structure, and (c) by inculcating a new ideology through carefully controlled childhood and adolescent socialization and education (and adult "reeducation"). Mao did the latter in China, as Jefferson did to a degree in the United States with the establishment of free public schools with heavily democratic and legal ideology—a very radical educational process for its day and one of the foremost structural-institutional differences between the United States and England.
2. *External* sources of power commonly intervene in changing societies. That is, an outside government may simply shore up artificially a weakened segment of a social structure or a weak regime, or undermine a strong element of the social structure and overthrow a strong regime. Sparta and Athens regularly did this to smaller city-states during the Peloponnesian Wars.

   The United States continues to act in this way in Latin America, shoring up the feudal and military segments and weakening capitalist-democratic ones, while actively repressing the communist elements wherever possible. Under Kennedy, the United States shored up the capitalist-democratic classes, exiled the feudal leaders, and repressed the communist leaders—but both then and now, we intervened to alter the political and social structure.

   The Soviet Union has played a similar role in repressing the capitalist-democratic elements and shoring up the communist regimes of Eastern Europe. In the case of Poland, Russia has suppressed a genuine charismatic leader, Lech Walesa, whose charismatized mass movement, *Solidarity*, would have swept him to power, and in this case, because the consonant social structure—newly consonant, as the university-educated "new middle class" and the gymnasium-educated working class formed a united majority—would have allowed him to routinize his charisma in a democratic-socialist direction something like that of Sweden and West Germany under the Social Democratic Party, if we take Walesa's rhetoric at face value. This case clearly shows how an outside power can eradicate or repress charisma even when it has massive support.

An outside society may influence change within another society through *diffusion* of ideas, rather than direct political interference. If these ideas are consonant with the direction of change, they may help groups within that society effect change. If the ideas are nonconsonant, they may produce confusion, instability, and disorder, rather than the desired change. The Napoleonic ideals produced confusion in Germany, for instance, whereas these same French ideals helped reinforce the polity of the newly founded United States.

Sometimes external attempts at alteration of the social structure and polity are so nonconsonant that even massive force and propaganda fail to produce the desired change. The United States' role in Nicaragua is a case in point, as is the Russian role in Czechoslovakia, Hungary, and Poland. The short-term Spartan occupation of Athens after the Peloponnesian Wars also failed to establish oligarchy in that city-state.

D. Can force be used to maintain a democratic regime or alter the social structure towards consonance with a democratic political system? A charismatic leader may attempt to alter the social structure so as to inculcate democratic ideology and reinforce democratic institutions. The problem involved here is that the utilization of force to eliminate nondemocratic segments of the social structure (and shore up democratic segments), may set an anti-democratic precedent within the historical tradition and therefore undermine the tradition it sought to establish. Hypocritical actions are not lost on a population, and democratic political institutions may be too fragile to survive a population's cynicism about them.

Most critical in this regard, however, is the insurmountable fact that if a coercive-repressive-propagandistic political system is established during a period that is supposed to be transitional to democracy, such institutions will not "wither away," and power-leaders may arise, succeeding the charismatic leader, who simply utilize the despotic political systems for their own ends. Thus, the institutionalization of force for the purpose of change in a democratic direction becomes its own major impediment to change in that direction. This has been the Marxist-Leninist dilemma in Russia and in China, in which a "true democracy" on a classless base was to be the ultimate goal of the transition, but where the despotic communist state, once entrenched, prevents transition in this direction.

However, it is not impossible to use force temporarily, if the social structure is fairly consonant with a democratic direction of change, and if democratic political institutions are established and legitimated as superordinate over the purveyors of force. A charismatic leader may give over the control of force (military, police, judicial, economic) to an emerging democratic political system. If this system becomes established as the state and the charismatic dictatorship is dismantled and majority segments of the population accept the new state, then a forced transition in a democratic direction becomes possible. Cromwell did this in England. Napoleon partially succeeded in this in France.

Finally, if force is directed at *minority* segments of the population, while majority segments of the population are protected by, and absorbed into, the emerging democratic polity, then democratic institutions may survive—the exercise of force being accepted by the majority segments as protection of democracy against small, well-organized, anti-democratic elements of society. Betancourt accomplished this in Venezuela, where force against the communist intellectuals and military dictators was used in defense of the democratic system he helped to establish.

The danger in the utilization of force to attain democratic alterations is monumental, yet the reality in some cases supports the possibility. There is a fine line here between the use of force and the possibility of this use degenerating into entrenched institutionalized despotism. If the events in Venezuela showed that some force could be used to preserve a transition to democracy, events in Uruguay and Chile have shown how easily such attempts may degenerate into permanent despotism, with the concomitant loss of democratic institutions for long periods.

IV. Charismatic leaders may lead a society in a *modernist* or *conservative* (nativist) direction.

A. *Modernist:* First, there may be alternative models of modernization. In Weberian theory, there is no unilinear direction of change. Today, for instance, there are capitalist-democratic, neo-fascist, communist, and democratic-socialist models of industrialization, all exhibiting themselves as models of modernization. These alternative models will be more or less consonant or nonconsonant with the social structure of any given society undergoing a change. Therefore, the success or failure of charismatic authority is again related to:

1. The model of modernization chosen and its consonance or nonconsonance with the social structure *as it stands*, or
2. The ability of the charismatic leader to alter a nonconsonant social structure in the direction consonant with the desired model of modernization.

B. *Conservative* (Nativist): A conservative leader may preserve the society as it exists in the transitional period, but usually cannot preserve the society in the form in which it existed prior to the period of change. As Mannheim has suggested, such a conservative leader usually steps in at the point when the society has already changed.[48] Any attempt to return it to its old form usually ends up producing further alterations, albeit different alterations than the modernists had hoped for.

Mannheim notwithstanding, however, conservative charismatic leaders (such as Hitler and the Ayatollah Khomeini) are able to preserve *some* elements of the old social structure—classes, ideas, religious institutions, and so forth—though often in odd juxtaposition both with themselves and innovative forms. The result is a mix of old and new elements, with some old elements accentuated at the price of others. This creates a *new* social structure. In fact, in Weberian terms, it often results in long-term "civilizational" peculiarities, such as German militarism, Latin machismo, American laissez-faire, Japanese "feudal"-industrialism, and Iranian Islamic "socialism." These peculiarities produce a "nativist" quality within the conservative trend, linked only to the particular cultural nexus in question and quite inexplicable apart from it.

Sometimes the conservative nature of the charismatic authority structure produces another crisis when the charismatic leader leaves office. By inhibiting change, the charismatic leader simply forestalled the transition, thus the crisis is generated anew. Perón did this in Argentina; Khomeini may have done it in Iran.

V. Although charisma is not, in Weberian terms, primarily a psychological element but rather an authority structure, nevertheless the *personality* of the charismatic leader may permanently affect the new political system which emerges:

A. A charismatic leader may move the society in a peculiar direction which then becomes institutionalized—with either positive or negative results for that society in the long run. For instance, Mao Zedong's emphasis on agrarian communism, over against urban-industrial communism, at first had positive results for China, but then acted as a major inhibition to China's development, sending China into a second crisis of transition. Gandhi's charisma helped to produce a democratic humanistic government in India, but it also engendered a state that turned out to be too weak to act effectively. It took Nehru many years to create the kind of democratic state that could function in India, and in this he had been sharply inhibited by Gandhi's charisma.

George Washington's two term presidency set a continuing example in the United States which was emulated until the days of Roosevelt, and has now become law. Comparatively, Napoleon crowning himself as emperor set the opposite precedent in France; a precedent which hurt French democratic stability. The charismatic

Napoleon could possibly have helped France by establishing a limited-tenure democratic succession procedure if he had done otherwise, for the reign of terror was over and his external wars had helped to stabilize France. Finally, the Ayatollah's surprising success at reinstitutionalizing Islamic beliefs has set a precedent in Iran that could have long-term effects on Iranian structural and political conditions.

B. The charismatic leader may affect the amount and kind of force utilized during and after the transition period. This can vary from a charismatic leader using the *minimum* amount of force necessary to produce order, stability, and change—such as that used by Cromwell and Mao and Betancourt—to the utilization of *unbelievable brutality* and terror *beyond that needed* to create order, stability, or change—such as that employed by Hitler.

Notes

INTRODUCTION

1. Weber, 1978a: 241-42.
2. Loewenstein, 1966: 79; Mommsen, 1965: 33.
3. Mills, 1959.
4. Edward Shils (1965), although attempting to extend Weber's theory, presents instead a Durkheimian conception of cohesion too static to capture the Weberian intent. Bensman and Givant, in this volume, present a full critique of Shils's position.
5. Thucydides, 1954; Plutarch, 1965.
6. Willner, 1984.
7. Aristotle, 1970: 154-88.
8. Durkheim, 1951; *see* Berger and Neuhaus, 1977.
9. Mommsen, 1974; Factor and Turner, 1984; Kilker, 1984.
10. It is important that the problematic of modernity not be attached to a particular political stance or nation-state. John Meyer, for example, rightly observes that "the power of modern culture—like that of medieval Christendom—lies in the fact that it is a shared and binding set of rules exogenous to any given society, and located not only in individual sentiments, but also in many world institutions." (1980: 117). The truth of this assertion can be illustrated by a report in the April 1985 issue of *News from Iceland*, the English-language Icelandic news monthly, on the rapid rise of Jón Baldvin Hannibalsoon to leadership of the leftist SDP. Einar Sigurdsson writes: "Hannibalsson's ascendance to the apex of the SDP seems to have inspired many voters. He is a charismatic leader and an eloquent speaker. With a populist flair he looks and acts like a leader on the television screen." Two elements are important: on the one hand, Iceland is a nation of little over a quarter of a million population; on the other, however, it is as modernized as any place in the world. Modernity, not "sheer size" (as we often hear as an armchair explanation of

why politicians in the United States must behave the way they do), is an explanatory variable in itself for its leadership styles.

11. This theme is explored in greater detail in Swatos, 1983. As an illustrative case in point, however: As we were preparing this volume we received two different advertisements from the Bloomingdale's department store chain. One, with a "Style Scandinavia" theme, invited us to "Come explore the charisma of Scandinavia." A summer sale issue featuring a Bermuda fashion theme asked that we "come save and be enchanted."

CHAPTER 1

1. Readers who wish to become further acquainted with this aspect of Weber's work may wish to consult his 1958a: 416-41.

2. Our translation from "Agrargeschichte des Altertums," *Handwörterbuch des Staatswissenschaften* 1: 182; *see* Weber, 1976b.

3. *See* Weber, 1978a: 1132-33.

4. *See* Weber, 1978a: 1116 ff.

5. Lecky, 1955 (vol. 1): 310.

6. *See* Weber, 1958a: 267-301.

7. Our translation; *see* Weber, 1978a: 254.

8. Gerth and Mills' volume was published prior to the English translation of *Wirtschaft und Gessellschaft*. In their text they translate the title as *Economics and Society*. [Editors].

9. *See* Gerth and Mills in Weber, 1958a: 32-44. [Editors].

10. *See* Weber, 1922: 132, 142.

CHAPTER 2

1. Willner and Willner, 1965: 78.

2. Loewenstein, 1966: 74-85; *see* B. Wilson, 1975.

3. Shils, 1965: 199-213.

4. *See* Apter, 1966: 303-6, also 168, 173-74, 233, 296-97, 323. For Apter's own reassessment, *see* Apter, 1968.

5. *See* Ake, 1966: 1-13. Ake raises many appropriate questions but does not seem aware that it is inappropriate to expect a legitimation of regular political institutions from charismatic leadership—these institutions exist already.

6. Lipset, 1963: 16-45; cf. the contrasting interpretation by Huntington, 1966: 408-14.

7. Weber's discussion tends to obscure the distinction between leadership and authority (*Herrschaft*), since he always analyzes the latter in terms of the chance that a command will be obeyed, and this criterion can be applied to leadership as well. In Weber's terminology charismatic authority in the sense of routinized charisma can be distinguished from charismatic authority in the sense of personal leadership, but that appears to leave no room for personal leadership that is not charismatic. I return to this question briefly at the end of this article. At any rate, the present discussion is confined to charismatic authority in the sense of personal leadership or what I call charismatic leadership. For an illuminating discussion of this point *see* Bierstedt, 1954: 71-72.

8. Weber, 1978a: 241.

9. The first of these points relates to the discussion by Loewenstein and Shils: Weber's statement is obviously conditional. Not the presence of "charisma" but its power to revolutionize the social order is judged to be greatest where traditions are well established. Weber also makes clear that "pure" charisma is incompatible with economic *routine*, not with material gain or possessions as such (1978a: 244-45).

10. Weber, 1978a: 242. The translation has been modified slightly, with emphasis added, as well as the sequence of Weber's specifications.

11. The phrase in quotation marks has been suggested by Rustow, 1967: 165. It is a succinct paraphrase of the miraculous element in the followers' perception of charisma.

12. Weber, 1978a: 447-48.

13. In a letter to Motilal Nehru, September 2, 1924; quoted in Fisher, 1967: 367.

14. According to Lee (1967), biographical data detrimental to Kim's official image have been suppressed, such as his flight to Siberia to escape the Japanese invasion, which makes his subsequent political prominence largely the result of Russian or Chinese influence. There is some question, of course, whether the manipulation of such details enters into people's awareness; but even in the absence of knowledge, suspicions and rumors can spread quickly if they project people's feelings.

15. It is probably more difficult to make testimonials to the leader appear genuine when these are given by his direct collaborators, because the secular context militates against the image of the disciple who is moved by unselfish devotion to duty and who partakes of the leader's charisma.

16. This paper originated in a symposium organized by the Association of Asian Studies which met in New York, 1966, under the chairmanship of Professor Rupert Emerson. Subsequently the editors of *Asian Survey* arranged for the publication of papers on four Asian leaders with this essay serving as an introduction (*Asian Survey*, Vol. VII, June 1967, pp. 341-352). I then made several revisions for its publication in the volume *State and Society: A Reader in Comparative Political Sociology* (Little, Brown & Co., 1968), and again for my book with Guenther Roth, *Scholarship and Partisanship* (University of California Press, 1971), from which this redaction occurs. In these republications I have included factual materials which originally appeared in separate essays by Professor Roger M. Smith, Dr. Margaret Fisher, Professor Chong-sik Lee, and Dr. Stuart R. Schram. I wish to thank the authors and the editors of *Asian Survey* for thier permission to use the materials from the articles in revised form.

CHAPTER 3

1. Shils, 1965: 201.
2. Weber, 1978a: 241-42.
3. Weber, 1978a: 1112-13.
4. Weber, 1978a: 1114 (trans., 1958a: 248-49).
5. Weber, 1952: 290-91.
6. Weber, 1978a: 440.
7. Weber, 1978a: 1142 (trans., 1958a: 251-52).
8. Weber, 1978a: 242-43.
9. The complete statement here referred to is perhaps Weber's most general

expression of his approach to the sociology of knowledge. It is: "Not ideas, but material and ideal interests, directly govern men's conduct. Yet very frequently the 'world images' that have been created by 'ideas' have, like switchmen, determined the tracks along which action has been pushed by the dynamic of interest" (1958a: 280).

10. Weber, 1978a: 1120.
11. Weber, 1978a: 248-49, 1139.
12. Weber, 1958a: 297; 1978a: 246-54, 1121-24.
13. Weber, 1978a: 1136.
14. Weber, 1978a: 248.
15. Weber, 1978a: 440.
16. Weber, 1978a: 1112-13.
17. Weber, 1978a: 1113.
18. Weber, 1978a: 243-44.
19. Weber, 1978a: 244.
20. Weber, 1978a: 1115 (trans., 1958a: 250).
21. Weber, 1978a: 1116.
22. Weber, 1978a: 1114 (trans., 1958a: 248).
23. Weber, 1978a: 242.
24. Shils (1965) states that Weber's "historicist concern to delineate the unique features of 'modern society' hindered his perception of the deeper and more permanent features of all societies" (203). He states that charisma is more "complicated" and more "protean" in the modern industrial society (213). Concerning Weber, Shils comments (202):

> He did not consider the more widely dispersed, unintense operation of the charismatic element in corporate bodies governed by the rational-legal type of authority. . . . Weber had a pronounced tendency to segregate the object of attributed charisma, to see it almost exclusively in its most concentrated and intense forms, and to disregard the possibility of its dispersed and attenuated existence. He tended indeed to deny the possibility that charisma can become an integral element in the process of secular institutionalization. (This might well be part of Weber's more general tendency to see the modern world as *entzaubert*, as devoid of any belief in the possibility of genuine charisma.)

A major premise for Shils is that "institutionalized" charisma exists in the modern world.

25. Shils, 1965: 201.
26. Shils, 1965: 201.
27. Shils, 1965: 203.
28. Shils, 1965: 204-13.
29. Shils, 1965: 206.
30. Shils, 1965: 203 (n. 7).
31. Shils, 1965: 203-204.
32. Shils, 1965: 201.
33. Shils, 1965: 202.
34. Shils, 1965: 207.
35. Shils, 1965: 204.
36. Shils, 1965: 206.
37. Shils, 1965: 207.
38. Shils, 1965: 210.

39. Shils, 1965: 210, 212.

40. Parsons, 1968: 669.

41. Claude Ake (1966: 8, 12) makes this criticism of the concept of charisma as used by Weber, Shils, Wallerstein, and Apter:

> . . . One will have to insist on an explanation of the process by which the masses identify with a particular leader in an atmosphere in which parochial loyalties largely determine the leader with whom the individual identifies. Unfortunately, the theory of charismatic legitimation says little about this process and this is why it is so difficult to relate it to phenomenal experience. [And he concludes:] Our critique has aimed to show that the theory of charismatic legitimation is still too incoherent to merit serious consideration as a realistic response to the problem of political integration.

42. McIntosh, 1970.

43. McIntosh, 1970: 902.

44. McIntosh, 1970: 902-903.

45. McIntosh, 1970: 909.

46. McIntosh, 1970: 909.

47. McIntosh, 1970: 909.

48. McIntosh, 1970: 910.

49. Weber, 1978a: 1132.

50. Weber, 1978a: 1132.

51. Weber, 1978a: 1132-33.

52. Weber, 1978a: 242.

53. Weber, 1958a: 309.

54. Friedrich, 1961: 15.

55. Apter, 1968; Bendix and Roth, 1971; Fagan, 1965; Runciman, 1963; Schram, 1967; Tucker, 1968; Willner and Willner, 1965.

56. McIntosh, 1970: 910.

57. We interpret this argument as being the major thrust of such essays as "The Social Psychology of the World Religions," "Religious Rejections of the World and Their Directions," "Science as a Vocation," and "Politics as a Vocation" (all in 1958a).

58. McIntosh, 1970: 910.

59. McIntosh, 1970: 911. A similar emphasis on identification and the need for transcendence with much less emphasis on the psychological dynamics (Freudian) is presented in Marcus, 1961. Marcus tends to combine Shils' emphasis on transcendence from the immediate, ordinary with Freudian psychological processes. *See*, too, Camic, 1980.

60. McIntosh, 1970: 911.

61. This would even apply, for example, when the Pope is termed "charismatic" by the media.

62. *See* Morin, 1960.

63. Bendix and Roth, 1971: 172.

64. Loewenstein, 1966: 86.

65. Bendix and Roth, 1971: 72.

66. Loewenstein, 1966: 84.

67. Loewenstein, 1966: 85-86.

68. Merton et al., 1946.

69. Apter, 1968.

70. Schram, 1967.
71. Tucker, 1968.
72. Fagan, 1965.
73. Willner and Willner, 1965.
74. For a discussion of symbolic leaders and symbolic leadership *see* Klapp, 1964.
75. Runciman, 1963.
76. McGinniss, 1968; Boorstin, 1962: 41-42, 249.
77. For an extended treatment of these themes, *see* Bensman and Lilienfeld, 1973 (esp. chap. 12).
78. Apter, 1955: 929-97; Ratnam, 1964: 352.
79. Blau, 1963: 309.
80. Apter, 1968: 766.
81. Weber, 1978a: 1111-12 (trans., 1958a: 245).
82. Weber, 1958a: 106, 370.
83. Friedrich (1961: 24) has actually used the term *pseudocharisma*, but he uses it to reject the suitability of the concept of charisma in all but a religious context. We agree with Friedrich's—and for different reasons, with Bendix's and Loewenstein's —notion that *pure* charisma is extremely rare in the modern world. But *pseudocharisma*, as we have defined it, is very common. Instead of using the term "pseudocharisma" to reject Weberian notions of charisma, we would use it to exend these notions, which we have repeatedly pointed out were foreshadowed by Weber himself. This, indeed, is one of the purposes of this essay.
84. Much of this chapter is derived from lectures and discussions with Hans Gerth. Its specific formulation and inadequacies, of course, are our own.

CHAPTER 4

1. *See* Diggins and Kann, 1981.
2. Sennett, 1980: 16, 22-23.
3. Weber, 1978a: 1112, 1118-20, 1132, 1139.
4. *See* Peters, 1967.
5. *See* Schaar, 1970.
6. Except as otherwise noted this list is drawn from Weber, 1978a: 1112-17.
7. Weber, 1958a: 295-97.
8. Weber, 1978a: 1122.
9. Weber, 1978a: 1146-47.
10. Schwartz, 1983: 19-20.
11. Weber, 1978a: 1126.
12. Weber, 1978a: 1128.
13. This list is drawn from Weber, 1978a: 1128-32.
14. Taylor, 1970: 595-97.
15. Schwartz, 1983: 21.
16. Wolin, 1981: 54-55.
17. Huntington, 1981: 216.
18. Bellah, 1975: x.
19. Diggins in Diggins and Kann, 1981: 21.
20. MacIntyre, 1981.

21. References to Bensman and Givant and to Glassman in this essay are to their essays that also appear in this volume.

CHAPTER 5

1. Weber, 1976a; 1958a: 302-22.
2. Poggi, 1983: 56; *see also* Marshall, 1981.
3. Little, 1969: 33-80, 226-37, 250-59.
4. Eisenstadt, 1968a, 1968b.
5. Mommsen (1965: 33) gives hints of this, arguing that Weber built his concept of charisma out of his Puritanism studies.
6. Abbott, 1872; Pond, 1862; Robbins, 1845; Schaff, 1857; Sears, 1844, 1863.
7. Weber, 1976a: 81-87, 112-14; *see also* Roth in Bendix and Roth, 1971: 18-19. Marshall (1981: 72) summarizes concisely and accurately: "Luther's conception of the calling is . . . of little significance for Weber's argument. . . . The really decisive religious figure in Weber's eyes is . . . John Calvin. It is Calvinism that is the true opponent of Catholicism." Thus F. G. Lee, a Catholic partisan writes (1886), "Where Christianity [i.e., Catholicism] has not rooted out Calvinism, Calvinism has rooted out Christianity."
8. Sears, 1863: 627.
9. On the contrast between virtuoso religiosity and charisma, *see* Hill, 1973; Swatos, 1981.
10. Sears, 1844: 442. Thus Luther clearly rejects any claim to a *unique* dispensation of divine grace or election. His "truth" was in what *was* written, not special revelation.
11. Although in the ironic twists history takes, Erasmus probably had more of an effect on Calvin; see Pond, 1862.
12. Robbins, 1845: 330-31.
13. In Robbins, 1845: 340 (emphasis added).
14. Schaff, 1857: 137, 126.
15. Poggi, 1983: 56.
16. *See* Little, 1969.
17. It is in no way necessary to accept any part of Martin Luther's person in order to accept Lutheranism, whereas Calvinism is entirely defeated if Calvin's personal election by God be rejected.
18. Schaff, 1857: 145.
19. Schluchter, 1981: 124; *see* Roth and Schluchter, 1979: 134.
20. *See* Swatos, 1979.
21. Schluchter, 1981: 124.
22. Haller, 1938: 84-85.
23. Troeltsch, 1931.
24. *See* Heller, 1981.
25. Poggi, 1983: 70.
26. This is not to say that Lutheranism had *no* social consequences, for of course it did—principally in breaking up the monastic foundations and their enormous wealth. *As an authority system*, however, it was essentially impotent.
27. In Robbins, 1845: 502.
28. Schaff, 1857: 128; *see* Acts 5: 29.

29. Robbins, 1845: 710-11 (emphasis added).

30. Robbins, 1845: 712-15 (emphasis added).

31. Mackinnon, 1962: 162-63.

32. Mackinnon (1962: 93) writes of Calvin's authority in a way that clearly demonstrates the structural rather than the "personality" basis for his dominance:

> Naturally a timid man and the victim of frequent illness, he knew neither fear nor hesitation when what he held to be the cause of God was at stake. Hence the commanding sense of his authority as God's minister. . . . Opposition to him is opposition to God and His Word. It was not permissible to doubt that *his interpretation* of the Word as preacher and theologian *was inerrant and must be received as the truth of God. This implied belief in himself was an indispensable part of his mission* (emphasis added).

33. Berger, 1963a: 130.

34. Osborne, 1961; Erikson, 1958.

35. Schaff, 1857.

36. There is some question as to just how poor Luther was and how wealthy Calvin was. Clearly there were marked differences in their families and upbringing. In general, however, the French bourgeoisie of the period was better off than its German counterpart. While class origins might account for some of their differences in lifestyle, it is still difficult to see why their *followers* would have treated the two differently in the kinds of descriptive narratives they provide of their lives—unless this is because of differences in relationship between leader and followers, i.e., different types of authority structures.

37. Schaff, 1857: 145.

38. One of the nagging problems in understanding Weber's Protestant Ethic thesis is that readers often make the superficial association between "Protestant Ethic," and the religious amalgam that is today termed "protestant." This is a very superficial approach to Weber's work, where the Protestant Ethic is much more clearly and carefully defined. The translation of the title of the work was most unfortunate, but can hardly be rectified at this point. Also unfortunate is the lack of scholarly attention paid to Weber's "anticritical" response to Rachfahl in 1910, the substantive portions of which are available in translation (Weber, 1978b). Here he clearly enumerates exactly what he thought he was doing in the Protestant Ethic essays and highlights again the contrast between Calvinism and Lutheranism. Evidence that this intent was understood by English-speaking readers of the German text prior to Parsons' translation of 1930 is provided by Forsyth's exposition of 1910. An example of the crass misunderstanding of Weber's work that continues to prevail in spite of the outstanding treatments by Marshall (1982) and Poggi (1983) is to be found in Zito's recent work (1984: 103). In the anticritical comments Weber clarifies what "the other side of the causal chain" is, as he does in the very text (1976a: 26-27) Zito misreads.

39. Schluchter, 1981.

40. Weber, 1978a: 1121.

41. For the sociopsychological aspect, *see* Poggi, 1983; 61-70; for more on the breakthrough to modernity, *see* Eisenstadt, 1968b. I am indebted to Paul Gustafson and Peter Kivisto for comments on an earlier draft of this essay, though neither is to be blamed for flaws that may remain.

CHAPTER 6

1. Eliade, 1963: 443-46.
2. Herberg, 1975: 19.
3. Eliade, 1961: 203.
4. Eliade, 1961: 203.
5. Rubenstein, 1978: 93-95
6. B. Wilson, 1975: 114.
7. Tucker, 1968.
8. Parsons, 1947: 64.
9. Smith, 1976: 16-17.
10. Smith, 1976: 58-59.
11. Heschel, 1966: 132-34.
12. Herberg, 1975: 40.
13. Katz, 1961: 227-28.
14. *See* Buber, 1966; Fackenheim, 1968; Heschel, 1973; Wiesel, 1978; Harris, 1985.
15. Fackenheim, 1968.
16. Fackenheim, 1968: 179.
17. Bosk, 1979.
18. Ben-Amos and Mintz, 1970: 28-31.
19. Dresner, 1960: 143.
20. Wiesel (1972: 154) has provided an intriguing variant interpretation of the Kotsker's behavior. He sees it as forewarning the Holocaust, hypothesizing:

> Could he [the Kotsker] have foreseen that one-hundred years after his retreat another fire would set the continent ablaze, and that its first victims would be Jewish men and women abandoned by God and by all mankind? Could it be that from that moment on he planned to fight fire with fire—attempting to prepare us, demanding that we be strong, intransigent, capable of resisting evil no matter what form it takes?

21. Dresner, 1960: 147 (emphasis added).
22. Shmueli, 1969: 5.
23. Weiner, 1957: 326.
24. Loftland, 1977: 318.
25. Dibelius, n.d.: 108-9.
26. Beckford, 1973: 323.
27. In Bryant and Hodges, 1978: 65.
28. *Divine Principle*, 1973: 128.
29. Savad, 1976: 134ff.
30. Bromley and Shupe, 1979: 126-27.
31. This problematic continues to vex the Unification movement as a result of the Reverend Moon's arrest in the United States on tax evasion charges. It is worth noting, however, that practically all major religious groups in the United States filed briefs on the Reverend Moon's behalf as the case was appealed (unsuccessfully).
32. Weber, 1978a: 1114 (trans., 1958a: 249).
33. Loftland, 1977: 312-13.
34. *See*, e.g., Acts 5: 35-37.

CHAPTER 7

1. *See* Wolf, 1969.
2. Weber, 1958a: 296.
3. Weber, 1978a: 241.
4. Bendix, 1960: 301.
5. Gramsci, 1971.
6. Bendix, 1960: 301.
7. Weber, 1978a: 456, 1115, 1146 (some trans., 1958a).
8. Weber, 1978a: 244.
9. Bendix, 1962: 300.
10. Weber, 1978a: 244, 1113 (some trans., 1958a).
11. *See* Eisenstadt, 1968b.
12. Weber, 1978a: 246.
13. Weber, 1976a: 182.
14. In Katouzian, 1981: 238-39.
15. Abrahamian, 1980: 21-22.
16. Graham, 1979: 36-37.
17. Halliday, 1978: 170-71.
18. Halliday, 1978.
19. In Helmut, 1975: 22.
20. *See* Halliday, 1978; Kazomi, 1980.
21. Fischer, 1980: 186-87.
22. Tehranian, 1980: 20.
23. Abrahamian, 1980: 23.
24. Graham, 1979: 22-24.
25. Keddie, 1981: 244-45.
26. In Abrahamian, 1980: 25.
27. The absence of such programs of systematic terror in Western societies may in turn account for the differences in perspective on "terrorism" that pertain between citizens of Middle Eastern states and those of, say, the United States.
28. In such a Weberian theory of revolution (i.e., one based upon charisma), the charismatic leader constitutes a necessary "spark" that is largely missing from the "spontaneous combustion" theory of Marxism.
29. In Floor, 1983.
30. Dekmejian, 1980: 2.
31. IRP, 1978(99): 7.
32. *Newsweek*, 1978: 80.
33. In Bill, 1982: 38.
34. In Arani, 1980: 9.
35. IRP, 1978(6): 2.
36. *See* Abrahamian, 1982b: 93; Fischer, 1980a: 111.
37. *See* the discussion of the "law of biographical analogy" in Berger's paper above; the same process seems to be operating here.
38. IRP, 1978(100): 1-2.
39. IRP, 1980(286): 80 (emphasis added).
40. IRP, 1979(368): 10.
41. This was also true of Calvinism *in statu nascendi* but altered in routinization

because of different civilizational contexts, and especially in reference to different understandings of wealth in each system.

42. Weber, 1978a: 625.
43. IRP, 1979(453): 1.
44. In Abrahamian, 1982a: 530.
45. Weber, 1978a: 463, 527, 569, 594.
46. IRP, 1979(371): 16.
47. In Katouzian, 1981: 362.
48. IRP, 1978(23): 3.

CHAPTER 8

1. *See* Bendix's paper above.
2. "Disenchantment" is taken up by Swatos in the following essay.
3. Weber, 1978a: 956-1002; Mumford, 1966: 188-212.
4. Mills, 1956; see also Djilas, 1974.
5. Weber, 1978a: 1006-68, 1159, 1212-1363.
6. Weber, 1978a: 241-42.
7. Examples of this phenomenon abound. In the modern world, Bobby Kennedy, Raul Castro, and Mao Zedong's wife come easily to mind.
8. Weber, 1978a: 1135.
9. Shils, 1965.
10. *See* Bensman and Givant, above.
11. Lévi-Strauss, 1967.
12. Weber, 1978a: 941, 641-76.
13. *See* Berger, 1969.
14. Walter, 1972.
15. During periods of anarchy or anomie orgies of violence do emerge. It is difficult to explain such violence without involving some theory of animal aggression. However, one must always do so in the context of a *balanced* conception of "human nature" which includes the conscious mind of humans and the cultural norms and values of human societies, along with the animal side of our being. The biosociologists and sociobiologists do not emphasize the human side of human nature, therefore their theories are as incomplete as those social theories which ignore the animal nature of human beings. We do not need a revival of "social Darwinism" to offset an "oversocialized" conception of human beings.
16. *See* Weber, 1951.
17. McLuhan, 1965, 1967.
18. Mills, 1956.
19. *See* Glassman, 1979.
20. Mills, 1956.
21. *See* Alan Berger's discussion of the Reverend Moon's charisma, above.

CHAPTER 9

1. Weber, 1978a: 1117.
2. Weber, 1978a: 227, 1116.

3. This point is also made, but toward rather different ends, in essays on charisma, religion, and revolution by Roth (in Roth and Schluchter, 1979: 119-65).

4. *See* Eisenstadt, 1978: 4-5.

5. Levine, 1981.

6. *See* Abramowski, 1982; Little, 1974; G. Mueller, 1977; Lidz, 1979; and Schluchter in Roth and Schluchter, 1979: 11-64.

7. In Weber, 1958a: 51.

8. Eisenstadt, 1968a: liv; *see* Abramowski, 1982.

9. *See* Schluchter in Roth and Schluchter, 1979: 43-44.

10. Mommsen, 1965: 24.

11. Weber, 1978a: 975.

12. Mommsen, 1965: 37-38.

13. Weber, 1958a: 129-56; *see* Schluchter in Roth and Schluchter, 1979: 113-16. Also Weber, 1958a: 71-72, 350-57, 1976a: 105, 1976b, 1978a: 1393-1405; Mommsen, 1974: 109-15; and Mitzman, 1970: 6. All demonstrate the continuity of the discussion of *Zauber* and *Entzauber* throughout Weber's work.

14. *See* Abramowski, 1982.

15. Weber, 1958b: 80.

16. Weber, 1958a: 128.

17. *See* Schluchter in Roth and Schluchter, 1979: 65-112.

18. Geertz, 1977: 150.

19. Weber did not invent the concept of "charisma," of course, but as Shils (1975: 128) notes, it "underwent its most important extension and formulation" in his work.

20. Gustafson, 1967: 68.

21. Weber, 1978a: 215-16.

22. Weber, 1978a: 262-66.

23. Weber's use of charisma is in connection with types of legitimate domination. The "electric pesonalities" of popular entertainment figures, for example, have no relationship to the general intention of his work—unless they carry over into the political sphere directly. It is, of course, possible to speak of a charismatic figure in (e.g.) the arts in the Weberian sense, if one means by that a person who brings about fundamental change in "the way things are done" (*see* Hammond and Hammond, 1979). Such a person is not likely to be a *political* hero, however.

24. Eisenstadt, 1968a: xx.

25. *See* Weber, 1978a: 1121-23; Friedland, 1964; Waddell, 1972; Camic, 1980.

26. *See* Hill, 1972: 172-80.

27. Shils, 1975: 122.

28. Dow, 1969; Berger, 1963b; Runciman, 1963; Constas, 1961.

29. *See* Bendix, 1965: 20.

30. Shils, 1975: 257, 261.

31. Eisenstadt, 1968a: xxix.

32. Shils, 1975: 97, 127; emphasis added.

33. Dow, 1969: 317.

34. On the "absent center," *see* Lemert, 1975.

35. Shils, 1975: 98.

36. Vinson, 1977.

37. *See* B. Wilson, 1975, 1976.

38. Weber, 1978a: 1129-30.
39. Lowenthal, 1968; Adorno, 1978; Marcuse, 1964; Boorstin, 1978.
40. Turner, 1974.
41. Weber (quoting Goethe), 1976a: 182.
42. In 1985, for example, one network "preempted" President Reagan's State of the Union address for a basketball game. That same night ABC, which did televise the address live advertised its programming as follows: "8:00 Fall Guy / 9:00 State of the Union / 10:00 Dynasty." A vocal overlay informed potential viewers that the middle program was "The President's State of the Union Address." The Democratic response to the address was preempted by "Dynasty." A presidential news conference was preempted by another basketball game later the same winter. During this period, thanks to the marvels of computers, the President wrote to many Americans "personally," offering the opportunity to become members of the Republican Presidential Task Force. A variety of trinkets and memorabilia would be sent to contributors.
43. Loewenstein, 1966: 84-86.
44. Weber, 1978a: 1209.
45. Weber, 1978a: 227.
46. Weber, 1978a: 243-44, 1115.
47. Hill, 1973: 2.
48. A less than sharp distinction in Shils' work (1975: 91-107) between the modern patrimonial virtuoso and the charismatic leader is what makes him more sanguine about "mass society" than I am—or so, at least, it seems to me.
49. *See* Cawelti, 1970; Nelson, 1976.
50. *See* Antonio, 1979.
51. *See* Weber, 1958a: 137-56; Holland, 1977; Buck, 1980.
52. Wallerstein, 1974: 98, 356.
53. Kimball and McClellan, 1962: 156.
54. Genovese, 1969: 241-42, 244.
55. *See* Goudzwaard, 1979: 71-77, 209.
56. *See* Bendix, 1960: 451.
57. Jaspers, 1964: 222-23, 261.
58. From time to time one hears that Weber thought of himself as becoming a "charismatic" figure. Nothing could be farther from the truth. In the "vocation" essays, he repeatedly emphasizes the everyday, daily demands, average people, and so forth, and clearly sees himself in this context. Marx, by contrast, has many charismatic self-images (*see* E. Wilson, 1940: 209, for examples).
59. Weber, 1978a: 267.
60. E. Wilson (1940: 195ff.) rightly points out that Marx did not begin as a "force" theorist—indeed, in *The Holy Family* it is difficult to tell the difference between his position and Weber's voluntarism. "*History does nothing,*" Marx writes, "It is rather *man*—real, living man—who acts, possesses and fights in everything. It is by no means 'History' which uses man as a means to carry out *its* ends, as if it were a person apart; rather History is *nothing* but the activity of man in pursuit of his ends." Marx became a force theorist as time went on, particularly as he interacted with Engels, whereas Weber became increasingly skeptical of such theories as his work matured.
61. Gellner, 1974: 195.

62. On the task of sociology to subvert "bad faith," *see* Berger, 1963a: 142-45.

63. Weber, 1958a: 128.

64. *See* Berger, 1970, 1979.

65. Berger and Neuhaus, 1977.

66. As recent books by Goudzwaard (1979), Ogilvy (1979), Rifkin and Howard (1979), and Miller (1980) indicate, it is not impossible for some of this reordering to take place in contexts related to the category "religion." It is a mistake, however, to infer from this that a "resacralization" or "reenchantment" *of the world* is in process. For Weber "religion" and "enchantment" are two quite different categories. It is possible for religion to undergo institutional metamorphosis without thereby producing an enchanted world (see Swatos, 1983).

67. So Weber concludes "Science as a Vocation" (1958a: 156). I wish to express appreciation to Vatro Murvar, Bill Mayrl, Paul Gustafson, Solon Kimball, Bill Wentworth, and especially Bob Antonio for their comments on earlier drafts. Larry Moore and Priscilla Swatos provided specific assistance in preparing the paper. A substantial portion of the work on the essay was completed while I was supported by a National Endowment for the Humanities stipend in the Department of Anthropology at the University of Florida.

CHAPTER 10

1. Weber, 1978a: 266.
2. Hitler, 1939: 391.
3. Zoller, 1949: 17-19.
4. Baynes, 1942: 44.
5. Domarus, 1963: 570.
6. Deuerlein, 1968: 235; Speer, 1970: 19.
7. *Der Hitler Prozess*, 1924: 120.
8. Jochmann, 1960: 53.
9. Frank, 1953: 315.
10. Domarus, 1963: 727.
11. Domarus, 1963: 712.
12. Domarus, 1963: 502.
13. Schaumburg-Lippe, 1963: 131.
14. Schirach, 1967: 98.
15. This similarity has been shown by Herr, 1968. But the inference that such a similarity substantiates an alliance between the Nazis and the Catholic church is not convincing. The role of charisma in Hitler's leadership is completely neglected.
16. Domarus, 1963: 762, 893.
17. *See Reichkanzlei* 43 II/172, Bundesarchiv, Coblenz, West Germany; Schuhmacher-Sammlung 245 I, Bundesarchiv.
18. *See* the summary statistics in Schweitzer, 1984: 74.
19. Seraphim, 1956: 97.
20. Picker, 1965: 154, 168. It has been established that this racial interpretation of Christ by Hitler goes back to the year 1924; *see* Nolte, 1961.
21. Picker, 1965: 186.
22. For details of this image building, supplementing the charismatic appeal, *see* Bramstedt, 1965: 197-229.

23. Brugge in Poliakov and Wulf, 1959: 48.
24. Goebbels, 1941: 101.
25. On these songs, *see* Gamm, 1962.
25. For an extensive history of these events, but without any reference to charisma, *see* K. Mueller, 1969.
27. *See* Schweitzer, 1970.
28. Domarus, 1963: 745.
29. Domarus, 1963: 760.
30. *Völkischer Beobachter*, March 16, 1938, Munich issue No. 75, p. 1.
31. Domarus, 1963: 432.
32. Domarus, 1963: 597.
33. On the sociological theory of reciprocity, but without reference to charisma, *see* Gouldner, 1973.
34. "Dictatorial" in this context means a capacity and utilized opportunities of a few to exploit and rule, receiving rights and benefits one-sidedly, without consent of the giving, and by imposing conformity upon the majority in the situation.
35. In Stalin's personality cult and purges, the culprits had to accuse themselves of various crimes, glorify the leader, and then were executed. Hitler's personality cult did not necessarily culminate in *repeated* purges.
36. Fraenkel, 1941.
37. Weber, 1978a: 243.
38. Weber, 1978a: 1149.
39. Toland, 1976: 764.
40. Gilbert, 1964: 251.
41. IMT, 1949: 146.

CHAPTER 11

1. Salomon, 1945: 596. Roth is largely correct in arguing (in Bendix and Roth, 1971: 245) that Weber's criticism of historical materialism is only part of a larger attack on evolutionism.
2. Cassirer, 1959: 5; *see also* Crocker, 1959; Goldman, 1973; Hazard, 1954.
3. Lichtheim, 1971.
4. Contrary to Jay's contention (1973: 120).
5. *See*, e.g., Tenbruck's questioning (1980) of the claim that the central theme of *Economy and Society* concerns the origins of Occidental rationalism; *see also* Friedland's specific critique of the concept of charisma (1964).
6. Weber, 1978a: 1209.
7. Lefebvre, 1947: 211.
8. In Hampson, 1983: 243.
9. Weber, 1978a: 1117.
10. Schluchter, 1981: 54.
11. Schluchter, 1981: 124; *see* Weber, 1978a: 1112.
12. In Roth and Schluchter, 1979: 134.
13. Berger, 1969: 107.
14. Berger, 1969: 110-11.
15. Weber, 1978a: 499; Berger, 1969: 52-80.
16. *See*, e.g., Stark, 1967.

17. Marx, 1963: 155.
18. Barker, 1980: 228.
19. Weber, 1978a: 26.
20. Roth, 1976: 316.
21. Dow, 1978: 83.
22. Dow, 1978: 87.
23. Dow, 1978: 91.
24. Anderson, 1976: 42
25. This is the description offered by Pachter, 1984: 295.
26. Gouldner, 1973: 414.
27. Lukács, 1968: ix.
28. Lukács, 1971: 80.
29. Lukács, 1968: 98.
30. Ferrarotti, 1982: 71.
31. Lukács, 1968: 34, 149.
32. Lukács, 1968: 231.
33. Lukács, 1968: 10.
34. Lukács, 1968: 193.
35. Lukács, 1968: 193.
36. Lukács, 1968: 149.
37. Lukács, 1968: 76.
38. Lukács, 1968: 70.
39. Lukács, 1968: 41.
40. Anderson, 1976: 54.
41. Lichtheim, 1970: 115; for a more sympathetic assessment, *see* Mészáros, 1972: 76.
42. Marcuse, 1964: 123.
43. Marcuse, 1966: viii.
44. Robinson, 1969: 157.
45. Marcuse, 1961: 7; *see also* 1970: 1-61.
46. Marcuse, 1961: 32.
47. Marcuse, 1961: 184.
48. Schoolman, 1975: 101.
49. Schoolman, 1975: 115.
50. Marcuse, 1964: 1.
51. Marcuse, 1964: 231.
52. Giddens, 1982: 151.
53. Marcuse, 1968: 225.
54. As Tar (1977: 80) observes, during the 1940s, the work of Horkheimer and Adorno could justifiably be seen as a united undertaking informed by the same philosophic principles.
55. Benjamin, 1968: 259-60.
56. Griesman, 1976: 495.
57. Jay, 1973: 47.
58. Jay, 1973: 43.
59. Horkheimer and Adorno, 1972: 3.
60. Horkheimer, 1974: 176.
61. Tar, 1977: 82.

62. Adorno, 1981: 48.
63. Horkheimer and Adorno, 1972: 120-67.
64. Berman, 1978: 60.
65. Habermas, 1983: 107-8.
66. Horkheimer, 1974: 175.
67. Horkheimer, 1972: 131.
68. Lukács, 1971: 22.
69. Tar, 1977: 115.
70. In Tar, 1977: 48.
71. These tendencies are especially evident in his later works; e.g., 1969 and 1972.

EPILOGUE

1. Mills, 1959.
2. *See*, too, Marx, 1964a: 48.
3. Weber, 1978a: 246-99, 1111-56.
4. Weber, 1976a: 183.
5. *See* Weber, 1981, 1976b; 1978: 311-85.
6. Kalberg, 1985.
7. Weber, 1978a: 926-39, 1212-1372; 1951, 1958c.
8. Weber, 1976a: 183.
9. Plato, 1956: 356-415; Aristotle, 1970: 154-88.
10. Machiavelli, 1952; Hobbes, 1931.
11. Marx, 1964a, 1964b; Durkheim, 1964.
12. Aristotle, 1970: 9-18, 154-88.
13. Weber, 1978a: 212-99, 901-39, 956-98, 1111-56.
14. *See* Casanova (1984) for a concise presentation and analysis of Benjamin Nelson's "civilizational" interpretation of Weber.
15. Glassman, 1969.
16. Weber, 1976a.
17. Tawney, 1912; Bernstein, 1963.
18. Acton, 1907.
19. Weber, 1976a; Tawney, 1926.
20. There were, of course, both Roman Catholic and Anglican churches, but a radically different sociocultural structure militated against their having anything like the influence they had either in the old country or in Latin American dependencies. *See* Swatos, 1979.
21. Moore, 1968; Acton, 1907.
22. *See* Bell's essay above.
23. Durkheim, 1951; Merton, 1938.
24. Weber, 1951.
25. Weber, 1951; *see* Glassman, 1986.
26. Weber, 1951.
27. Weber, 1958a: 116-21.
28. Weber, 1978a: 576-627.
29. Sadat was indeed murdered for traveling to Jerusalem, but Mubarik has continued his general policies successfully.
30. Glassman, 1969.

31. Bolivar, Zapata, Perón—none of these charismatic figures could routinize his charisma.

32. Mills, 1960.

33. Glassman, 1969.

34. Petras and Zeitlin, 1968.

35. Arbenz of Guatemala was ousted by the CIA in 1954, but even he was not a full-fledged Marxist-Leninist.

36. Collier and Horowitz, 1984. It was basically this same "external" strategy the Reagan administration used in Grenada, but with the Kennedy loss firmly in mind.

37. Mannheim, 1955; Almond and Coleman, 1960.

38. Weber, 1958a: 386-95; Rosenberg, 1980.

39. Tawney, 1912.

40. Weber, 1978a: 1111-56.

41. Mommsen, 1974; Eden, 1984; Factor and Turner, 1984.

42. Factor and Turner, 1984; Keynes, 1920.

43. Even Perón envisioned Mussolini more than Hitler as his role model.

44. Glassman, 1969.

45. Ortega y Gasset, 1957.

46. Bernstein, 1963; Tawney, 1926.

47. Lipset, 1963: 17-68.

48. Mannheim, 1955.

Bibliography

Abbott, Granville S. 1872. "Calvin and Calvinism." *Bibliotheca Sacra* 30: 401-21.

Abrahamian, Ervand. 1980. "Structural causes of the Iranian revolution." *MERIP Report* 87 (10 May): 21-26.

———. 1982a. *Iran Between the Revolutions*. Princeton: Princeton University Press.

———. 1982b. "Middle East Annual, 1982." Unpublished manuscript.

Abramowski, Günter. 1982. "Meaningful life in a disenchanted world: rational science and ethical responsibility—an interpretation of Max Weber." *Journal of Religious Ethics* 10: 121-34.

Acton, John. 1907. *A History of Freedom*. London: Macmillan.

Adorno, Theodor. 1978. *Minima Moralia*. New York: Schocken.

———. 1981. *Prisms*. Cambridge, Mass.: MIT Press.

Ake, Claude. 1966. "Charismatic legitimation and political integration." *Comparative Studies in Society and History* 9: 1-13.

Almond, Gabriel, and James Coleman. 1960. *The Politics of Developing Areas*. Princeton: Princeton University Press.

Anderson, Perry. 1976. *Considerations of Western Marxism*. London: New Left Books.

Antonio, Robert J. 1979. "The contradiction of domination and production in bureaucracy: the contribution of organizational efficiency to the decline of the Roman empire." *American Sociological Review* 44: 895-912.

Apter, David E. 1955. *The Gold Coast in Transition*. Princeton: Princeton University Press.

———. 1966. *Ghana in Transition*. New York: Atheneum.

———. 1968. "Nkrumah, charisma, and the coup." *Daedalus* 97: 757-92.

Arani, Sharif. 1980. "Iran: from the Shah's dictatorship to Khomeini's demogogic theocracy." *Dissent* 27: 9-26.

Aristotle. 1970. *Politics*. New York: Oxford Unviersity Press.

Barker, Martin. 1980. "Kant as a problem for Weber." *British Journal of Sociology* 31: 224-45.

Baynes, Norman H., ed. 1942. *The Speeches of Adolf Hitler* I. New York: Oxford University Press.

Beckford, James A. 1973. "A Korean evangelistic movement in the west." *International Conference on Sociology of Religion*. Paris: Centre National de la Recherche Scientifique.

Bellah, Robert N. 1975. *The Broken Covenant: American Civil Religion in Time of Trial*. New York: Seabury.

Ben-Amos, Dan, and Jerome Mintz, eds. 1970. *In Praise of the Baal Shem Tov*. Bloomington: Indiana University Press.

Bendix, Reinhard. 1960. *Max Weber: An Intellectual Portrait*. Garden City, N.Y.: Doubleday.

______. 1965. "Max Weber's sociology today." *International Social Science Journal* 17: 9-22.

Bendix, Reinhard, and Guenther Roth. 1971. *Scholarship and Partisanship*. Berkeley: University of California Press.

Benjamin, Walter. 1968. *Illuminations*. New York: Schocken.

Bensman, Joseph and Robert Lilienfeld. 1973. *Craft and Consciousness*. New York: Wiley.

Berger, Peter L. 1963a. *Invitation to Sociology*. Garden City, N.Y.: Doubleday.

______. 1963b. "Charisma and religious innovation: the social location of Israelite prophecy." *American Sociological Review* 28: 940-50.

______. 1969. *The Sacred Canopy*. Garden City, N.Y.: Doubleday.

______. 1970. *A Rumor of Angels*. Garden City, N.Y.: Doubleday.

______. 1979. *The Heretical Imperative*. Garden City, N.Y.: Doubleday.

Berger, Peter L., and Thomas Luckmann. 1967. *The Social Construction of Reality*. Garden City, N.Y.: Doubleday.

Berger, Peter L., and Richard J. Neuhaus. 1977. *To Empower People*. Washington: American Enterprise Institute.

Berman, Marshall. 1978. " 'All that is solid melts into air': Marxism, modernism, and modernization." *Dissent* 25: 54-73.

Bernstein, Eduard. 1963. *Cromwell and Communism: Socialism and Democracy in the Great English Revolution*. New York: Schocken.

Bierstedt, Robert. 1954. "The problem of authority." Pp. 67-81 in Monroe Berger, Theodore Abel, and Charles Page (eds.), *Freedom and Control in Modern Society*. New York: Van Nostrand.

Bill, James. 1982. "Power and religion in revolutionary Iran." *Middle East Journal* 36: 22-47.

Blau, Peter. 1963. "Critical remarks on Weber's theory of authority." *American Political Science Review* 57: 305-16.

Boorstin, Daniel J. 1962. *The Image*. New York: Atheneum.

______. 1978. *The Republic of Technology*. New York: Harper & Row.

Bosk, Charles. 1979. "The routinization of charisma: the case of the zaddik." *Sociological Inquiry* 49: 150-67.

Bramstedt, Ernest. 1965. *Goebbels and National Socialist Propaganda 1925-1945*. East Lansing: Michigan State University Press.

Bromley, David, and Anson D. Shupe, Jr. 1979. *"Moonies" in America: Cult, Church and Crusade.* Beverly Hills, Calif.: Sage.

Bryant, M. Darrol, and Susan Hodges (eds.). 1978. *Exploring Unification Theology.* New York: Rose of Sharon.

Buber, Martin. 1966. *Hasidism and Modern Man.* New York: Harper & Row.

Buck, Roy C. 1980. "Power of 'the word' in tourism promotion." Pp. 161-78 in D. E. Harkins, E. L. Shafer, and J. M. Rovelstad, eds., *Tourism Marketing and Management Issues.* Washington: George Washington University Press.

Camic, Charles. 1980. "Charisma." *Sociological Inquiry* 50: 5-23.

Casanova, Jose V. 1984. "Interpretations and misinterpretations of Max Weber: the problem of rationalization." Pp. 141-53 in Ronald M. Glassman and Vatro Murvar, eds., *Max Weber's Political Sociology.* Westport, Conn.: Greenwood.

Cassirer, Ernst. 1959. *The Philosophy of the Enlightenment.* Princeton: Princeton University Press.

Cawelti, John. 1970. *Six-Gun Mystique.* Bowling Green, Ohio: BGU Popular Press.

Collier, Peter, and David Horowitz. 1984. *The Kennedys.* New York: Summit.

Constas, Helen. 1961. "The U.S.S.R.—from charismatic sect to bureaucratic society." *Administrative Science Quarterly* 6: 282-98.

Crocker, Lester. 1959. *An Age of Crisis.* Baltimore: Johns Hopkins University Press.

Dekmeijian, Richard. 1980. "The anatomy of Islamic revival." *Middle East Journal* 34: 1-12.

Der Hitler Prozess. 1924. *Der Hitler Prozess.* Munich: Deutscher Volksverlag.

Deuerlein, Ernst. 1968. *Der Aufstieg der NSDAP.* Düsseldorf: Rauch.

Dibelius, Martin, n.d. *From Tradition to Gospel.* New York: Scribners.

Diggins, John P., and Mark E. Kann, eds. 1981. *The Problem of Authority in America.* Philadelphia: Temple University Press.

Divine Principle. 1973. *Divine Principle.* Washington: Holy Spirit Association for the Unification of World Christianity.

Djilas, Milovan. 1974. *The New Class.* New York: Praeger.

Domarus, Max. 1963. *Hitler Reden und Proklamationen 1932-1945.* Würzburg: Schmidt.

Dow, Thomas. 1969. "The theory of charisma." *Sociological Quarterly* 10: 306-18.

______. 1978. "An analysis of Weber's work on charisma." *British Journal of Sociology* 29: 83-93.

Dresner, Samuel H. 1960. *The Zaddik.* London: Abelard Schuman.

Durkheim, Emile. 1951. *Suicide.* New York: Free Press.

______. 1964. *The Division of Labor in Society.* New York: Free Press.

Eden, Robert. 1984. *Political Leadership and Nihilism: A Study of Weber and Nietzsche.* Tampa: University Presses of Florida.

Eisenstadt, S. N. 1968a. "Charisma and institution building." Pp. ix-lvi in Max Weber, *On Charisma and Institution Building.* Chicago: University of Chicago Press.

______, ed. 1968b. *The Protestant Ethic and Modernization.* New York: Basic Books.

______. 1978. *Revolution and the Transformation of Societies.* New York: Free Press.

Eliade, Mircea. 1961. *The Sacred and the Profane.* New York: Harper & Row.

______. 1963. *Patterns in Comparative Religion.* Cleveland: World.

Erikson, Erik. 1958. *Young Man Luther*. New York: Norton.

Fackenheim, Emil L. 1968. *Quest for Past and Future: Essays in Jewish Theology*. Boston: Beacon.

Factor, Regis A., and Stephen P. Turner. 1984. "Weber, the Germans, and 'Anglo-Saxon convention': liberalism as technique and form of life." Pp. 39-54 in Ronald M. Glassman and Vatro Murvar, eds., *Max Weber's Political Sociology*. Westport, Conn.: Greenwood.

Fagan, Richard. 1965. "Charismatic authority and the leadership of Fidel Castro." *Western Political Quarterly* 18: 275-84.

Ferrarotti, Franco. 1982. *Max Weber and the Destiny of Reason*. New York: Sharpe.

Fischer, Michael M. J. 1980a. *Iran from Religious Dispute to Revolution*. Cambridge, Mass.: Harvard Unviersity Press.

______. 1980b. "Becoming Mullah." *Iranian Studies* 13: 83-119.

Fisher, Margaret. 1967. "India's Jawaharlal Nehru." *Asian Survey* 7: 363-73.

Floor, Willem M. 1983. "The revolutionary character of the ulama: wishful thinking or reality?" Pp. 73-97 in Nikki Keddie, ed., *Religion and Politics in Iran*. New Haven: Yale University Press.

Forsyth, P. T. 1910. "Calvinism and capitalism." *Contemporary Review* 97: 728-41.

Fraenkel, Ernst. 1941. *The Dual State*. New York: Oxford University Press.

Frank, Hans. 1953. *Im Angesicht des Galgens*. Gräfelfing: Beck.

Friedland, William H. 1964. "For a sociological concept of charisma." *Social Forces* 43: 18-26.

Friedrich, Carl J. 1961. "Political leadership and the problem of charismatic power." *Journal of Politics* 23: 3-24.

Gamm, Hans Jochen. 1962. *Der braune Kult*. Hamburg: Rutten and Loening.

Geertz, Clifford. 1977. "Centers, kings, and charisma." Pp. 150-71 in Joseph Ben-David and Terry Nichols Clark, eds., *Culture and Its Creators*. Chicago: University of Chicago Press.

Gellner, Ernest. 1974. *Legitimation of Belief*. New York: Cambridge University Press.

Genovese, Eugene D. 1969. *The World the Slaveholders Made*. New York: Random House.

Giddens, Anthony. 1982. *Profiles and Critiques in Social Theory*. Berkeley: University of California Press.

Gilbert, M. 1964. *Nuremberg Diary*. New York: Signet.

Glassman, Ronald M. 1969. *The Political History of Latin America*. New York: Funk & Wagnalls.

______. 1986. *The New Middle Class and Democracy*. Forthcoming.

Goebbels, Joseph. 1941. *Die Zeit ohne Beispiel*. Munich: Eher.

Goldman, Lucien. 1973. *The Philosophy of the Enlightenment*. Cambridge, Mass.: MIT Press.

Goudzwaard, Bob. 1979. *Capitalism and Progress*. Toronto: Wedge.

Gouldner, Alvin W. 1973. *For Sociology: Renewal and Critique in Sociology Today*. New York: Basic Books.

Graham, Robert. 1979. *Iran: The Illusion of Power*. New York: St. Martin's.

Gramsci, Antonio. 1971. *The Prison Notebooks*. New York: International Press.

Griesman, H. C. 1976. " 'Disenchantment of the world': romanticism, aesthetics, and sociological theory." *British Journal of Sociology* 27: 495-507.

Gustafson, Paul M. 1967. "UO-US-PS-PO: a restatement of Troeltsch's church-sect typology." *Journal for the Scientific Study of Religion* 6: 64-68.

Habermas, Jürgen. 1983. *Philosophical-Political Profiles*. Cambridge, Mass.: MIT Press.

Haller, William. 1938. *The Rise of Puritanism*. New York: Columbia University Press.

Halliday, Fred. 1978. "Iran: economic contradiction." *MERIP Report* 69 (July-August): 9-19.

Hammond, Phillip E., and Sandra N. Hammond. 1979. "The internal logic of dance." *Journal of Social History* 12: 591-608.

Hampson, Norman. 1983. *Will and Circumstance*. Norman: University Oklahoma Press.

Harris, Lis. 1985. "A reporter at large: holy days." *The New Yorker* 61 (September 16, 23, 30): 41-101, 57-100, 73-110.

Hazard, Paul. 1954. *European Thought in the Eighteenth Century*. New Haven: Yale University Press.

Heller, Agnes. 1981. *Renaissance Man*. New York: Schocken.

Helmut, Richard. 1975. "America's Shah, Shahansh's Iran." *MERIP Report* 40 (September): 3-19.

Herberg, Will. 1975. *Judaism and Modern Man*. New York: Atheneum.

Herr, Friedrich. 1968. *Der Glaube des Adolf Hitler*. Munich: Bechtel.

Heschel, Abraham, J. 1966. *The Insecurity of Freedom*. New York: Farrar, Straus, and Giroux.

______. 1973. *A Passion for Truth*. New York: Farrar, Straus, and Giroux.

Hill, Michael. 1972. *A Sociology of Religion*. New York: Basic Books.

______. 1973. *The Religious Order*. London: Heinemann.

Hitler, Adolf. 1939. *Mein Kampf*. Munich: Eher.

Hobbes, Thomas. 1931. *Leviathan*. London: Dent.

Holland, Joe. 1977. *The American Journey*. New York: IDOC.

Horkheimer, Max. 1974. *Eclipse of Reason*. New York: Seabury.

______, and Theodor Adorno. 1972. *Dialectic of Enlightenment*. New York: Seabury.

Huntington, Samuel P. 1966. "Political modernization: America vs. Europe." *World Politics* 18: 400-30.

______. 1981. *American Politics: The Promise of Disharmony*. Cambridge, Mass.: Harvard University Press.

IMT. 1949. *The Trial of Major War Criminals* XXIX. Nuremberg: International Military Tribunal.

IRP. 1978-1980. *Jumhuri-I-Islami*. Tehran: Islamic Republican Party.

Jaspers, Karl. 1964. *Three Essays: Leonardo, Descartes, and Max Weber*. New York: Harcourt, Brace & World.

Jay, Martin. 1973. *The Dialectical Imagination*. Boston: Little, Brown.

Jochmann, Werner. 1960. *Im Kampf um die Macht*. Frankfurt: Europaische Verlagsanstalt.

Kalberg, Stephen. 1985. "Ideal interests in the work of Max Weber," Pp. 46-47 in Robert J. Antonio and Ronald M. Glassman, eds., *A Weber-Marx Dialogue*. Lawrence: University Press of Kansas.

Katouzian, Homa. 1981. *The Political Economy of Iran, 1926-79*. New York: NYU Press.

Katz, Jacob. 1961. *Tradition and Crisis: Jewish Society at the End of the Middle Ages*. New York: Schocken.

Kazomi, F. 1980. "Urban migrants and the revolution." *Iranian Studies* 13: 257-79.

Keddie, Nikki. 1981. *Roots of Revolution*. New Haven: Yale University Press.

Keynes, John Maynard. 1920. *The Economic Consequences of the Peace*. New York: Harcourt, Brace and Howe.

Kilker, Ernest. 1984. "Max Weber and the possibilities for democracy." Pp. 55-65 in Ronald M. Glassman and Vatro Murvar, eds., *Max Weber's Political Sociology*. Westport, Conn.: Greenwood.

Kimball, Solon T., and James E. McClellan, Jr. 1962. *Education and the New America*. New York: Random House.

Klapp, Orrin. 1964. *Symbolic Leaders*. Chicago: Aldine.

Lecky, W. E. H. 1955. *History of the Rise and Influence of the Spirit of Rationalism in Europe*. New York: Braziller.

Lee, Chong-sik. 1967. "Kim Il-sŏng of North Korea." *Asian Survey* 7: 374-82.

Lee, Frederick George. 1886. *King Edward the Sixth, Supreme Head*. London: Burns and Oates.

Lefebvre, George. 1947. *The Coming of the French Revolution*. Princeton: Princeton University Press.

Lemert, Charles C. 1975. "Social structure and the absent center." *Sociological Analysis* 36: 95-107.

Levine, Donald N. 1981. "Rationality and freedom." *Sociological Inquiry* 51: 5-26.

Lévi-Strauss, Claude. 1967. "The social psychological aspects of chieftanship in a primitive tribe." Pp. 48-75 in Ronald Cohen and John Middleton, eds., *Comparative Political Systems*. Garden City, N.Y.: Natural History Press.

Lichtheim, George. 1970. *George Lukács*. New York: Viking.

______. 1971. *From Marx to Hegel*. New York: Seabury.

Lidz, Victor M. 1979. "Secularization, ethical life, and religion in modern societies." *Sociological Inquiry* 49: 191-217.

Lipset, Seymour Martin. 1963. *The First New Nation*. New York: Basic Books.

Little, David. 1969. *Religion, Order, and Law*. New York: Harper & Row.

______. 1974. "Max Weber and the comparative study of religious ethics." *Journal of Religious Ethics* 2: 5-40.

Loewenstein, Karl. 1966. *Max Weber's Political Ideas in the Perspective of Our Time*. Amherst: University of Massachusetts Press.

Loftland, John. 1977. *Doomsday Cult*. New York: Irvington.

Lowenthal, Leo. 1968. *Literature, Popular Culture and Society*. Palo Alto, Calif.: Pacific Books.

Lukács, Georg. 1968. *History and Class Consciousness*. Cambridge, Mass.: MIT Press.

______. 1971. *The Theory of the Novel*. Cambridge, Mass.: MIT Press.

Machiavelli, Niccolò. 1952. *The Prince*. New York: New American Library.

MacIntyre, Alasdair, 1981. *After Virtue: A Study in Moral Theory*. Notre Dame, Ind.: University of Notre Dame Press.

Mackinnon, James. 1962. *Calvin and the Reformation*. New York: Russell & Russell.

Mannheim, Karl. 1955. *Ideology and Utopia*. New York: Harcourt, Brace.

Marcus, John. 1961. "Transcendence and charisma." *Western Political Quarterly* 14: 236-41.

Marcuse, Herbert. 1961. *Eros and Civilization.* Boston: Beacon.

———. 1964. *One-Dimensional Man.* Boston: Beacon.

———. 1966. *Reason and Revolution.* Boston: Beacon.

———. 1968. *Negations: Essays in Critical Theory.* Boston: Beacon.

———. 1969. *An Essay on Liberation.* Boston: Beacon.

———. 1970. *Five Lectures.* Boston: Beacon.

———. 1972. *Counterrevolution and Revolt.* Boston: Beacon.

Marshall, Gordon. 1981. *In Search of the Spirit of Capitalism.* New York: Columbia University Press.

Marx, Karl. 1963. *Early Writings.* New York: McGraw-Hill.

———. 1964a. *The German Ideology.* New York: International Publishers.

———. 1964b. *The Communist Manifesto.* New York: International Publishers.

McGinniss, Joe. 1968. *The Selling of the President 1968.* New York: Pocket Books.

McIntosh, Donald. 1970. "Weber and Freud: on the nature and sources of authority." *American Sociological Review* 35: 901-11.

McLuhan, Marshall. 1965. *Understanding Media.* New York: McGraw-Hill.

———. 1967. *The Medium is the Message.* New York: Bantam Books.

Merton, Robert K. 1938. "Social structure and *anomie.*" *American Sociological Review* 3: 672-82.

———, Marjorie Fiske, and Alberta Curtis. 1946. *Mass Persuasion.* New York: Harper.

Mészáros, István. 1972. *Lukács' Concept of Dialectic.* London: Merlin.

Meyer, John W. 1980. "The world polity and the authority of the nation-state." Pp. 109-37 in Albert Bergesen, ed., *Studies of the Modern World-System.* New York: Academic Press.

Miller, Donald E. 1980. *The Case for Liberal Christianity.* San Francisco: Harper & Row.

Mills, C. Wright. 1956. *The Power Elite.* New York: Oxford University Press.

———. 1959. *The Sociological Imagination.* New York: Oxford University Press.

———. 1960. *Listen, Yankee: The Revolution in Cuba.* New York: McGraw-Hill.

Mitzman, Arthur. 1970. *The Iron Cage.* New York: Knopf.

Mommsen, Wolfgang. 1965. "Max Weber's political sociology and his philosophy of world history." *International Social Science Journal* 17: 23-45.

———. 1974. *The Age of Bureaucracy.* Oxford: Blackwell.

Moore, Barrington. 1968. *The Social Origins of Dictatorship and Democracy.* Boston: Beacon.

Morin, Edgar. 1960. *The Stars.* New York: Grove Press.

Mueller, Gert H. 1979. "The notion of rationality in the work of Max Weber." *Archives Européenes de Sociologie* 20: 149-71.

Mueller, Klaus-Jurgen. 1969. *Das Heer und Hitler.* Stuttgart: Deutsche Verlagsanstalt.

Mumford, Lewis. 1966. *The Myth of the Machine.* New York: Harcourt, Brace and World.

Murvar, Vatro. 1983. *Max Weber Today—An Introduction to a Living Legacy: Selected Bibliography.* Brookfield: Max Weber Colloquia and Symposia at the University of Wisconsin-Milwaukee.

Nelson, John Wiley. 1976. *Your God is Alive and Well and Appearing in Popular Culture.* Philadelphia: Westminster.

Newsweek. 1978. " 'I cry for them.' " *Newsweek* 96 (6 November): 80.

Nolte, Ernst. 1961. "Eine frühe quelle zu Hitlers antisemitismus." *Historische Zeitschrift* 192: 584-606.

Ogilvy, James. 1979. *Many Dimensional Man*. New York: Harper & Row.

Ortega y Gasset, José. 1957. *The Revolt of the Masses*. New York: Norton.

Osborne, John. 1961. *Luther*. London: Faber.

Pachter, Henry. 1984. *Socialism and History*. New York: Columbia University Press.

Parsons, Talcott. 1947. "Introduction." Pp. 3-86 in Max Weber, *The Theory of Social and Economic Organization*. New York: Oxford University Press.

______. 1968. *The Structure of Social Action*. New York: Free Press.

Peters, R. S. 1967. "Authority (1)." Pp. 83-96 in Anthony Quinton, ed., *Political Philosophy*. New York: Oxford University Press.

Petras, James, and Maurice Zeitlin. 1968. *Latin America: Reform or Revolution*. Greenwich, Conn.: Fawcett.

Picker, Henry. 1965. *Hitlers Tischgespräche*. Stuttgart: Sewald.

Plato. 1956. *The Republic*. New York: Penguin.

Plutarch. 1965. *Lives*. New York: Penguin.

Poggi, Gianfranco. 1983. *Calvinism and the Capitalist Spirit*. Amherst: University of Massachusetts Press.

Poliakov, L., and J. Wulf. 1959. *Das Dritte Reich und seine Denker*. Berlin: Arani.

Pond, Enoch. 1862. "The life of Erasmus." *Bibliotheca Sacra* 19: 106-32.

Ratnam, K. J. 1964. "Charisma and political leadership." *Political Studies* 12: 345-58.

Rifkin, Jeremy, with Ted Howard. 1979. *The Emerging Order*. New York: Putnams.

Robbins, R. D. C. 1845. "Life of John Calvin." *Bibliotheca Sacra* 2: 329-56.

Robinson, Paul. 1969. *The Freudian Left*. New York: Harper & Row.

Rosenberg, Hans. 1968. *Aristocracy, Bureaucracy, Autocracy*. Cambridge, Mass.: Harvard University Press.

Roth, Guenther. 1976. "History and sociology in the work of Max Weber." *British Journal of Sociology* 27: 306-18.

______, and Wolfgang Schluchter. 1979. *Max Weber's Vision of History*. Berkeley: University of California Press.

Rubenstein, Richard L. 1978. *The Cunning of History—The Holocaust and the American Future*. New York: Harper & Row.

Runciman, W. G. 1963. "Charismatic legitimacy and one-party rule in Ghana." *Archives Européenes de Sociologie* 4: 148-65.

Rustow, Dankwart. 1967. *The World of Nations*. Washington: Brookings Institution.

Salomon, Albert. 1945. "German sociology." Pp. 586-614 in George Gurvitch and Wilbert Moore, eds., *Twentieth Century Sociology*. New York: Philosophical Library.

Savad, Mark H. 1965. "Study of a Modern Religious Movement—The Unification Church." Unpublished masters thesis, George Washington University.

Schaar, John H. 1970. "Legitimacy in the modern state." Pp. 276-327 in Philip Green and Sanford Levinson, eds., *Power and Community: Dissenting Essays in Political Science*. New York: Vintage.

Schaff, P. 1857. "John Calvin." *Bibliotheca Sacra* 13: 125-46.

Schaumburg-Lippe, Prinz su. 1963. *Dr. Goebbels*. Wiesbaden: Limes.

Schirach, Baldur von. 1967. *Ich glaubte an Hitler*. Hamburg: Mosaik.

Schluchter, Wolfgang. 1981. *The Rise of Western Rationalism*. Berkeley: University of California Press.

Schoolman, Morton. 1975. "Marcuse's 'second dimension.' " *Telos* 23: 89-115.

Schram, Stuart. 1967. "Mao Tse-tung as a charismatic leader." *Asian Survey* 7: 383-88.

Schwartz, Barry. 1983. "Geroge Washington and the whig conception of heroic leadership." *American Sociological Review* 48: 18-33.

Schweitzer, Arthur. 1970. "Parteidiktatur und überministerielle führergewalt." *Jahrbuch für Sozialwissenschaft* 21: 49-74.

______. 1984. *The Age of Charisma*. Chicago: Nelson-Hall.

Sears, B. 1844. "Reformers before the reformation." *Bibliotheca Sacra* 1: 425-43.

______. 1863. "The fathers and founders of the Lutheran church." *Bibliotheca Sacra* 20: 636-49.

Sennett, Richard. 1980. *Authority*. New York: Knopf.

Seraphim, Hans G. 1956. *Das politische Tagebuch Alfred Rosenbergs*. Göttingen: Musterschmidt.

Shils, Edward. 1965. "Charisma, order, and status." *American Sociological Review* 30: 199-213.

______. 1975. *Center and Periphery*. Chicago: University of Chicago Press.

Shmueli, Efraim. 1969. "The appeal of Hasidism for American Jewry today." *Journal of Jewish Sociology* 11: 5-20.

Smith, Huston. 1976. *Forgotten Truth: The Primordial Tradition*. New York: Harper & Row.

Speer, Albert. 1970. *Inside the Third Reich*. New York: Macmillan.

Stark, Werner. 1967. "Max Weber and the heterogony of purposes." *Social Research* 34: 249-64.

Swatos, William H., Jr. 1979. *Into Denominationalism: The Anglican Metamorphosis*. Storrs, Conn.: Society for the Scientific Study of Religion.

______. 1981. "Church-sect and cult: bringing mysticism back in." *Sociological Analysis* 42: 17-26.

______. 1983. "Enchantment and disenchantment in modernity: the significance of 'religion' as a sociological category." *Sociological Analysis* 44: 321-38.

Tar, Zoltán. 1977. *The Frankfurt School*. New York: Wiley.

Tawney, R. H. 1912. *The Agrarian Problem in the 16th Century*. New York: Longmans Green.

______. 1926. *Religion and the Rise of Capitalism*. New York: Harcourt.

Taylor, A. J. P. 1965. *English History: 1914-1945*. New York: Oxford University Press.

Tehranian, Majid. 1980. "Communication and revolution." *Iranian Studies* 13: 5-31.

Tenbruck, Frederich. 1980. "The problem of thematic unity in the works of Max Weber." *British Journal of Sociology* 31: 316-51.

Thucydides. 1954. *The Peloponnesian Wars*. New York: Penguin.

Toland, John. 1976. *Adolf Hitler*. Garden City, N.Y.: Doubleday.

Troeltsch, Ernst. 1931. *The Social Teachings of the Christian Church*. New York: Macmillan.

Tucker, Robert C. 1968. "The theory of charismatic leadership." *Daedalus* 97: 731-56.

Turner, Victor. 1974. *Dramas, Fields, and Metaphors.* Ithaca, N.Y.: Cornell University Press.

Vinson, Donald E. 1977. "Charisma." *International Journal of Contemporary Sociology* 14: 269-75.

Waddell, R. G. 1972. "Charisma and reason." Pp. 1-10 in Michael Hill, ed., *A Sociological Yearbook of Religion in Britain* V. London: SCM.

Wallerstein, Immanuel. 1974. *The Modern World-System* I. New York: Academic Press.

Walter, E. V. 1972. *Terror and Resistance.* New York: Oxford University Press.

Weber, Max. 1922. *Gesammelte Aufseatze zur Wissenschaftslehre.* Tübingen: Mohr.

______. 1927. *General Economic History.* Glencoe, Ill.: Free Press.

______. 1951. *The Religion of China.* Glencoe, Ill.: Free Press.

______. 1952. *Ancient Judaism.* New York: Free Press.

______. 1958a. *From Max Weber.* New York: Oxford University Press.

______. 1958b. *The Rational and Social Foundations of Music.* Carbondale: Southern Illinois University Press.

______. 1958c. *The Religion of India.* Glencoe, Ill.: Free Press.

______. 1976a. *The Protestant Ethic and the Spirit of Capitalism.* New York: Scribners.

______. 1976b. *the Agrarian Sociology of Ancient Civilizations.* London: New Left Books.

______. 1978a. *Economy and Society.* Berkeley: University of California. Used by permission.

______. 1978b. "Anticritical last word on *The Spirit of Capitalism.*" *American Journal of Sociology* 83: 1105-31.

Weiner, Herbert. 1957. "The Lubovitcher movement: II." *Commentary* 23: 316-27.

Wiesel, Elie. 1972. *Souls on Fire.* New York: Random House.

______. 1978. *Four Hasidic Masters.* South Bend, Ind.: Notre Dame University Press.

Willner, Ann Ruth. 1984. *The Spellbinder: Charismatic Political Leadership.* New Haven: Yale University Press.

______, and Dorothy Willner. 1965. "The rise and role of charismatic leaders." *Annals of the American Academy of Political and Social Science* 358: 77-89.

Wilson, Bryan R. 1975. *The Noble Savages.* Berkeley: University of California Press.

______. 1976. *Contemporary Transformations of Religion.* New York: Oxford University Press.

Wilson, Edmund. 1940. *To The Finland Station.* Garden City, N.Y.: Doubleday.

Wolf, Eric. 1969. *Peasant Wars of the Twentieth Century.* New York: Harper & Row.

Wolin, Sheldon. 1981. "The idea of the state in America." Pp. 41-55 in John P. Diggins and Mark E. Kann, eds., *The Problem of Authority in America.* Philadelphia: Temple University Press.

Zito, George V. 1984. *Systems of Discourse.* Westport, Conn.: Greenwood.

Zoller, Albert, ed. 1949. *Hitler Privat: Erlebnisbericht seiner Geheimsekretarin.* Düsseldorf: Droste.

Index

Adorno, Theodor, 137, 167, 171, 174-77, 220
Ake, Claude, 18, 206, 209
Anglicanism, 76, 77, 221
Anomie, 64, 86, 88, 187, 215
Apter, David, 18, 48, 49, 53, 206, 209
Argentina, 105, 195-96, 202
Aristotle, 5, 181-82, 186, 189, 197

Batista, Juan, 192-93
Bellah, Robert, 68
Bendix, Reinhard, 47-48, 103, 115, 179, 183, 210
Benjamin, Walter, 174
Berger, Peter L., 135, 144-45; quoted, 79
Besht (Israel ben Eliezar, Ba'al Shem Tov), 89
Betancourt, Rómulo, 201, 203
Bismarck, Otto von, 194
Bolivar, Simon, 183-85, 195, 197, 222
Buber, Martin, 87-88
Buddha, 43, 93
Bureaucracy (bureaucratic authority, bureaucratization), 5-7, 11-13, 19, 30, 33, 43, 44, 45, 47-54, 58, 59, 62-69, 79, 81, 86, 99, 103-4, 116, 121-22, 126-44 passim, 168-69, 180, 188, 190, 193-95

Caesar, Julius, 14, 197
Caesarism, 14, 62, 103, 116, 156, 180, 197. *See also* Charisma, demagogic; Charisma, dictatorial
Calvin, John, 14, 31, 43, 73-89, 211-12
Calvinism, 5, 15, 73-89, 186, 211-12, 214
Capitalism, 74, 111, 132, 143, 169-74, 184-201
Carter, James E., 125, 142
Castro, Fidel, 48, 122, 190, 192-93, 195, 198
Center-periphery distinction, 35-36, 39, 41, 135-36, 142
Charisma: definition of, 3, 12, 19-20, 27; demagogic, 47, 53; depersonalized, 4, 31, 81, 115; dictatorial, 147, 156, 158, 161-62, 219; genuine ("pure," "natural"), 4, 6, 20-21, 25, 30-39, 45-46, 49-62 passim; 83, 115, 119-20, 122, 134-37, 148, 153, 157-58, 189, 191, 193, 195, 198, 207, 210; hereditary, 4, 18, 30-36 passim, 41, 65, 98, 117, 135; heroic (*see*

heroes); impersonalization of, 77, 79-81, 166; lineage, 4, 17, 31, 34, 36, 41, 117; manufactured, 4, 6-7, 18, 23-24, 47, 55, 61, 65-66, 70, 115-27, 137-38, 141, 193, 198; of an office, 4, 18, 31-36 passim, 41-42, 51, 58, 76, 118, 124, 135, 137; plebiscitary, 5-6, 43, 62-63, 138, 155-60; providential, 153-55, 157; routinization of, 4-5, 13-14, 18-19, 21, 31-34, 42, 46, 53, 60, 76-77, 80, 98, 115, 134-36, 140, 142-43, 168, 171, 176, 179-80, 183, 185, 189-99, 206, 214; supernatural, 149-51, 153, 157; and warrior leaders, 5, 12, 29-30, 33, 41, 46, 58, 191

Charisma of Reason, 88, 139, 164-76

Charisma of rhetoric, 64-69, 137-38

Chaing Kai-shek, 189, 198

Chile, 105, 201

China: ancient, 34, 41, 121, 132, 188; kings of, 30-31; modern, 187-90, 198-202, 207

Churchill, Winston, 63, 122

Communism, 7, 23, 116, 127, 190-93, 196, 199, 201-2

Cromwell, Oliver, 14, 197-98, 201, 203

Cuba, 192-93. *See also* Castro, Fidel

Democracy, democratization, 5-7, 13-14, 17, 53, 59-64, 70, 81, 89, 116, 119, 135-38, 155-60, 164, 173, 180, 184-203 passim

Despotism, 5, 180, 194, 200

Devekuth, 89-90, 96

Disenchantment (enchantment, *entzauberung*), 6-7, 11, 44, 48, 53, 66, 70, 83-84, 87, 96, 99, 104, 115, 129-45 passim, 163, 166, 168, 175, 206, 208, 215, 216, 218

Divine Principle, 93-98

Dow, Thomas, 135-36, 167-68

Durkheim, Emile, 86, 182, 205

Economy and Society, 8, 14, 129, 144, 164-65, 167, 219

Egypt, 190-92

Eisenstadt, S. N., 73, 130, 134-36

Eisner, Kurt, 43, 47. *See also* Charisma, demagogic

England, 63, 77, 139, 184-87, 191-201 passim

Enlightenment (historical movement), 11, 85, 88, 163-64, 174-75

Erasmus, 74, 211

Fagan, Richard, 48-49

Fascism, 7, 51, 140-41, 189, 195-96, 201

Ford, Gerald, 125

France: colonialism of, 191, 197; Hitler and, 155; and Napoleonic era, 200-203; revolution in, 51, 54, 165, 184, 187, 198

Freud, Sigmund (Freudianism), 27, 41, 51, 57, 85, 171-73, 209

Friedrich, Carl, 43, 210

Fromm, Eric, 171-72

Gandhi, Mohandas, 17, 21-23, 187, 202

Gemeinschaft (pseudo-*Gemeinschaft*), 48-51, 55, 138

Geneva, 76-79

Germany, 30, 74-75, 85, 148-62, 194-96, 198-202, 212

Gerth, Hans H., 8, 77, 130, 134, 206, 210

Ghana, 18, 48

Gramsci, Antonio, 103

Guatemala, 193

Halakha, 84, 89, 91, 96

Hasidism, 5, 83-84, 88-92, 96-99, 135

Hegel, Georg F. (Hegelianism), 85, 164, 168, 171, 173-74, 195

Heroes (hero worship), 4, 12-14, 20, 27, 33-38, 42, 43, 58, 60-70, 137-40, 145, 153-55, 157, 160, 187, 191, 195-96, 216

Hitler, Adolf, 5-6, 17, 43, 101, 122, 147-62, 193-95, 198, 202-3, 218-19, 222

Hobbes, Thomas, 182, 189

Horkheimer, Max, 164, 174-77, 220

Huntington, Samuel P., 68, 206

IBM (International Business Machines), 137
Iceland, 205
Ideal typology, 3, 14-15, 133-35, 140-41
Import Substitution Industrialization (ISI), 105-6
India, 13, 20-23, 186, 202
Indonesia, 191, 197
Infantilization, 83, 87, 99, 122, 128
Iran, 101-12, 139, 142, 194, 202-3
Islam, 89, 101, 106-12, 139, 190-92, 202-3

Jaspers, Karl, 143, 171
Jefferson, Thomas, 187, 199
Jesus Christ, 5, 12, 29, 33, 43, 93-94, 97-99, 140, 152-53, 166, 186, 218

Kennedy, John Fitzgerald, 67, 124, 193, 199, 222
Khomeini, Ayatollah Ruhollah, 5, 101-2, 104, 108-12, 194, 202-3
Kim Il-Sŏng, 23-24, 207
King, Martin Luther, Jr., 186
Knox, John, 76-77
Korea, 23-24, 92-94
Kotsker (Menachem Mendl of Kotsk), 84, 89, 213
Kuomintang, 189

Lenin, V. I. (Leninism), 17, 43, 48, 51, 170, 192-93, 197-98, 200, 222
Liberalism, 11-12, 63, 141-42, 153, 166, 193, 195
Lichtheim, George, 164, 171
Lincoln, Abraham, 14, 187
Little, David, 73, 76
Loewenstein, Karl, 3, 17, 19, 47-48, 138, 207, 210
Lukács, Georg, 164, 168-77 passim
Luther, Martin, 31, 43, 74-89, 167, 211-12
Lutheranism, 74-89, 211-12

Machiavelli, Nicolò, 51, 65, 116, 182, 189
MacIntyre, Alasdair, 68-69
Madison, James, 68
Magic, 7, 11, 20, 22, 31, 33-34, 41, 89, 118, 130, 138-39, 166. *See also* Disenchantment
Mandarins, 31, 121, 188
Mao Zedong, 48, 187, 189-90, 199, 202-3, 215
Marcuse, Herbert, 137, 164, 171-77 passim
Marshall, Gordon, 211-12
Marx, Karl, 51, 142-44, 163-74 passim, 182, 217
Marxism, 51, 141-43, 152-53, 163, 168-69, 171, 174, 177, 181, 192-93, 197, 200, 214, 222
Mass media, 6, 18, 23-24, 46-50, 66, 70, 115, 122-28, 133, 137-39, 149, 209
McIntosh, Donald, 41-42, 44-46
Mendl, Menachem. *See* Kotsker
Merton, Robert K., 48, 55
Mills, C. Wright, 8, 77, 130, 134, 173, 179, 206
Minh, Ho Chi, 197
Mohammed, 98, 110
Mommsen, Wolfgang, 3, 6, 131
Moon, Sun Myung, 7, 84, 92-99, 140, 213, 215
Moonies, Moonism. *See* Unification Church
Mormonism, 12
Moses, 93, 109, 140
Moslem brotherhood, 190, 192, 197
Music, 12, 132-33, 138, 154, 175, 195, 218
Mussolini, Benito, 43, 194, 222

Napoleon I, 12, 14, 200-203
Nasser, Gamal Abdal, 190-92
Nazism, 75, 86, 140, 143, 149-59. *See also* Hitler, Adolf
Nehru, Jawaharlal, 20-23, 202
Nixon, Richard M., 124, 139
Nkrumah, Kwame, 18, 48-49, 197

Pahlevi, Mohammed Reza, 102, 104-12
Parsons, Talcott, 40, 212

Perón, Evita, 195-96
Perón, Juan, 195-96, 202, 222
Poggi, Gianfranco, 73, 76, 80, 212
Poland, 199-200
Prophecy, prophets: exemplary, 21-23, 28, 109, 111; in general, 3, 5, 11-14, 20-22, 28-29, 32-33, 36-37, 41, 79, 104, 109, 137, 142, 145, 151-53, 159
Protestant Ethic and the Spirit of Capitalism (Protestant ethic theory), 31, 73, 75, 79, 81, 104, 190, 212
Pseudocharisma, 6, 7, 48, 51, 53, 55, 61, 66-67, 99, 137-38, 194, 210. *See also* Charisma, manufactured
Puritanism, 68, 73, 76, 77, 211

Rationality (rational-legal authority, rationalization), 11-12, 19, 31, 33-34, 37, 41-46, 49-59 passim, 64, 66, 68-70, 80, 83, 88, 91, 96, 102-4, 108-9, 111, 115, 118-19, 124-32, 135-46, 163-64, 167, 169, 180, 188, 208
Reagan, Ronald, 7, 68, 123, 125, 217, 222
Reich, Wilhelm, 171-72
Reisman, David, 6, 173
Renaissance, 13, 77, 185
Revolution, 7, 12, 19, 30-36, 40-41, 44, 47, 51-54, 58-65, 69, 77, 79, 86, 101-3, 108-9, 111-12, 118, 129, 134-42, 160, 165-66, 170-71, 187, 194, 207, 214, 216. *See also* under names of specific countries and leaders
Robespierre, Maximilien Marie Isidore, 139, 165, 198
Robinson, Paul, 171
Roheim, Géza, 171
Roosevelt, Franklin Delano, 5, 17, 48, 122, 202
Roosevelt, Theodore, 43, 63
Roth, Guenther, 8, 77, 165-67, 207 216, 219
Runciman, W. G., 49, 135

Sadat, Anwhar, 191, 221
Salomon, Albert, 163
Sartre, Jean-Paul, 171
Schluchter, Wolfgang, 77, 165-66
Schram, Stuart, 48, 207
Schwartz, Barry, 61-63, 70
Scientism, 84, 87, 96-99
Scotland, 76-77
Secularization, 42-44, 107, 131, 136, 144, 166
Sennett, Richard, 57-58, 61
Shah of Iran, 102, 104-12
Shils, Edward A., 17-19, 27, 35-42, 44-46, 135-37, 142, 205, 207-9, 216-17
Simmel, Georg, 168-69
Smith, Joseph, 12, 186
Sohm, Rudolf, 12, 28
Stalin, Josef (Stalinism), 123, 168, 177, 198, 219
Stardom ("stars"), 6, 46, 50, 123-25, 133
Sukarno, 197
Sun Yatzen, 187-89, 197-98
Sweden, 76, 199
Switzerland, 74

Tehran, 101, 107
Tradition (traditional authority, traditionalism), 5, 14, 19, 30, 33-34, 41-42, 59-60, 64-65, 74-75, 79-92, 96-98, 102-4, 107, 111-12, 116, 118, 121, 126, 129-30, 135-44, 167, 175, 187, 194
Tucker, Richard, 48, 49
Turner, Victor, 137-38

Unification Church (Holy Spirit Association for the Unification of World Christianity, Moonies), 7, 83-84, 87-88, 92-99, 135, 213. *See also* Moon, Sun Myung
Union of Soviet Socialist Republics (USSR), 101, 102, 132, 142-43, 171, 189, 191-93, 195, 199-200, 207. *See also* under names of individual leaders
United States of America: and the Civil War, 187; in general, 101-2, 105-10, 140, 143, 145, 173, 185, 189, 192-93,

195-202, 206; politics of, 43, 62, 67-68; presidency of, 6, 19, 123, 127; religion in, 83-86, 98; and the War of Independence, 62, 184-87, 197, 200. *See also* under names of individual leaders

Venezuela, 201
Virtuosos, 14, 61, 74, 81, 139, 211, 217

Walesa, Lech, 199
Wallerstein, Immanuel, 141, 209
Walter, E. V., 119
Washington, George, 14, 19, 61, 63, 183-87, 197, 202
Wiesel, Elie, 88, 213
Willner, Ann Ruth, 5, 17, 48
Willner, Dorothy, 17, 48
Wirtschaft und Gesselleschaft, 8, 206. *See also Economy and Society*
Wittich, Claus, 8
Wolin, Sheldon, 67

Zaddikim, 84, 88-92, 96-99. *See also* Hasidism
Zapata, Emilio, 197, 222
Zwingli, Ulrich, 74

About the Contributors

Richard S. Bell has taught in the sociology program of the University of Maryland system and is the author of a number of papers and articles in political sociology.

Reinhard Bendix is a professor in the Political Science Department of the University of California at Berkeley. He is the author of the widely known volume *Max Weber: An Intellectual Portrait*. His latest work is *Kings or People: Power and the Mandate to Rule.*

Joseph Bensman is Distinguished Professor of Sociology at City College and the Graduate Center of the City University of New York. With Robert Lilienfeld he is the author of *Craft and Consciousness.*

Alan L. Berger is a member of the Religion Department and chairs the interdisciplinary Jewish Studies Program at Syracuse University. He recently published a book entitled *Crisis and Covenant: The Holocaust in American Jewish Fiction.*

H. H. Gerth was for many years professor of sociology at the University of Wisconsin. As an émigré from Germany, he translated Max Weber's works into English and helped interpret them to American readers. He is best known for his collaborative works with C. Wright Mills, *From Max Weber* and *Character and Social Structure.* A posthumous collection of his papers has appeared, edited by Joseph Bensman, Arthur Vidich, and Nobuko Gerth: *Politics, Character and Culture: Perspectives from Hans Gerth.*

Michael Givant is a member of the sociology faculty at Adelphi University, Garden City, New York. He has written numerous articles on a variety of sociological topics.

Michael S. Kimmel is Assistant Professor of Sociology at Rutgers University. He is the author of *Absolutism and its Discontents: Fiscal Crisis and Political Opposition in 17th Century France and England*, and is currently working on two books, *Paths to Modernity: Industrialization and Development in Comparative and Historical Perspective* and *Revolution in the Sociological Imagination*.

Peter Kivisto is a member of the Sociology Department of Augustana College, Rock Island, Illinois, with interests in social theory, deviance, and ethnic relations. He has recently published *Immigrant Socialists in the United States: The Case of Finns and the Left*.

C. Wright Mills was more than just a sociologist. For many scholars, he was the charismatic leader of the 1950s and 1960s radical crusade. A Weberian, rather than a Marxist, he nevertheless stimulated a deep-seated critique of the United States' domestic and foreign policies. His books *White Collar*, *The Power Elite*, and *The Sociological Imagination*, though controversial, have become classics in sociology. With Hans Gerth, with whom he was associated at Wisconsin before moving to Columbia, he produced *From Max Weber* and *Character and Social Structure*.

Rahmat Tavakol is a doctoral candidate in sociology at Rutgers Unviersity. He is currently writing a dissertation on "The Social and Economic Foundations of the Radicalization of Islam: Iran, 1960-1980."

Ronald M. Glassman is Associate Professor of Sociology at William Paterson College of the State University of New Jersey. He is also convener of the North American Max Weber Colloquium and the outgoing chairman of the Section on Comparative-Historical Sociology of the American Sociological Association. His books include *The Political History of Latin America*, *Democracy and Despotism in Primitive Society*, *A Weber-Marx Dialogue* (edited with Robert J. Antonio), *Max Weber's Political Sociology* (edited with Vatro Murvar), *Conflict and Control* (edited with Arthur Vidich), and, forthcoming, *The New Middle Class and Democracy*.

William H. Swatos, Jr., is a member of the faculty of the Department of Sociology of Northern Illinois University. His major areas of interest are the sociology of religion and classical sociological theory. He is a member of the Board of Directors of the Religious Research Association and the Executive Council of the Association for the Sociology of Religion, also serving as book review editor of that association's journal, *Sociological Analysis*. He is the author of numerous articles and two monographs: *Into Denominationalism: The Anglican Metamorphosis* and *Faith of the Fathers: Science, Religion, and Reform in the Development of Early American Sociology*.